amazing
GRACE

Our Daily Bread
Devotional Collection

Our Daily Bread
Publishing.

INTRODUCTION

Grace. What a beautiful word.

Like *mercy*, its partner word in Scripture, *grace* has the feel of a tender, unexpected hug or a whispered "I love you." It's a warm blanket, a strong shield, and a safe shelter—unfathomable and unforgettable.

Grace is such a warm and inviting word that parents often use it to name their daughters. My beautiful granddaughters, Kaitlyn and Mollie, both have Grace as their middle name. I love the sound of it.

The New International Version of the New Testament uses the word *grace* 114 times. A quick look at what it means in a few of these passages reveals some exciting insights.

- The "grace of God" was on Jesus (Luke 2:40). God was pouring out His divine favor on this perfect, flawless, growing child as His parents took Him home to Nazareth. Imagine the effect of God the Father cascading His grace into the life of His "only begotten Son" as Jesus prepared to face the next thirty or so years on earth.

- Jesus was "full of grace," according to John 1:14. So full of graciousness and compassion that He willingly left heaven's glories and entered earth's troubled realm as a human—expressly to die on our behalf. This grace is impossible for us to fully understand, but something for which we are unspeakably grateful.

- This grace is not only reserved for the divine. Acts 6:8 tells us that Stephen, one of the chosen seven who served the early church, was "a man full of God's grace." In him, people saw the God-given goodness, humility, and virtue of a person who would be dedicated to God's service.

When we continue this kind of study throughout the New Testament, we come away with a growing appreciation for the value and importance of grace.

We reflect on that grand passage in Ephesians which reminds us that it is "by grace you have been saved" (2:8). Because of Jesus's sacrifice on the cross, grace can bestow on us the greatest of all gifts—salvation from the penalty of our sin. Grace makes it possible to experience Jesus's promised "life . . . to the full" (John 10:10) and to anticipate eternal existence with God.

Grace is indeed amazing!

We can never grow tired of reveling in its benefits in our daily lives and looking forward to its forever reward when we see Jesus.

In this book, I've dug deep into the archives of *Our Daily Bread* articles from past decades to discover a treasure trove of readings to lift our hearts in praise at the grace God has bestowed on believers. From our legacy writers who founded the devotional all the way to our present-day array of authors, the message remains the same.

We'll be challenged daily to take advantage of the plentiful opportunities for service and worship that come to us as recipients of God's grace. We'll be moved with gratitude and challenged to action as we read about how this beautiful gift intersects our life.

And, as always in *Our Daily Bread*, this volume covers a variety of biblical teachings to help us grow closer to Jesus and live as shining lights in the world.

As a bonus for those who enjoy the great songs of the faith and to help you reflect on God's goodness, grace, and mercy to us, I've included twelve song stories—one for each month. These stories will help you appreciate the grand hymns of our faith. Whether these songs are new to you or are old favorites, you'll be encouraged by the background blessings these stories provide.

You'll also notice several references to the glorious song that shares its title with this book: *Amazing Grace*. Woven throughout the pages you'll read vignettes that reveal greater depth to the story of John Newton and his great hymn. It's a story that reminds us of the great gulf between our sinfulness and God's amazing grace—unveiling again the reality that only Jesus can bridge this gap.

Grace. What an amazing gift! As you read, my prayer is that God's grace will flow more and more into your life as you seek to know Him better and serve Him more.

Dave Branon

SONGS OF GRACE

JANUARY

"Amazing Grace"

John Newton and William Walker

*'Twas grace that taught my heart to fear,
and grace my fears relieved.*

God's Amazing Grace Transforms a Slave-Trader

Out of one of the most wretched activities mankind has ever en-
gaged in came one of the most beautiful hymns of faith and grace
ever written.

John Newton spent much of his adult life captaining ships that
transported hundreds of captured Africans to lives of slavery. Even
after Newton confessed to faith in Christ, a decision he made while
aboard a storm-ravaged ship, he continued to captain slave ships.

It's hard for us to fathom how the culture of his time accepted
slavery as a legitimate activity—and why he let that culture convince

Sources: "Amazing Grace," Wikipedia, http://tinyurl.com/b3wy67kj; "John Newton" PBS.org. http://tinyurl.com/2ss4kfmn; "The Creation of 'Amazing Grace,'"
Library of Congress, http://tinyurl.com/4h3smhhr; Johnson, Daniel, "We've Sung
'Amazing Grace' for 250 Years. We've Only Just Begun," *Christianity Today Online*,
http://tinyurl.com/mr27uem9; "21 Renditions of 'Amazing Grace' So Good You'll
Get Goosebumps," *Church Pops*, http://tinyurl.com/2s4zbaka; all accessed November 6, 2023.

him to continue contributing to it. After coming to faith, Newton treated his captive passengers with some concern and kindness, but he continued to ply his despicable trade for several years.

An illness forced him ashore when he was twenty-eight years old, and he took a job with the customs office in Liverpool. His faith was new and mysterious, so he began to study his beliefs more thoroughly. By the time he was nearly forty years old, he had become a minister.

In 1772, at the age of forty-seven, Newton worked with poet William Cowper on the words of what would become perhaps the greatest hymn of the faith. Newton wrote the song to accompany a sermon he was preparing for New Year's Day. *The Dictionary of American Hymnology* describes the song as Newton's "autobiography in verse."

The words for "Amazing Grace" were first published in a book Newton and Cowper produced in 1779 under the title *Olney Hymns*. (Olney was the town where Newton pastored.) In 1835, American composer William Walker added the music we know so well to Newton's words. He chose a melody called "New Britain," which immediately became popular and has stood the test of time.

Nineteenth-century evangelist Dwight L. Moody and his song leader–singer Ira Sankey helped popularize the song further as they presented the song in churches around the United States. And the Sacred Harp Choir made the song's first recording in 1922.

Ironically, given Newton's career before he became a minister, the song became a spiritual sung by Black Christians. Singers such as Mahalia Jackson used it as an anthem of the American Civil Rights movement in the 1960s.

Newton eventually came to recognize the atrocity of human slavery, especially under the influence of British statesman William Wilberforce, the driving force behind the abolition of slave trade among the English. In 1788, Newton published an essay titled "Thoughts upon the African Slave Trade" in which he condemned the practice. In one essay, Newton wrote, "I was once an active instrument in a business at which my heart now shudders."

Amazing grace. How sweet the sound. It saved a wretch like John Newton. Like you. Like me. Like all who trust in Jesus. Grace relieves our fears and sets us free.

Amazing Grace

Amazing grace (how sweet the sound)
That saved a wretch like me!
I once was lost, but now I'm found,
Was blind, but now I see.

'Twas grace that taught my heart to fear,
And grace my fears relieved;
How precious did that grace appear
The hour I first believed!

GOD'S AMAZING GRACE

Ephesians 2:1–10

You were dead in your transgressions and sins. —Ephesians 2:1

Not everyone who knows the hymn "Amazing Grace" knows what *grace* means.

One day, when evangelist Dwight L. Moody (1837–1899) was studying the meaning of God's grace, he dashed into the street and shouted to the first man he saw, "Do you know grace?" Mystified, the man replied, "Grace who?" One can imagine that Moody eagerly explained grace—that God has compassion on sinful people and freely offers forgiveness and new life to all who put their faith in Christ.

I heard of a man who had lived a troubled life and died without understanding the message of God's grace. A minister had talked to him and encouraged him to consider putting his faith in Jesus, but his response was, "I'm too undeserving." He didn't know that God's grace is *for* the undeserving.

In Paul's letter to the Ephesians, he bluntly described their lives before Jesus as being "dead in your transgressions and sins" (2:1). Then he used two hope-filled words: "But God" (v. 4 NKJV). This contrast helped Paul introduce God's grace to the people—a grace that provides forgiveness and new life through Christ. Salvation, he explained, is through faith, not works, so no one can boast (vv. 8–9).

Let's help others understand that God's salvation is for sinners only—and this includes all of us. This is what makes God's grace so amazing!   *Joanie Yoder*

God's grace is reserved for the undeserving.

IN THE BEGINNING

Genesis 1:1–15

In the beginning God created the heavens
and the earth. —Genesis 1:1

Talk about great opening lines! You can't do better than the Bible does. In just ten words, Genesis 1:1 answers the age-old question of the origin of the universe. But what's even more important, that opening verse introduces us to the majestic One who is behind it all.

As another new year commences, it seems appropriate to turn to the beginning of the Bible and read the account of how the eternal God spoke the world into existence.

Of course, God as Creator is just one of many descriptions of the Almighty the Bible reveals to us. This is why it might be a good idea to use the new year to study God—to find out more about who He is.

For instance, in this great beginning chapter, we are awestruck by His power as He moves across the face of the earth, fashioning it as He wants, and furnishing it with plants, animals, and humans.

As the year moves along, why not make a special effort to know God more intimately? The best way to do this is to read the Bible every day and ask, "What does this tell me about God?" You know Him as the majestic, almighty Creator through Genesis 1, but He is so much more.

Use this year to get to know God as never before.   *Dave Branon*

**It might be a good idea to use the new year to study
God—to find out more about who He is.**

A WIDE, SWEEPING GRACE

Isaiah 44:21–23

I have swept away your offenses. —Isaiah 44:22

Alexa, Amazon's voice-controlled device, has an interesting feature: it can erase everything you say. Whatever you've asked Alexa to do, whatever information you've asked Alexa to retrieve, one simple sentence ("Delete everything I said today") sweeps it all clean, as if it never happened. It's too bad that the rest of our life doesn't have this capability. Every misspoken word, every disgraceful act, every moment we wish we could erase—we'd just speak the command, and the entire mess would disappear.

There's good news, though. God does offer each of us a clean start. Only, He goes far deeper than merely deleting our mistakes or bad behavior. God provides redemption, a deep healing that transforms us and makes us new. "Return to me," He says, "I have redeemed you" (Isaiah 44:22). Even though Israel rebelled and disobeyed, God reached out to them with lavish mercy. He "swept away [their] offenses like a cloud, [their] sins like the morning mist" (v. 22). He gathered all their shame and failures and washed them away with His wide, sweeping grace.

God will do the same with our sin and blunders. There's no mistake He can't mend, no wound He can't heal. God's mercy heals and redeems the most painful places in our soul—even the ones we've hidden for so very long. His mercy sweeps away all our guilt and washes away every regret. *Winn Collier*

God's mercy heals and redeems the most painful places in our soul.

HOW TO STAND FIRM

Jude 1:24–25

To him who is able to keep you from stumbling. —Jude 1:24

It was a cold, icy winter's day, and my mind was focused on getting from my warm vehicle to a warm building. The next thing I knew, I was on the ground with my knees turned inward and my lower legs turned outward. Nothing was broken, but I was in pain. The pain would get worse as time went by, and it would be weeks before I was whole again.

Who among us hasn't taken a spill of some sort? Wouldn't it be nice to have something or someone to keep us on our feet all the time? While there are no guarantees of surefootedness in the physical sense, there is One who stands ready to assist us in our quest to honor Christ in this life and prepare us to stand joyfully before Him in the next.

Every day we face temptations (and even false teachings) that seek to divert us, confuse us, and entangle us. Yet, it's not ultimately through our own efforts that we remain on our feet as we walk in this world. How assuring to know that when we hold our peace if tempted to speak angrily, or opt for honesty over deceit, or choose love over hate, or select truth over error—we experience God's power to keep us standing (Jude 1:24). And when we appear approved before God when Christ returns, the praise that we offer now for His sustaining grace will echo throughout eternity (v. 25).

Arthur Jackson

**There is One who stands ready to assist
us in our quest to honor Christ.**

GRACE FOR TRIALS

Deuteronomy 31:1–8

[The Lord] will never leave you nor forsake you. Do not
be afraid; do not be discouraged. —Deuteronomy 31:8

Annie Johnson Flint (1866–1932) was crippled by severe arthritis
just a few years after high school. She never walked again and
relied on others to help care for her needs. Because she became rather
well-known for her poetry and hymns, she received many visitors,
including a deaconess who felt discouraged about her own ministry.
When the visitor returned home, she wrote to Annie, wondering why
God allowed such hard things in her life.

In response, Annie sent a poem that began: "God hath not
promised skies always blue, flower-strewn pathways all our lives
through. . . ." Annie knew from experience that suffering often occurred but that God would never abandon those He loves. Instead,
He promised to give "grace for the trials, help from above, unfailing sympathy, undying love." You may recognize this poem as the
hymn "What God Hath Promised."

Moses also suffered and faced strife, but he knew God's presence
was with him. When he passed his leadership of the Israelites to
Joshua, he told the younger man to be strong and courageous, because "the LORD your God goes with you" (Deuteronomy 31:6).
Moses, knowing that the people of Israel would face formidable enemies as they entered and took the promised land, said to Joshua,
"Do not be afraid; do not be discouraged" (v. 8).

Followers of Jesus will face hardship and strife in this fallen world,
but we have God's Spirit to encourage us. He'll never leave us.

Amy Boucher Pye

Moses said to Joshua, "Do not be afraid."

A GOOD WORK

Psalm 139:13–24

He who began a good work in you will carry it on to
completion until the day of Christ Jesus. —Philippians 1:6

As a teenager, Charles Spurgeon (1834–1892) wrestled with God. He'd grown up going to church, but what was preached seemed bland and meaningless. It was a struggle for him to believe in God, and Charles, in his own words, "rebelled and revolted." One night a fierce snowstorm forced the sixteen-year-old Spurgeon to seek shelter in a tiny Methodist church. The preacher's sermon seemed directed at him personally. In that moment, God won the wrestling match, and Charles gave his heart to Jesus.

Spurgeon later wrote, "Long before I began with Christ, He began with me." In fact, our life with God doesn't begin with the moment of salvation. The psalmist notes that God "created [our] inmost being," knitting us together in our mother's womb (Psalm 139:13). The apostle Paul writes, "Even before I was born, God chose me and called me by his marvelous grace" (Galatians 1:15 NLT). And God doesn't stop working with us when we're saved: "He who began a good work in you will carry it on to completion" (Philippians 1:6).

We're all works in progress in the hands of a loving God. He leads us through our rebellious wrestling and into His warm embrace. But His purpose with us then is only beginning. "For God is working in you, giving you the desire and the power to do what pleases him" (Philippians 2:13 NLT). Rest assured, we're His good work regardless of how old we are or what stage of life we're in.

Kenneth Petersen

We're all works in progress in the hands of a loving God.

CELEBRATING CREATIVITY

Genesis 1:16–21

God said, "Let the water teem with living
creatures." —Genesis 1:20

A rarely seen jellyfish waltzed with the currents, four thousand feet deep in the ocean near Baja California. Its body shone with fluorescent shades of blue, purple, and pink—bright against the backdrop of black water. Elegant tentacles waved gracefully with each pulsing of its bell-shaped hood. As I watched the amazing footage of the Halitrephes maasi jellyfish on a *National Geographic* video, I reflected on how God chose the specific design of this beautiful, gelatinous creature. He also fashioned the more than 2,000 other types of jellyfish scientists have identified.

Though we acknowledge God as Creator, do we slow down long enough to truly consider the profound truth revealed in the first chapter of the Bible? Our amazing God brought forth light and life into the creatively diverse world He crafted with the power of His word. He designed "the great creatures of the sea and every living thing with which the water teems" (Genesis 1:21). Scientists have discovered only a fraction of the wondrous creatures the Lord created in the beginning.

God also intentionally sculpted each person in the world, giving purpose to every day of our lives before we drew our first breaths (Psalm 139:13–16). As we celebrate the Lord's creativity, we can also rejoice over the many ways He helps us use our imagination and creativity for His glory.   *Xochitl Dixon*

**God intentionally sculpted each person in the
world, giving purpose to every day of our lives.**

SINKING INTO GRACE

Psalm 127:1–2

[God] grants sleep to those he loves. —Psalm 127:2

Finally, on January 8, 1964, seventeen-year-old Randy Gardner did something he hadn't done for eleven days and twenty-five minutes: he nodded off to sleep. He wanted to beat the *Guinness Book of World Records* standard for how long a human could stay awake. By drinking soft drinks and hitting the basketball court and bowling alley, Gardner rebuffed sleep for a week and a half. Before finally collapsing, his sense of taste, smell, and hearing went haywire. Decades later, Gardner suffered from severe bouts of insomnia. He set the record but also confirmed the obvious: sleep is essential.

Many of us struggle to get a decent night's rest. Unlike Gardner, who deprived himself intentionally, we might suffer sleeplessness for several reasons, including a mountain of anxieties: the fear of what we need to accomplish, the dread of others' expectations, or the distress of living at a frantic pace. Sometimes it's hard for us to turn off the fear and relax.

The psalmist tells us that "unless the LORD builds the house," we labor in vain (Psalm 127:1). Our toiling and relentless efforts are useless unless God provides what we need. Thankfully, God does provide what we need. He "grants sleep to those he loves" (v. 2). And God's love extends to all of us. He invites us to release our anxieties to Him and sink into His rest, into His grace.

Winn Collier

God invites us to release our anxieties to Him.

HE FIRST LOVED US

1 John 4:10–19

We love because he first loved us. —1 John 4:19

It's easy to be fond of nice people. It's natural to see virtue in our own family. However, to love a rebellious, obnoxious outsider is not easy. To have genuine, unselfish regard for unlovable people is rare. In fact, it's impossible apart from the grace of the Lord Jesus Christ.

In light of this, God's love for mankind is amazing beyond our imagination. Knowing exactly how wicked human beings would become—how they would lie, steal, act immorally, and manifest hateful and unkind attitudes—God still loved us so much that He gave His only Son for our salvation. He loved us from before the foundation of the world, and He loves us still—even though there's nothing in us to attract His favor.

A young mother was sewing while her little girl was playing with her dolls. After some time, the youngster came to her mom and asked for a hug. "Why do you want me to hold you?" Mom asked. "Because I love you!" she replied.

"What about your dolls?" her mother teased. "Don't you love them too?"

"Yes," she responded. "But I love you more! Know why? 'Cause you loved me when I was too little to love you back!"

Doesn't this sound like God's love for us? The apostle John summarized this truth in that brief but wonderful sentence: "We love because he first loved us" (1 John 4:19). If God hadn't taken the initiative, we'd have no inclination to seek Him. We would all perish eternally.

What gratitude pours into our hearts when we contemplate God's love for us!

Herb Vander Lugt

God loved us from before the foundation of the world.

ETCH A SKETCH FORGIVENESS

Psalm 103:7–13

As far as the east is from the west, so far has he removed
our transgressions from us. —Psalm 103:12

The little red rectangular box was magical. As a kid, I could play with it for hours. When I turned one knob on the box, I could create a horizontal line on its screen. Turn the other knob . . . and voila!—a vertical line. When I turned the knobs together, I could make diagonal lines, circles, and creative designs. But the real magic came when I turned my Etch A Sketch toy upside down, shook it a little, and turned it right side up. A blank screen appeared, offering me the opportunity to create a new design.

God's forgiveness works much like that Etch A Sketch. He wipes away our sins, creating a clean canvas for us. Even if we remember wrongs we committed, God chooses to forgive and forget. He's wiped them out and doesn't hold our sins against us. He doesn't treat us according to our sinful actions (Psalm 103:10) but extends grace through forgiveness. We have a clean slate—a new life awaiting us when we seek God's forgiveness. We can be rid of guilt and shame because of His amazing gift to us.

The psalmist reminds us that our sins have been separated from us as far as the east is separated from the west (v. 12). That's as far away as you can get! In God's eyes, our sins no longer cling to us like a scarlet letter or a bad drawing. This is reason to rejoice and to thank God for His amazing grace and mercy.   *Katara Patton*

**We have a clean slate—a new life awaiting
us when we seek God's forgiveness.**

THE BEAUTY OF FELLOWSHIP

James 5:13–20

Confess your sins to each other and pray for each
other so that you may be healed. —James 5:16

"Hey, Poh Fang!" A church friend texted. "For this month's care group meeting, let's get everyone to do what James 5:16 says. Let's create a safe environment of trust and confidentiality, so we can share an area of struggle in our life and pray for each other."

For a moment, I wasn't sure how to reply. While our small-group members have known each other for years, we'd never really shared all our hurts and struggles openly with one another. After all, it's scary to be vulnerable.

But the truth is, we're all sinners and we all struggle. We all need Jesus. Authentic conversations about God's amazing grace and our dependency on Christ have a way of encouraging us to keep trusting in Him. With Jesus, we can stop pretending to have trouble-free lives.

So, I replied, "Yes! Let's do that!" Initially, it was awkward. But as one person opened up and shared, another soon followed. Although a few kept silent, there was understanding. No one was pressured. We ended the time by doing what the second part of James 5:16 says, "Pray for each other."

That day I experienced the beauty of fellowship with believers in Jesus. Because of our common faith in Christ, we can be vulnerable with each other and depend on Him and others to help us in our weaknesses and struggles.   *Poh Fang Chia*

We can be vulnerable with each other.

EACH DAY

Matthew 6:5–15

Give us today our daily bread. —Matthew 6:11

In 1924, a boy named Johnny, who loved to play basketball, completed the eighth grade in a small rural school. His father, rich in love but short on money for a graduation gift, gave Johnny a card on which he had written his own seven-point creed, and he encouraged his son to start following it daily. Three of the points were: Drink deeply from good books, especially the Bible. Make each day your masterpiece. Pray for guidance and give thanks for your blessings every day.

Jesus, in what we often call the Lord's Prayer (Matthew 6:9–13), taught us to approach our heavenly Father each day; it's not something to be said once and forgotten. Through prayer we offer God praise (v. 9); seek His kingdom and His will (v. 10); trust His provision (v. 11); and ask for His forgiveness, power, and deliverance (vv. 12–13).

Throughout his life, Johnny sought the Lord's strength to live each day for Him. He became a three-time All-American basketball player at Purdue University and one of the greatest college coaches of all time. When Coach John Wooden died at the age of ninety-nine, he was honored most of all for his character, his faith, and the many lives he touched.

By God's grace, may we make each day our masterpiece for Him.

David McCasland

"Pray for guidance and give thanks for your blessings every day." —Joshua Wooden

KEEP YOUR GUARD UP

Deuteronomy 4:1–9

Be careful, and watch yourselves closely. —Deuteronomy 4:9

A man and several friends went through a ski resort gate posted with avalanche warning signs and started snowboarding. On the second trip down, someone shouted, "Avalanche!" But the man couldn't escape and perished in the cascading snow. Some criticized him, calling him a novice. But he wasn't; he was an "avalanche-certified backcountry guide." One researcher said that skiers and snowboarders with the most avalanche training are more likely to give in to faulty reasoning. "[The snowboarder] died because he was lulled into letting his guard down."

As Israel prepared to go into the promised land, God wanted His people to keep their guard up—to be careful and alert. So, He commanded them to obey all His "decrees and laws" (Deuteronomy 4:1–2) and to remember His past judgment on those who disobeyed (vv. 3–4). They needed to "be careful" to examine themselves and keep watch over their inner lives (v. 9). This would help them keep their guard up against spiritual dangers from without and spiritual apathy from within.

It's easy for us to let our guard down and fall into apathy and self-deception. But God can give us strength to avoid falling in life and forgiveness by His grace when we do. By following Him and resting in His wisdom and provision, we can keep our guard up and make good decisions!   *Marvin Williams*

God can give us strength to avoid falling in life.

SLOW-FASHIONED GRACE

Colossians 3:12–17

Clothe yourselves with compassion, kindness, humility,
gentleness and patience. —Colossians 3:12

Have you heard of #slowfashion? The hashtag captures a movement focused on resisting "fast fashion"—an industry dominated by cheaply made and quickly disposed of clothes. In fast fashion, clothes go out of style nearly as quickly as they appear in stores—with some brands disposing of large quantities of their products every year.

The slow fashion movement encourages people to slow down and take a different approach. Instead of being driven by the need to always have the latest look, slow fashion encourages us to select fewer well-made and ethically sourced items that will last.

As I reflected on #slowfashion's invitation, I found myself wondering about other ways I fall into a "fast fashion" way of thinking—always looking for fulfillment in the latest trend. In Colossians 3, however, Paul says finding *true* transformation in Jesus isn't a quick fix or a fad. It's a lifetime of quiet, gradual transformation in Christ.

Instead of needing to clothe ourselves with the world's latest status symbols, we can exchange our striving, replacing it with the Spirit's clothing of "compassion, kindness, humility, gentleness and patience" (v. 12). We can learn patience with each other on the slow journey of Christ transforming our hearts—a journey that leads to lasting peace (v. 15). *Monica La Rose*

**True transformation in Jesus is a lifetime of
quiet, gradual transformation in Christ.**

WHOSE PRISONER?

Ephesians 3:1–9

This grace was given me: to preach to the Gentiles
the boundless riches of Christ. —Ephesians 3:8

A story is told of Scottish minister Alexander Whyte (1836–1921), who was able to look at the bleakest situation and find something to be thankful for. On a dark Sunday morning when the weather was freezing, wet, and stormy, one of his deacons whispered, "I am sure the preacher won't be able to thank God for anything on a day like this. It's absolutely horrible outside!" The pastor began the service by praying, "We thank Thee, O God, that the weather is not always like this."

The apostle Paul also saw the best in every situation. Consider his circumstances as he wrote to the church in Ephesus while he awaited trial before the Roman emperor Nero. Most people would have concluded that he was a prisoner of Rome. But Paul saw himself as a prisoner of Christ. He thought of his hardship as an opportunity to take the gospel to the gentiles.

These words of Paul should challenge us: "Although I am less than the least of all the Lord's people, this grace was given me: to preach to the Gentiles the boundless riches of Christ" (Ephesians 3:8). Paul, a prisoner of Christ, saw himself as being given the privilege to serve God and present the "riches of Christ" to many.

Whose prisoner are we?   *Albert Lee*

**Paul thought of his hardship as an opportunity
to take the gospel to the gentiles.**

THE WORLD OF MORE

Romans 5:1–11

Eye has not seen . . . the things which God has prepared
for those who love Him. —1 Corinthians 2:9 NKJV

My cable company sent a postcard inviting me to check out its
latest improvements in TV channels. The card indicated that
I needed to contact the company to get the necessary new digital
equipment and explained how to hook it up and activate it. After
that, the ad said I was just to "sit back and enjoy the World of More."

The card made me think of the "World of More" that Christians are privileged to live in. When God transports people from
the darkness of sin "into His wonderful light" (1 Peter 2:9), a whole
new life opens up.

Romans 5 tells us some of the *more* that we have in Christ: We
have been "reconciled to [God] through the death of his Son" (v. 10)
and therefore have "peace with God through our Lord Jesus Christ"
(v. 1). We have access to God and His grace (v. 2). Rejoicing in trouble is now possible because we understand that it's an opportunity to
grow in our character through trusting Him (vv. 3–4). Additionally,
the Holy Spirit, who has been given to live in us, pours the love of
God into our hearts (v. 5). And sin no longer has the same hold on
us (6:18).

As Christians, we have unlimited access to a real "World of
More." Wouldn't it be selfish not to invite others to join us in this
special world? *Anne Cetas*

We have unlimited access to a real "World of More."

GIVING THANKS

John 11:32–44

Jesus looked up and said, "Father, I thank you
that you have heard me." —John 11:41

A tragedy left a family with a void that nothing could fill. A toddler chasing a cat wandered into the road and was run over by a delivery truck. A four-year-old watched in shocked silence as her parents cradled the lifeless body of her little sister. For years, the cold emptiness of that moment encased the family in sadness. Feelings were frozen. The only comfort was numbness. Relief was unimaginable.

Author Ann Voskamp was the four-year-old, and the sorrow surrounding her sister's death formed her view of life and God. The world she grew up in had little concept of grace. Joy was an idea that had no basis in reality.

As a young mother, Voskamp set out to discover the elusive thing the Bible calls *joy*. The words for *joy* and *grace* come from the Greek word *chairo*, which she found out is at the center of the Greek word for thanksgiving. Could it be that simple? she wondered. To test her discovery, Voskamp decided to give thanks for a thousand gifts she already had. She started slowly, but soon gratefulness was flowing freely.

Just as Jesus gave thanks before, not after, raising Lazarus from the dead (John 11:41), Voskamp discovered that giving thanks brought to life feelings of joy that had died along with her sister. Joy comes from thanksgiving.   *Julie Ackerman Link*

Giving thanks brought to life feelings of joy that had died.

GETTING WHAT YOU WANT

Psalm 21:1–7

Take delight in the LORD, and he will give you
the desires of your heart. —Psalm 37:4

A certain airline pilot had a peculiar habit. Whenever he took off from his hometown of Minneapolis, he would ask the co-pilot to take the controls. Then he would stare intently out the window for a few moments.

Finally, the copilot's curiosity got the best of him, so he asked, "What do you always look at down there?"

"See that boy fishing on that riverbank?" the pilot asked. "I used to fish from that same spot when I was a kid. Whenever a plane flew over, I would watch it until it disappeared and wish that I could be the pilot." With a sigh he added, "Now I wish I could be back down there fishing."

It's natural to spend time thinking about where we'd like to be or what we'd like to have. But we must evaluate our desires to make sure they're consistent with what God says will truly satisfy.

King David found satisfaction by putting first things first. His joy was rooted in the strength of the Lord and the salvation He provided (Psalm 21:1–2). It was because David sought the Lord that God gave him the desires of his heart (37:4).

When our desires conform to God's will, we're not likely to waste time wishing for things that can't satisfy. Real joy comes not in getting what we want, but in wanting to be close to God. *David Egner*

**We must evaluate our desires to make sure they are
consistent with what God says will truly satisfy.**

ANCHORED IN TRUTH

Isaiah 22:15–20, 22–25

I will drive him like a peg into a firm place. —Isaiah 22:23

My family lives in a nearly century-old house with a lot of character, including wonderfully textured plaster walls. A builder cautioned me that with these walls, to hang a picture up I'd have to either drill the nail into a wood support or use a plaster anchor for support. Otherwise, I'd risk the picture crashing to the ground, leaving an ugly hole behind.

The prophet Isaiah used the imagery of a nail driven firmly into a wall to describe a minor biblical character named Eliakim. Unlike the corrupt official Shebna (Isaiah 22:15–19), as well as the people of Israel—who looked to themselves for strength (vv. 8–11)—Eliakim trusted in God. Prophesying Eliakim's promotion to palace administrator for King Hezekiah, Isaiah wrote that Eliakim would be driven like a "peg into a firm place" (v. 23). Being securely anchored in God's truth and grace would also allow Eliakim to be a support for his family and his people (vv. 22–24).

Yet Isaiah concluded this prophecy with a sobering reminder that no person can be the ultimate security for friends or family—we all fail (v. 25). The only completely trustworthy anchor for our lives is the Lord (Psalm 62:5–6; Matthew 7:24). As we care for others and share their burdens, may we also point them to Jesus, the anchor who will never fail.
Lisa M. Samra

The only completely trustworthy anchor for our lives is Jesus.

GRACE IN OUR HEARTS

Ephesians 2:4–10

Words from the mouth of the wise are
gracious. —Ecclesiastes 10:12

A few years ago, four-star General Peter Chiarelli (the No. 2 general in the US Army at that time) was mistaken for a waiter by a senior presidential advisor at a formal Washington dinner. As the general stood behind her in his dress uniform, the senior advisor asked him to get her a beverage. She then realized her mistake, and the general graciously eased her embarrassment by cheerfully refilling her glass and even inviting her to join his family for dinner in the future.

The word *gracious* comes from the word *grace*, and it can mean an act of kindness or courtesy, like the general's. But it has an even deeper meaning to followers of Christ. We are recipients of the incredible free and unmerited favor—grace—that God has provided through His Son, Jesus (Ephesians 2:8).

Because we have received grace, we are to show it in the way we treat others—for example, in the way we speak to them: "Words from the mouth of the wise are gracious" (Ecclesiastes 10:12). Grace in our hearts pours out in our words and deeds (Colossians 3:16–17).

Learning to extend the grace in our hearts toward others is a by-product of the life of a Spirit-filled follower of Christ Jesus—the greatest grace-giver ever.   *Cindy Hess Kasper*

**Because we have received grace, we are to
show it in the way we treat others.**

GOD LEADS US ALONG

Psalm 23

He guides me along the right paths for
his name's sake. —Psalm 23:3

The British hymn writer William Cowper (1731–1800) often suffered great mental anguish. At times, he even considered taking his own life.

One night while in such a mood, he hailed a horse-driven cab and asked to be taken to the Thames River. However, the city of London was blanketed with such a thick fog that the driver lost his way. At last Cowper leaped impatiently from the buggy, determined to find his watery grave unassisted. Groping through the fog, he was astonished when he discovered that he was back at his own doorstep! Falling to his knees, he thanked the Lord for the fog He had sent over London, which had prevented him from committing suicide.

Knowing that God in His grace had misdirected the cab driver, Cowper wrote these memorable words: "God moves in a mysterious way His wonders to perform; He plants His footsteps in the sea, and rides upon the storm. You fearful saints, fresh courage take; the clouds you so much dread are big with mercy, and shall break in blessing on your head!"

God has a purpose in everything that comes into your life and mine. We may not be able to comprehend the "why" of things at the present, but someday in heaven we shall see how God led us even in times of great distress. *Henry Bosch*

God has a purpose in everything that comes into your life.

NEW SONGS

Psalm 40:1–10

He put a new song in my mouth, a hymn
of praise to our God. —Psalm 40:3

The song of the humpback whale is one of the strangest in nature. It is a weird combination of high- and low-pitched groanings. Those who have studied the humpback whale say their songs are noteworthy because these giants of the deep are continually changing them. New patterns are added, and old ones are eliminated so that over a period of time the whale actually sings a whole new song.

There's a sense in which the Christian should be continually composing new songs of praise around the fresh mercies of God. Unfortunately, many of us just keep singing the "same old song." Most certainly, we must repeatedly affirm the fundamentals of our faith. But as the psalmist tells us, the works of God's deliverance in the lives of His people are many, and they give us reason to express our praise to Him in new ways. His works are more than we can count (Psalm 40:5).

We need to ask: Is our testimony of God's saving grace expressed in the same rote way year after year? Let's continually fill our hearts and minds with new songs as we enjoy fresh experiences of the mercies of the cross and of Christ's resurrection power.

The gospel story never changes. Thank God for that. But the songs of our praise should be endlessly new.   *Mart DeHaan*

The songs of our praise should be endlessly new.

SPOTTING GOD

Isaiah 26:3–4

You will keep in perfect peace those whose minds are
steadfast, because they trust in you. —Isaiah 26:3

A pirouette is a graceful spin that's executed by ballerinas and contemporary dancers alike. As a child, I loved to do pirouettes in my modern dance class, whirling round and round until I was dizzy in the head and fell to the ground. As I got older, a trick I learned to help me maintain my balance and control was "spotting"—identifying a single point for my eyes to return to each time I made a full circle spin. Having a single focal point was all I needed to master my pirouette with a graceful finish.

We all face many twists and turns in life. When we focus on our problems, however, the things we encounter seem unmanageable, leaving us dizzy and heading toward a disastrous fall. The Bible reminds us that if we keep our minds steadfast, or focused, on God, He'll keep us in "perfect peace" (Isaiah 26:3). Perfect peace means that no matter how many turns life takes, we can remain calm, assured that God will be with us through our problems and trials. He's the "Rock eternal" (v. 4)—the ultimate "spot" to fix our eyes on—because His promises never change.

May we keep our eyes on Him as we go through each day, going to Him in prayer and studying His promises in the Scriptures. May we rely on God, our eternal Rock, to help us move gracefully through all of life.   *Kimya Loder*

**If we keep our minds steadfast, or focused, on
God, He'll keep us in "perfect peace."**

EXTENDING GRACE TO OTHERS

Acts 4:32–35

God's grace was so powerfully at work in them all that there
were no needy persons among them. —Acts 4:33–34

Our son spent the early years of his life in a children's home prior
to our adopting him. Before leaving the cinderblock building together to go home, we asked to collect his belongings. Sadly, he had
none. We exchanged the clothes he was wearing for the new items
we'd brought for him, and we also left some clothing for the other
children. Even though I was grieved by how little he had, I rejoiced
that we could now help meet his physical and emotional needs.

A few years later, we saw a person asking for donations for families in need. My son was eager to donate his stuffed animals and a
few coins to help them. Given his background, he might have (un-
derstandably) been more inclined to hold tightly to his belongings.

I'd like to think the reason for his generous response was the same
as that of the early church: "God's grace was so powerfully at work
in them all" that nobody in their midst had need (Acts 4:33–34).
The people willingly sold their own possessions to provide for one
another's needs.

When we become aware of the needs of others, whether material
or intangible, may God's grace be so powerfully at work in us that
we respond as they did, willingly giving from our hearts to those
in need. This makes us vessels of God's grace as fellow believers in
Jesus, "one in heart and mind" (v. 32).   *Kirsten Holmberg*

**When we become aware of the needs of others, may
we respond willingly, giving from our hearts.**

STRENGTHENED THROUGH SUFFERING

1 Peter 5:1–11

May the God of all grace, . . . after you have suffered a
while, . . . strengthen, and settle you. —1 Peter 5:10 NKJV

Church services sometimes end with a benediction. A common
one is taken from Peter's concluding remarks in his first epis-
tle: "May the God of all grace, who called us to His eternal glory
by Christ Jesus, after you have suffered a while, perfect, establish,
strengthen, and settle you" (1 Peter 5:10 NKJV). Sometimes omitted
in the benediction is the phrase "after you have suffered a while."
Why? Perhaps because it is not pleasant to speak of suffering.

It should not surprise us, however, when suffering comes our
way. The apostle Paul, who knew well what it was to suffer, wrote:
"All who desire to live godly in Christ Jesus will suffer persecution"
(2 Timothy 3:12 NKJV).

If we live a life of submission to God (1 Peter 5:6) and resisting
the devil (v. 9), we can expect to be maligned, misunderstood, and
even taken advantage of. But the apostle Peter says there is a purpose for such suffering. It is to "restore you and make you strong,
firm and steadfast" (v.10).

God's path for our Christian growth often leads us through dif-
ficulties, but they fortify us to withstand life's future storms. May
God help us to be faithful as we seek to boldly live a life that honors
Him.   *C. P. Hia*

Suffering will "restore you and make you strong,
firm and steadfast." —1 Peter 5:10

HE MAKES US NEW

John 6:5–13

Gather the pieces that are left over. —John 6:12

As a traveling executive, Shawn Seipler wrestled with an odd question. What happens to leftover soap in hotel rooms? Thrown out as trash for landfills, millions of soap bars could instead find new life, Seipler believed. So, he launched Clean the World, a recycling venture that has helped more than eight thousand hotels, cruise lines, and resorts turn millions of pounds of discarded soap into sterilized, newly molded soap bars. Sent to people in need in more than one hundred countries, the recycled soap helps prevent countless hygiene-related illnesses and deaths.

As Seipler said, "I know it sounds funny, but that little bar of soap on the counter in your hotel room can literally save a life."

The gathering up of something used or dirty to give it new life is also one of the most loving traits of our Savior, Jesus. In that manner, after He fed a crowd of five thousand with five small barley loaves and two small fish, He still said to His disciples, "Gather the pieces that are left over. Let nothing be wasted" (John 6:12).

In our lives, when we feel "washed up," God sees us not as wasted lives but as His miracles. Never throwaways in His sight, we have divine potential for new kingdom work. "Therefore, if anyone is in Christ, the new creation has come: The old has gone, the new is here!" (2 Corinthians 5:17). What makes us new? Christ within us.

Patricia Raybon

**The gathering up of something used or dirty to give it
new life is one of the most loving traits of our Savior.**

YOU ARE NEEDED!

Ephesians 4:11–16

The body is not made up of one part but
of many. —1 Corinthians 12:14

The story is told about an important rehearsal for a grand orato-
rio. In front of the musicians and singers stood the famed conductor. As he wielded the baton, the music of the mighty chorus,
along with the thundering strains of the organ, the rolling of the
drums, the vibrant tones of the horns, and the beautiful notes of
the stringed instruments filled the building.

Suddenly, the conductor commanded, "Stop! Where is the
piccolo?"

One musician in that vast company of choir and orchestra had
fallen silent. The ear of the highly trained director missed the tiny
note, for the sound was imperfect without it.

Perhaps you have, at one time, said, "There's really nothing I can
do for Christ. My talents are too small." However, if by faith you
have trusted in the Savior, the Holy Spirit has placed you into the
body of Christ, the church. And you do have tasks to fulfill.

In the human body, "the eye cannot say to the hand, 'I don't need
you!' And the head cannot say to the feet, 'I don't need you!'" In fact,
"those parts of the body that seem to be weaker are indispensable"
(1 Corinthians 12:21–22). In the church, the body of Christ, you
are important as well! There's something for you to do! Paul says in
Ephesians 4:16 that we are held together "as each part does its work."

As we seek to complete the task the Lord has empowered us to
do, we can give thanks for the amazing grace that has transformed
us. Then we can let God's Spirit make us useful for His glory.

Paul Van Gorder

**Each believer must complete the task the
Lord has empowered him or her to do.**

GRACE AND CHANGE

Exodus 2:11–15

Moses was afraid and thought, "What I did must
have become known." —Exodus 2:14

The crime was shocking, and the man who committed it was sentenced to life in prison. In the years that followed, the man—in solitary confinement—began a process of mental and spiritual healing. This led to repentance and a restored relationship with Jesus. These days he's been allowed limited interactions with other inmates. And, by God's grace, through his witness some fellow prisoners have received Christ as Savior—finding forgiveness in Him.

Moses, though now recognized as a great man of faith, also committed a shocking crime. After he witnessed "an Egyptian beating a Hebrew," he looked "this way and that" and "killed the Egyptian" (Exodus 2:11–12). Despite this sin, God in His grace wasn't done with His imperfect servant. Later, He chose Moses to free His people from their oppression (3:10). In Romans 5:14, we read, "Death reigned from the time of Adam to the time of Moses, even over those who did not sin by breaking a command." But in the following verses Paul states that "God's grace" makes it possible for us, regardless of our past sins, to be changed and made right with Him (vv. 15–16).

We might think that some error we've made disqualifies us from knowing God's forgiveness and being used for His honor. But because of His grace, in Jesus we can be changed and set free to help others be saved for eternity. *Tom Felten*

**God's grace makes it possible for us, regardless
of our past sins, to be changed.**

SUPERNATURAL SURVEILLANCE

Matthew 6:1–6, 16–18

Your Father, who sees what is done in secret,
will reward you. —Matthew 6:18

Not far from my house, authorities have rigged a camera to snap pictures of drivers who race through red lights. The offenders later receive in the mail a ticket along with a "red-light photo," which is visual proof of their traffic violation.

Sometimes I think of God in the same way I think of that camera—He's up there, just waiting to catch me doing the wrong thing. While God does see our sin (Hebrews 4:13), He sees and takes interest in our good deeds as well. Due to His supernatural surveillance, God sees the size of our sacrifice when we give money to the church or to those in need (Mark 12:41–44). He hears our private prayers (Matthew 6:6). And when we fast, we can carry on as usual, being assured that our "Father . . . sees . . . in secret" (v. 18).

Knowing that God sees everything frees us from thinking about the watchful eyes of others. When we do what is right, we need no applause from onlookers; when we sin, we do not need to worry about our reputation once we settle the issue with God and anyone we've harmed. We can rest, knowing that "the eyes of the LORD range throughout the earth to strengthen those whose hearts are fully committed to him" (2 Chronicles 16:9). *Jennifer Benson Schuldt*

While God does see our sin, He sees and takes interest in our good deeds as well.

BEARING THE BURDEN OF WRONGS

1 Peter 3:8–14

Do not repay evil with evil. —1 Peter 3:9

On January 30, 2018, almost thirty-eight years after his conviction, Malcolm Alexander walked out of prison a free man. DNA evidence cleared Alexander, who had steadfastly maintained his innocence amid a myriad of court proceedings that were tragically unjust. An incompetent defense attorney (later disbarred), shoddy evidence, and dubious investigative tactics all put an innocent man in prison for nearly four decades. When he was finally released, however, Alexander showed immense grace. "You cannot be angry," he said. "There's not enough time to be angry."

Alexander's words are evidence of a deep grace in his life. If injustice robbed us of thirty-eight years of our lives and destroyed our reputations, we would likely be angry— furious even. Although Alexander spent many long, heartbreaking years bearing the burden of wrongs inflicted upon him, he wasn't undone by the evil. Rather than exerting his energy trying to get revenge, he exhibited the posture Peter instructs: "Do not repay evil with evil or insult with insult" (1 Peter 3:9).

The Scriptures go a step further: rather than seeking vengeance, the apostle Peter tells us we are to bless others (v. 9). We extend forgiveness, the hope of well-being, for those who have unjustly wronged us. Without excusing their evil actions, we can meet them with God's scandalous mercy. On the cross, Jesus bore the burden of our wrongs, that we might receive grace and extend it to others—even those who have wronged us.   *Winn Collier*

We are to extend forgiveness, the hope of well-being, for those who have unjustly wronged us.

GRACE: THE HEART OF THE GOSPEL

Romans 4:13–18

It was not through the law that Abraham and his offspring
received the promise that he would be heir of the world, but
through the righteousness that comes by faith. —Romans 4:13

What makes Christianity different from all the other religions of the world? Years ago, that very question was discussed at a conference. Some of the participants argued that Christianity is unique in teaching that God became man. But someone objected, saying that other religions teach similar doctrines. What about the resurrection? No, it was argued, other faiths believe that the dead rise again. The discussion grew heated.

C. S. Lewis, a strong defender of Christianity, came in late, sat down, and asked, "What's the rumpus about?" When he learned that it was a debate about the uniqueness of Christianity, he immediately commented, "Oh, that's easy. It's grace."

How right he was! The very heart of the gospel is the supreme truth that God accepts us with no conditions whatever when we put our trust in the atoning sacrifice of His incarnate Son. Although we are helplessly sinful, God in grace forgives us completely. It's by His infinite grace that we are saved, not by moral character, works of righteousness, commandment keeping, or churchgoing. When we do nothing else but accept God's total pardon, we receive the guarantee of eternal life (Titus 3:4–7).

Grace is good news indeed. What a gospel! What a Savior!

Vernon Grounds

**Although we are helplessly sinful, God
in grace forgives us completely.**

FEBRUARY

"All Hail the Power of Jesus' Name"

Edward Perronet and John Rippon

Hail Him who saves you by His Grace.

What Can the Power of Jesus's Name Do?

Let's start with a story—a missionary story. They are often the most heartwarming.

Reverend E. P. Scott's heart was burdened for the people of India. In the early 1800s, Edward and his wife Anna left Britain's shores to witness to those who had never heard the gospel. While in India, they discovered there was a mountain tribe known for its savagery. The Indian people who heard of Rev. Scott's desire to reach out to this people group advised him not to go. It was too dangerous.

As Scott gathered his violin and a small bag for the two-day walk to the village, his friends told him, "We will never see you again."

Sources: "History of Hymns: 'All Hail the Power of Jesus' Name,'" Discipleship Ministries of The United Methodist Church, http://tinyurl.com/3e3bm49w; "The Story Behind the Song—'All Hail the Power of Jesus' Name,'" *Church Choir Music,* http://tinyurl.com/5y6d7pnx; all accessed November 6, 2023.

When Scott finally reached the area where the people lived, a circle of menacing tribesmen surrounded him, pointing their spears at him. He fell to his knees, carefully picked up his violin, closed his eyes, and began to play and sing, in the Indian dialect, "All hail the power of Jesus' name, let angels prostrate fall." When he got to the third verse—"Let every nation, every tribe . . ."—he opened his eyes.

The men had lowered their spears as tears ran down their faces.

Scott was invited into the village, where he stayed for two years, proclaiming the gospel of grace through Jesus Christ.

"All Hail the Power of Jesus' Name" first appeared in print in 1779 in a publication called the *Gospel Magazine*, produced by Augustus M. Toplady, the man who wrote "Rock of Ages."

Speaking of connections, Edward Perronet, the writer of the hymn, was a friend of John Wesley. Wesley, a well-known preacher, encouraged Perronet to do a little preaching of his own. Perronet was not interested.

One day, however, when they were at the same church, Wesley announced, "Brother Perronet will now speak." Standing before the rather large congregation, Perronet proclaimed, "I will now deliver the greatest sermon ever preached on earth." Upon that proclamation, he opened his Bible, read Jesus's Sermon on the Mount, and sat down.

When Perronet first wrote the original version of "All Hail the Power" in 1779, it had eight verses. He titled it "On the Resurrection, the Lord Is King." The original words have been altered greatly over the years from that original version. Perronet wrote no music for his verses, so churches of the day would adapt the words to fit a common tune.

Later, other writers added parts of the current song. The portion that says, "Oh that, with yonder sacred throng, we at his feet may fall, join in the everlasting song, and crown Him Lord of all" was written in 1787 by John Rippon.

The tune we sing now, known by the title "Miles Lane," was composed by William Shrubsole, an organist in London.

Perronet's song, which touched the hearts of a group of men in India so long ago and continues to touch hearts today, has been called "The National Anthem of Christendom."

All Hail the Power of Jesus's Name

All hail the power of Jesus's name!
Let angels prostrate fall;
Bring forth the royal diadem,
And crown Him Lord of all;
Bring forth the royal diadem,
And crown Him Lord of all.

O seed of Israel's chosen race
Now ransomed from the fall;
Hail Him who saves you by His grace,
And crown Him Lord of all;
Hail Him who saves you by His grace,
And crown Him Lord of all.

Let ev'ry kindred, every tribe,
On this terrestrial ball;
To Him all majesty ascribe,
And crown Him Lord of all;
To Him all majesty ascribe,
And crown Him Lord of all.

TRUST IN HIS NAME

Psalm 9:7–12

Those who know your name trust in you, for you, LORD,
have never forsaken those who seek you. —Psalm 9:10

When I was a child, there was a time I dreaded going to school. Some girls were bullying me by subjecting me to cruel pranks. So, during recess, I'd take refuge in the library, where I read a series of Christian storybooks. I remember the first time I read the name "Jesus." Somehow, I knew this was the name of someone who loved me. In the months that followed, whenever I'd enter school fearful of the torment that lie ahead, I'd pray, "Jesus, protect me." I'd feel stronger and calmer, knowing He was watching over me. In time, the girls grew tired of bullying me and stopped.

Many years have passed, and trusting His name continues to sustain me through difficult times. Trusting His name is believing that what He says about His character is true, allowing me to rest in Him.

David too knew the security of trusting in God's name. When he wrote Psalm 9, he'd already experienced God as the all-powerful ruler who is just and faithful (vv. 7–8, 10, 16). David thus showed his trust in God's name by going into battle against his enemies, trusting not in his weapons or military skill, but in God ultimately coming through for him as "a refuge for the oppressed" (v. 9).

As a little girl, I called on His name and experienced how He lived up to it. May we always trust His name—Jesus—the name of the One who loves us.

Karen Huang

Trusting His name is believing that what He says about His character is true, allowing us to rest in Him.

GOD'S GENTLE GRACE

Ephesians 4:2–15

Be completely humble and gentle; be patient, bearing
with one another in love. —Ephesians 4:2

"Tell all the truth but tell it slant," the nineteenth-century American poet Emily Dickinson wrote. She was suggesting that because God's truth and glory are far "too bright" for vulnerable human beings to understand or receive all at once, it's best for us to receive and share God's grace and truth in "slant"—gentle, indirect—ways. For "the Truth must dazzle gradually, or every man be blind."

The apostle Paul made a similar argument in Ephesians 4 when he urged believers to be "completely humble and gentle" and to "be patient, bearing with one another in love" (v. 2). The foundation for believers' gentleness and grace with each other, Paul explained, is Christ's gracious ways with us. In His incarnation (vv. 9–10), Jesus revealed himself in the quiet, gentle ways people needed in order to trust and receive Him.

And He continues to reveal himself in such gentle, loving ways—gifting and empowering His people in just the ways they need to continue to grow and mature—"so that the body of Christ may be built up until we all reach unity in the faith and in the knowledge of the Son of God and become mature" (vv. 12–13). As we grow, we become less vulnerable to looking elsewhere for hope (v. 14) and more confident in following Jesus's example of gentle love (vv. 15–16).

Monica La Rose

Jesus continues to reveal himself in such gentle, loving ways.

"SELF" IN THE BALANCE

James 4:1–10

For by the grace given me I say to every one of you: Do not think of yourself more highly than you ought. —Romans 12:3

A man stepped on the scales in a penny arcade and was delighted with the statement on the card he received from the weighing device. Handing it to his wife, he said, "Here, look at this!" She took it and read aloud, "You are dynamic, a born leader, handsome, and much admired by women for your personality." Giving it a second look, she added, "Hmmm, I see it's got your weight wrong too!" We may smile at that crestfallen egotist; yet he portrays a danger we all face: pride.

Indeed, there's nothing that stunts the growth of God's people as much as self-assertion, self-conceit, and self-indulgence. This concentration on the "big I" manifests itself in several ways. There's the pride of nationality, of social status, or of mental or physical superiority. There's also a form of egotism that we may classify as self-pity. Such an individual feeds on attention and is easily upset if not constantly pampered by others.

We need Paul's admonition not to think too highly of ourselves. Rather, we should accurately measure our God-given abilities and praise Him for anything He finds usable.

Do you want a new infusion of power in your life? Then walk in submissive fellowship with the Lord, for He gives grace to the humble (James 4:6).   *Henry Bosch*

We should accurately measure our God-given abilities and praise God for anything He finds usable.

TRUE GREATNESS

Mark 10:35–45

Whoever wants to become great among you
must be your servant. —Mark 10:43

Some people feel like a small pebble lost in the immensity of the Grand Canyon. But no matter how insignificant we judge ourselves to be, we can be greatly used by God.

In a sermon early in 1968, Martin Luther King Jr. quoted Jesus's words from Mark 10 about servanthood. Then he said, "Everybody can be great, because everybody can serve. You don't have to have a college degree to serve. You don't have to make your subject and your verb agree to serve. You don't have to know about Plato and Aristotle to serve. . . . You only need a heart full of grace, a soul generated by love."

When Jesus's disciples quarreled about who would get the places of honor in heaven, He told them: "Whoever wants to become great among you must be your servant, and whoever wants to be first must be slave of all. For even the Son of Man did not come to be served, but to serve, and to give his life as a ransom for many" (Mark 10:43–45).

I wonder about us. Is this our understanding of greatness? Are we gladly serving, doing tasks that may be unnoticed? Do we serve to please our Lord rather than to gain the applause of people? If we are willing to be a servant, we can achieve true greatness.

Vernon Grounds

**"Everybody can be great, because everybody
can serve." —Martin Luther King Jr.**

PLODDING FOR GOD

Hebrews 6:9–12

We want each of you to show this same diligence
to the very end, so that what you hope for
may be fully realized. —Hebrews 6:11

The people raised in the English village with William Carey (1761–1834) probably thought he wouldn't accomplish much, but today he's known as the father of modern missions. Born to parents who were weavers, he became a not-too-successful teacher and cobbler while teaching himself Greek, Hebrew, and Latin. After many years, he realized his dream of becoming a missionary to India. But he faced hardship, including his child's death, his wife's mental-health problems, and for many years the lack of response from those he served.

What kept him serving amid difficulties as he translated the entire Bible into six languages and parts of it into twenty-nine others? "I can plod," he said. "I can persevere in any definite pursuit." He committed to serving God no matter what trials he encountered.

This kind of continued devotion to Christ is what the writer to the Hebrews counseled. He called for those reading his letter to not "become lazy" (Hebrews 6:12), but to "show this same diligence to the very end" (v. 11) as they sought to honor God. He reassured them that God "will not forget your work and the love you have shown" (v. 10).

During William Carey's later years, he reflected on how God consistently supplied his needs. "He has never failed in His promise, so I cannot fail in my service to Him." May God also empower us to serve Him day by day. *Amy Boucher Pye*

God "will not forget your work and the love
you have shown." —Hebrews 6:10

TELL IT!

Luke 8:26–39

The man went away and told all over town how
much Jesus had done for him. —Luke 8:39

The year was 1975 and something significant had just happened to me. I needed to find my friend Francis, with whom I shared a lot of personal matters, and tell him about it. I found him in his apartment hurriedly preparing to go out, but I slowed him down. The way he stared at me, he must have sensed I had something important to tell him. "What is it?" he asked. So, I told him simply, "Yesterday I surrendered my life to Jesus!"

Francis looked at me, sighed heavily, and said, "I've felt like doing the same for a long time now." He asked me to share what happened, and I told him how the previous day someone had explained the gospel to me and how I asked Jesus to come into my life. I still remember the tears in his eyes as he too prayed to receive Jesus's forgiveness. No longer in a hurry, he and I talked and talked about our new relationship with Christ.

After Jesus healed the man with an evil spirit in the Gerasenes, He told him, "Return home and tell how much God has done for you" (Luke 8:39). The man didn't need to preach a powerful sermon; he simply needed to share his story.

No matter what our conversion experience is, we can do what that man did: "[He] went away and told . . . how much Jesus had done for him" (v. 39). *Lawrence Darmani*

**The man who had been healed didn't need to preach a
powerful sermon; he simply needed to share his story.**

GRACE IS AMAZING

Ephesians 2:1–10

That in the coming ages he might show the
incomparable riches of his grace. —Ephesians 2:7

In his book *What's So Amazing About Grace?* Philip Yancey says
that "the world thirsts for grace in ways it does not even recognize." He writes, "Little wonder the hymn 'Amazing Grace' edged
its way onto the Top Ten charts two hundred years after composition." In the 1970s, both Judy Collins and a British military band
recorded versions of the song that made the Top Ten list.

The hymn's composer John Newton, who was once an infidel
and a slave trader, had been thirsty for grace. After he discovered the
grace of God, he never ceased to be amazed. And people have never
ceased singing his song, "Amazing Grace."

But what is grace? Paul summed up its countless virtues by calling them "incomparable riches" (Ephesians 2:7). He spelled out
some of those riches in Ephesians 2. Grace is God's favor bestowed
on undeserving people (v. 1); God's instrument for bringing salvation to each believer (v. 8); God's provision of spiritual fellowship
with others (vv. 5–6); and God's creative influence, equipping the
believer to fulfill God's purposes (v. 10).

God's grace is not only amazingly rich but it's also free. Yancey
points out, "Grace is free only because the giver himself has borne
the cost."

Let's drink deeply of God's amazing grace so we will be grace
dispensers to a thirsty world. *Joanie Yoder*

God's grace is not only amazingly rich but it's also free.

A BLIND MAN'S PLEA

Luke 18:35–43

Jesus, Son of David, have mercy on me! —Luke 18:38

Some years ago, a traveling companion noticed I was straining to see objects at a distance. What he did next was simple but life-changing. He took off his glasses and said, "Try these." When I put his glasses on, I was surprised that my blurred vision cleared up. Eventually, I went to an optometrist, who prescribed glasses to correct my vision problem.

Today's reading in Luke 18 features a man with no vision at all. Existing in total darkness had forced him to beg for a living. News about Jesus, the popular teacher and miracle worker, had reached the blind beggar's ears. So, when Jesus's travel route took Him near where the blind man was sitting, hope was ignited in his heart. "Jesus, Son of David, have mercy on me!" (v. 38) he called. Although he was without sight physically, the man possessed spiritual insight into Jesus's true identity and faith in Him to meet his need. Compelled by this faith, "he shouted all the more, 'Son of David, have mercy on me!'" (v. 39). The result? Jesus banished his blindness, and he went from begging for a living to blessing God because he could see (v. 43).

In moments or seasons of darkness, where do you turn? Upon what or to whom do you call? Eyeglass prescriptions help improve vision, but it's the merciful touch of Jesus, God's Son, that brings people from spiritual darkness into indescribable light.

Arthur Jackson

The former blind man went from begging for a living to blessing God because he could see.

HELP NEEDED

Hebrews 4:9–16

Let us then approach God's throne of grace with
confidence, so that we may receive mercy and find grace
to help us in our time of need. —Hebrews 4:16

During World War II, the British Isles represented the last line
of resistance against the sweep of Nazi oppression in Europe.
Under relentless attack and in danger of collapse, however, Britain
lacked the resources needed to see the conflict through to victory.
For that reason, British Prime Minister Winston Churchill went on
BBC Radio and appealed to the world: "Give us the tools, and we
will finish the job." He knew that without help from the outside,
the British could not endure the assault they were facing.

Life is like that. Often, we are inadequate for the troubles life
throws at us, and we need help from outside of ourselves. As members
of the body of Christ, that help can come at times from our
Christian brothers and sisters (Romans 12:10–13)—and this is a
wonderful thing. Ultimately, however, we seek help from our heavenly
Father. The good and great news is that our God has invited
us to come confidently before Him: "Let us then approach God's
throne of grace with confidence, so that we may receive mercy and
find grace to help us in our time of need" (Hebrews 4:16).

At such times, our greatest resource is prayer—for it brings us
into the very presence of God. There we find, in His mercy and
grace, the help we need.   *Bill Crowder*

Our God has invited us to come confidently before Him.

GRACE-FILLED WAITING

2 Corinthians 4:7–18

We do not lose heart. —2 Corinthians 4:16

Roger lost his job due to his company being downsized. For months he searched, applied for jobs, prayed, asked others to pray, and trusted God. Roger's and his wife Jerrie's emotions fluctuated, though. They saw God provide for them in unexpected ways and experienced His grace, but sometimes they worried that a job would never come. For fifteen long months, they waited.

Then Roger had three interviews with a company, and a week later the employment agency called and said, "Have you heard the saying, 'Sometimes clouds have a silver lining'? Well, you've got the job!" Jerrie told me later, "We wouldn't trade this hard experience for anything. It brought us closer together and closer to the Lord." Friends who had prayed rejoiced and gave thanks to God.

Paul wanted the Corinthian church to see the grace of God at work in his life, which could cause "thanksgiving to overflow to the glory of God" (2 Corinthians 4:15). His trials were so severe that he was "hard pressed on every side," "perplexed," "persecuted," and "struck down" (vv. 8–9). Yet he encouraged the people not to lose heart in their troubles (v. 16) but to trust God. During our difficulties, we can be drawn nearer to God and others, as Roger and Jerrie experienced, and praise will go to the Lord for His grace.

Anne Cetas

**He encouraged the people not to lose
heart in troubles but to trust God.**

UNEXPECTED WINNERS

Matthew 19:17–30

Many who are first will be last, and many who
are last will be first. —Matthew 19:30

Perhaps the most preposterous, spellbinding moment in the 2018
Winter Olympics was when the Czech Republic's world champion snowboarder Ester Ledecka won an event in a completely different sport: skiing! And she took the first-place gold medal even though she had the unenviable position of skiing 26th—a feat believed to be basically impossible.

Amazingly, Ledecka qualified to race the women's super-G—an event that combines downhill skiing with a slalom course. After she won by .01 of a second on borrowed skis, she was just as shocked as the media and other contestants who had assumed the winner would be one of the top skiers.

This is how the world works. We assume the winners will keep winning while all the others will lose. It was a jolt, then, when the disciples heard Jesus say how "hard [it is] for someone who is rich to enter the kingdom of heaven" (Matthew 19:23). Jesus turned everything upside down. How could being rich (a winner) offer a roadblock? Apparently, if we trust in what we have (what we can do, who we are), then it's not only hard but actually impossible to trust God.

The kingdom of God doesn't play by our rules. "Many who are first," Jesus says, "will be last, and many who are last will be first" (v. 30). And whether you're first or last, everything we receive is purely by grace—by God's unmerited favor. *Winn Collier*

The kingdom of God doesn't play by our rules.

THE IMMENSITY OF GOD'S LOVE

Psalm 8

When I consider . . . the moon and the stars, . . . what is
mankind . . . that you care for them? —Psalm 8:3–4

How big is the universe? If you ask an astronomer, he'll tell you
the universe contains trillions of stars and the most distant
galaxies are billions of light-years away. Not just thousands or millions or even billions of stars but trillions of them, spread out across
the vast expanse of space!

Incomprehensible figures like this make some people conclude it
is impossible to believe the Bible, for the earth and humans seem so
utterly insignificant. But these mind-boggling dimensions need not
shake our faith. Instead, they can increase our awe as we ponder the
message of divine grace. In Psalm 8, for example, the author marvels at God's creation and mankind's smallness, and then he breaks
out in praise for God's greatness and care for us.

How amazing that the Creator who made and upholds all this
immensity has focused His redemptive love on tiny creatures like
us—and sinful creatures at that! He cherishes us individually as if
each one were the sole object of His fatherly attention. It's amazing,
as Paul testified, that Christ "loved me and gave himself for me"
(Galatians 2:20).

Instead of shaking our faith, the findings of astronomy can fill
our souls with wonder. The immensity of God's creation reminds
us of the immensity of God's love.   *Vernon Grounds*

**The immensity of God's creation reminds
us of the immensity of God's love.**

A NEW BEGINNING

Psalm 120:1–121:2

Save me, LORD, from lying lips and from
deceitful tongues. —Psalm 120:2

"Christian consciousness begins in the painful realization that what we had assumed was the truth is in fact a lie," Eugene Peterson wrote in his powerful reflections on Psalm 120. Psalm 120 is the first of the Psalms of Ascents (Psalms 120–134) sung by pilgrims on their way to Jerusalem. And as Peterson explored this in *A Long Obedience in the Same Direction*, these psalms also offer us a picture of the spiritual journey toward God.

That journey can only begin with profound awareness of our need for something different. As Peterson puts it, "A person has to be thoroughly disgusted with the way things are to find the motivation to set out on the Christian way. . . . [One] has to get fed up with the ways of the world before he, before she, acquires an appetite for the world of grace."

It's easy to become discouraged by the brokenness and despair we see in the world around us—the pervasive ways our culture often shows callous disregard for the harm being done to others. Psalm 120 laments this honestly: "I am for peace; but when I speak, they are for war" (v. 7).

But there's healing and freedom in realizing that our pain can also awaken us to a new beginning through our only help, the Savior, who can guide us from destructive lies into paths of peace and wholeness (121:2). During each new day, let us seek Him and His ways.

Monica La Rose

**Our Savior can guide us from destructive lies
into paths of peace and wholeness.**

FOR LOVE'S SAKE

Romans 12:9–18

Be devoted to one another in love. Honor one
another above yourselves. —Romans 12:10

Running a marathon is about pushing yourself, physically and
mentally. For one high school runner, however, competing in
a cross-country race is all about pushing someone else. In every
practice and meet, fourteen-year-old Susan Bergeman pushes her
older brother, Jeffrey, in his wheelchair. When Jeffrey was twenty-
two months old, he went into cardiac arrest—leaving him with
severe brain damage and cerebral palsy. Today, Susan sacrifices personal running goals so Jeffrey can compete with her. What love
and sacrifice!

The apostle Paul had love and sacrifice in mind when he encouraged his readers to be "devoted to one another" (Romans 12:10).
He knew that the believers in Rome were struggling with jealousy,
anger, and sharp disagreements (v. 18). So he encouraged them to
let divine love rule their hearts. This kind of love, rooted in Christ's
love, would fight for the highest possible good of others. It would
be sincere, and it would lead to generous sharing (v. 13). Those who
love this way are eager to consider others more worthy of honor
than themselves (v. 16).

As believers in Jesus, we're running a race of love while helping
others finish the race too. Though it can be difficult, it brings honor
to Jesus. So, for love's sake, let's rely on Him to empower us to love
and serve others.   *Marvin Williams*

**As believers in Jesus, we're running a race of love
while helping others finish the race too.**

LAW AND GRACE

Galatians 3:1–12

For what the law was powerless to do because it was weakened
by the flesh, God did by sending his own Son in the
likeness of sinful flesh to be a sin offering. —Romans 8:3

L aw and grace are complete opposites. Notice the contrast.
The law prohibits; grace invites and gives.

The law condemns sinners; grace redeems them.

The law says, "Do," while grace says, "It's done."

The law curses; grace blesses.

The law slays sinners; grace makes them alive.

The law shuts every mouth before God; grace opens it in praise to Him.

The law condemns the best of people, while grace saves the worst.

The law says, "Pay what you owe." Grace says, "I freely forgive you all."

The law says, "The wages of sin is death." Grace declares, "The gift of God is eternal life."

The law says, "The soul that sins, it will die." Grace says, "Believe and live."

By the law is the knowledge of sin; by grace is redemption from sin. The law was given by Moses, but grace and truth came by Jesus Christ. The law demands obedience, while grace provides power to obey.

Here's the bottom line: The law puts us under bondage, while grace sets us free in the wonderful liberty of the sons of God!

"Christ is the culmination of the law so that there may be righteousness for everyone who believes" (Romans 10:4). Have you believed?

M. R. DeHaan

Grace sets us free in the wonderful liberty of the sons of God.

SHINING LIGHT

Matthew 5:13–16

Let your light shine before others, that they may see your good
deeds and glorify your Father in heaven. —Matthew 5:16

I felt nervous about a five-week prayer class I agreed to teach at
a local church. Would the students like it? Would they like me?
My anxiety was ill-focused, leading me to over-prepare lesson plans,
presentation slides, and class handouts. Yet with a week to go, I still
hadn't encouraged many people to attend.

In prayer, however, I was reminded that the class was a service
that shined light on God. Because the Holy Spirit would use the
class to point people to our heavenly Father, I could set aside my
nervousness about public speaking. When Jesus taught His disciples in His Sermon on the Mount, He told them, "You are the light
of the world. A town built on a hill cannot be hidden. Neither do
people light a lamp and put it under a bowl. Instead they put it
on its stand, and it gives light to everyone in the house" (Matthew
5:14–15).

Reading those words, I finally sent out a class announcement on
social media. Almost immediately, people started registering—expressing gratitude and excitement. Seeing their reactions, I reflected
more on Jesus's teaching: "Let your light shine before others, that
they may see your good deeds and glorify your Father in heaven"
(v. 16).

With that perspective, I taught the class with joy. I pray that my
simple deed becomes a beacon and encourages others to shine their
light for God as well.   *Patricia Raybon*

**One simple deed can be a beacon that
encourages others to shine for Jesus.**

PUT THIS ON EVERY DAY

Romans 13:11–14

Let us put aside the deeds of darkness and put
on the armor of light. —Romans 13:12

I was so excited to put on my new glasses for the first time, but after just a few hours I wanted to throw them away. My eyes ached and my head throbbed from adjusting to the new prescription. My ears were sore from the unfamiliar frames. The next day I groaned when I remembered I had to wear them. I had to repeatedly choose to use my glasses each day so my body could adjust to them. It took several weeks, but after that, I hardly noticed I was wearing them.

Putting on something new requires an adjustment, but over time we grow into it, and it suits us better. We may even see things we didn't see before. In Romans 13, the apostle Paul instructed Christ followers to "put on the armor of light" (v. 12) and practice right living. They had already believed in Jesus, but it seems they had fallen into "slumber" and become complacent (v. 11). They needed to "wake up" and take action, behave decently, and let go of all sin. Paul encouraged them to be clothed with Jesus and become more like Him in their thoughts and deeds (v. 14).

We don't begin to reflect the loving, gentle, kind, grace-filled, and faithful ways of Jesus overnight. It's a long process of choosing to "put on the armor of light" every day, even when we don't want to because it's uncomfortable. Over time, He changes us for the better.

Karen Pimpo

**Be clothed with Jesus and become more like
Him in our thoughts and deeds.**

SEVEN MINUTES OF TERROR

John 11:38–43

*Let us then approach God's throne of grace
with confidence.* —Hebrews 4:16

When the Mars rover *Perseverance* landed on that red planet on February 18, 2021, the men and women monitoring its arrival endured "seven minutes of terror." As the spacecraft ended its 292-million-mile journey, it went through a complex landing procedure it had to do on its own. Signals from Mars to Earth take several minutes, so NASA couldn't hear from *Perseverance* during the landing. Not being in contact was frightening for the team, who had put so much effort and resources into the mission.

Sometimes we may experience our own times of fear when we feel we're not hearing from God—we pray but we don't get answers. In Scripture, we find people getting answers to prayer quickly (see Daniel 9:20–23) and others not getting answers for a long time (see Hannah's story in 1 Samuel 1:10–20). Perhaps the most poignant example of a delayed answer—one that surely struck terror in the hearts of Mary and Martha—was when they asked Jesus to help their sick brother Lazarus (John 11:3). Jesus delayed, and their brother died (vv. 6–7, 14–15). Yet four days later, Christ answered by resurrecting Lazarus (vv. 43–44).

Waiting for answers to our prayers can be difficult. But God can comfort and help as we "approach [His] throne of grace with confidence, . . . that we may receive mercy and find grace to help us in our time of need" (Hebrews 4:16).   *Dave Branon*

**Waiting for answers to our prayers is difficult. But
God can comfort and help as we "approach [His]
throne of grace with confidence." —Hebrews 4:16**

A GOOD TESTIMONY

Hebrews 11:17–40

These were all commended for their faith, yet none of them
received what had been promised. —Hebrews 11:39

Some lists can be boring, but not the one in Hebrews 11. It's
an impressive list of Old Testament believers and their amazing accomplishments. However, the writer kept interspersing the
words "by faith," because his emphasis was strictly faith, not fame.
Through faith these people obtained a good testimony (v. 39), but
was there always a good outcome?

In verses 33–35, the writer highlighted those who by faith sub-
dued kingdoms, stopped the mouths of lions, and escaped the edge
of the sword. But then he mentioned "others" who were tortured
and killed—those for whom sudden reprieves never came (vv. 35–
38). Did they obtain a bad testimony? No! Verse 39 says that all of
them—both the delivered and the undelivered—obtained a good
testimony, for they all had acted in faith.

We can assume that each of them had asked the Lord for help.
But while some received deliverance, others received an answer similar to the one given to Paul when he pleaded for his "thorn" to be removed: "My grace is sufficient for you, for my power is made perfect
in weakness" (2 Corinthians 12:9).

Be greatly encouraged! Whenever you act in faith and in God's
strength, you are obtaining a good testimony before Him—no matter what the outcome.   *Joanie Yoder*

**Whenever you act in faith and in God's strength,
you are obtaining a good testimony before Him.**

DEMONSTRATING GRACE

Micah 7:18–20

You will tread our sins underfoot and hurl all our
iniquities into the depths of the sea. —Micah 7:19

"In moments where tragedy happens or even hurt, there are opportunities to demonstrate grace or to exact vengeance," the recently
bereaved man remarked. "I chose to demonstrate grace." Pastor Erik
Fitzgerald's wife had been killed in a car accident caused by an exhausted firefighter who fell asleep while driving home. Legal prosecu-
tors wanted to know whether he would seek the maximum sentence.
The pastor chose to practice the forgiveness he often preached about.
To the surprise of both him and the firefighter, the men eventually
became friends.

Pastor Erik was living out of the grace he'd received from God,
who'd forgiven him all of his sins. Through his actions, he echoed
the words of the prophet Micah, who praised God for pardoning sin
and forgiving when we do wrong (Micah 7:18). The prophet uses
wonderfully visual language to show just how far God goes in forgiving His people, saying that He will "tread our sins underfoot" and
hurl our wrongdoings into the deep sea (v. 19). The firefighter received a gift of freedom that day, which brought him closer to God.

Whatever difficulty we face, we know that God reaches out to
us with loving, open arms, welcoming us into His safe embrace. He
"delight[s] to show mercy" (v. 18). As we receive His love and grace,
He gives us the strength to forgive those who hurt us—even as Pastor Erik did.   *Amy Boucher Pye*

**God reaches out to us with loving, open arms,
welcoming us into His safe embrace.**

BRAIDED TOGETHER

Ecclesiastes 4:9–12

A cord of three strands is not quickly
broken. —Ecclesiastes 4:12

A friend gave me a houseplant she'd owned for more than forty years. The plant was equal to my height, and it produced large leaves from three separate spindly trunks. Over time, the weight of the leaves had caused all three of the stalks to curve down toward the floor. To straighten them, I put a wedge under the plant's pot and placed it near a window so the sunlight could draw the leaves upward and help cure its bad posture.

Shortly after receiving the plant, I saw one just like it in a waiting room at a local business. It also grew from three long skinny stalks, but they'd been braided together to form a larger, more solid core. This plant stood upright without any help.

Any two people may stay in the same "pot" for years, yet grow apart and experience fewer of the benefits God wants them to enjoy. When their lives are woven together with God, however, there is a greater sense of stability and closeness. Their relationship will grow stronger. "A cord of three strands is not quickly broken" (Ecclesiastes 4:12).

Like houseplants, marriages and friendships require nurturing. Tending to these relationships involves merging spiritually so that God is present at the center of each important bond. He's an endless supply of love and grace—the things we need most to stay happily united with each other. *Jennifer Benson Schuldt*

**When two lives are woven together with God, however,
there is a greater sense of stability and closeness.**

WORKING OFF BAD INFORMATION

Proverbs 23:9–12

Apply your heart to instruction and your ears to
words of knowledge. —Proverbs 23:12

On a trip to New York City, my wife and I wanted to brave a
snowy evening and hire a taxi for a three-mile ride from our
hotel to a Cuban restaurant. After entering the details into the taxi
service's app, I gulped hard when the screen revealed the price for
our short jaunt: $1,547.26. After recovering from the shock, I real-
ized I had mistakenly requested a ride to our home—several hundred miles away!

If you're working with the wrong information, you're going to
end up with disastrous results. Always. This is why Proverbs encourages us to "apply [our] heart to instruction and [our] ears to
words of knowledge"—God's wisdom (Proverbs 23:12). If we instead seek advice from those who are foolish, those who pretend to
know more than they do and who have turned their back on God,
we'll be in trouble. They "scorn . . . prudent words" and can lead us
astray with unhelpful, misguided, or even deceptive advice (v. 9).

Instead, we can bend our "ears to words of knowledge" (v. 12).
We can open our heart to receive God's liberating instruction, His
words of clarity and hope. When we listen to those who know the
deep ways of God through His Word, they help us receive and follow divine wisdom. God's wisdom will never lead us astray. It always
encourages and leads us toward life and wholeness.   *Winn Collier*

When we listen to those who know the deep
ways of God through His Word, they help
us receive and follow divine wisdom.

THIS IS GRACE

Acts 2:32–41

God has made this Jesus, whom you crucified,
both Lord and Messiah. —Acts 2:36

The classic Victor Hugo novel *Les Misérables* begins with paroled convict Jean Valjean stealing a priest's silver. He's caught, and he expects to be returned to the mines. But the priest shocks everyone when he claims he'd given the silver to Valjean. After the police leave, he turns to the thief and says, "You belong no longer to evil, but to good."

Such extravagant love points to the love that flowed from the fountain from which all grace comes. On the day of Pentecost, Peter told his audience that less than two months before, in that very city, they had crucified Jesus. The crowd was crushed and asked what they must do. Peter replied, "Repent and be baptized, every one of you, in the name of Jesus Christ for the forgiveness of your sins" (Acts 2:38). Jesus had endured the punishment they deserved. Now their penalty would be forgiven if they put their faith in Him.

Oh, the irony of grace. The people could only be forgiven because of Christ's death—a death they were responsible for. How gracious and powerful is our God! He has used humanity's greatest sin to accomplish our salvation. If God has already done this with the sin of crucifying Jesus, we may assume there's nothing He can't turn into something good. Trust the One who "in all things . . . works for the good of those who love him" (Romans 8:28).

Mike Wittmer

**How gracious and powerful is our God! He has used
humanity's greatest sin to accomplish our salvation.**

GATHERING STRENGTH IN GOD

2 Corinthians 12:2–10

When I am weak, then I am strong. —2 Corinthians 12:10

Grainger McKoy is an artist who studies and sculpts birds, capturing their grace, vulnerability, and power. One of his pieces is titled *Recovery*. It shows the single right wing of a pintail duck, stretched high in a vertical position. Below, a plaque describes the bird's recovery stroke as "the moment of the bird's greatest weakness in flight, yet also the moment when it gathers strength for the journey ahead." Grainger includes this verse: "My grace is sufficient for you, for my power is made perfect in weakness" (2 Corinthians 12:9).

The apostle Paul wrote these words to the church at Corinth. Enduring a season when he was overwhelmed with personal struggle, Paul begged God to remove what he described as "a thorn in my flesh" (v. 7). His affliction might have been a physical ailment or spiritual opposition. Like Jesus in the garden the night before His crucifixion (Luke 22:39–44), Paul repeatedly asked God to remove his suffering. The Holy Spirit responded by assuring him that He would provide the needed strength. Paul learned, "When I am weak, then I am strong" (2 Corinthians 12:10).

Oh, the thorns we experience in this life! Like a bird gathering its strength for the journey ahead, we can gather up God's strength for what we're facing. In His strength, we find our own.   *Elisa Morgan*

The Holy Spirit responded to Paul by assuring him that He would provide the needed strength.

EXPECT AND EXTEND MERCY

Luke 18:9–14

God, have mercy on me, a sinner. —Luke 18:13

When I complained that a friend's choices were leading her deeper into sin and how her actions affected me, the woman I prayed with weekly placed her hand over mine. "Let's pray for all of us."

I frowned. "All of us?"

"Yes," she said. "Aren't you the one who always says Jesus sets our standard of holiness, so we shouldn't compare our sins to the sins of others?"

"That truth hurts a little," I said, "but you're right. My judgmental attitude and spiritual pride are no better or worse than her sins."

"And by talking about your friend, we're gossiping. So—"

"We're sinning." I lowered my head. "Please, pray for us."

In Luke 18, Jesus shared a parable about two men approaching the temple to pray in very different ways (vv. 9–14). Like the Pharisee, we can become trapped in a circle of comparing ourselves to other people. We can boast about ourselves (vv. 11–12) and live as though we have the right to judge and the responsibility or the power to change others.

But when we look to Jesus as our example of holy living and encounter His goodness firsthand, like the tax collectors, our desperate need for God's grace is magnified (v. 13). As we experience the Lord's loving compassion and forgiveness personally, we'll be forever changed and empowered to expect and extend mercy, not condemnation, to others.

Xochitl Dixon

When we look to Jesus as our example of holy living, our desperate need for God's grace is magnified.

A SERMON AT SUNRISE

2 Corinthians 5:17–21

Go into all the world and preach the gospel
to all creation. —Mark 16:15

Walking along the shores of the Gulf of Mexico as the sun is beginning to rise over the eastern horizon is a wonderful way to start the day. In the quietness of the morning hour, the communion one experiences with the God of creation is most blessed.

Once as I was enjoying such a morning, I saw a middle-aged man partially submerged in the water. "Good morning!" he called. As he struggled to his feet, I could see that he was experiencing excruciating pain. He seemed to want to talk, so I listened. What a story of bitterness and resentment!

Having studied law and about to enter practice, he was called into military service. While serving, he contracted an illness that left him maimed in body and embittered in soul. As he poured out his heart, he expressed the whole gamut of human emotion—charging me and the whole world with guilt for his condition. Slapping the water with his hands in anger, the tears began streaming down his cheeks as he continued to complain.

Finally, I asked, "Wouldn't you like to trust Christ right now as your Savior?" "Yes, I would," he responded. So, right there, standing knee deep in the Gulf of Mexico, we bowed our heads and prayed. When we finished, he looked up and said, "No one has ever talked with me this way before." He had never been confronted personally with the gospel of God's grace!

What a reminder to be open to any opportunity to talk about our Savior!   *Richard DeHaan*

Be open to any opportunity to talk about our Savior!

A STEWARD OF GRACE

1 Corinthians 15:1–11

Each of you should use whatever gift you have received to serve
others, as faithful stewards of God's grace. —1 Peter 4:10

I remember the week when I had several opportunities to show
grace. I wasn't flawless, of course, but I was pleased with the way
I handled one situation in particular. Instead of getting angry, I had
said, "I understand how that could have happened. I've certainly
made my share of mistakes." And I left it at that.

According to my own grading scale, I deserved a high score. Not
perfect, but close. Lurking in the back of my mind (I hate to admit)
was the thought that maybe by being gracious I could expect to be
treated that way at some future date.

The following Sunday morning our congregation was singing "Amazing Grace," and suddenly the audacity of my attitude
came through to me in the words, "Amazing grace! How sweet the
sound—that saved a wretch like me."

What in the world was I thinking?! The grace we show to others
is not our own. The only reason we can "give" grace to anyone is
because God has already given it to us. We can pass along only that
which we have received from Him.

Good stewards look for opportunities to pass along to others what
we have received from the Lord. May all of us be "faithful stewards of
God's grace" (1 Peter 4:10).   *Julie Ackerman Link*

**The only reason we can "give" grace to anyone
is because God has already given it to us.**

POWER IN PRAISE

2 Chronicles 20:15–22

Praise the LORD, for His mercy endures
forever. —2 Chronicles 20:21 NKJV

Willie Myrick was kidnapped from his driveway when he was nine years old. For hours, he traveled in a car with his kidnapper, not knowing what would happen to him. During that time, Willie decided to sing a song called "Every Praise." As he repeatedly sang the words, his abductor spewed profanity and told him to shut up. Finally, the man stopped the car and let Willie out—unharmed.

As Willie demonstrated, truly praising the Lord requires us to concentrate on God's character while forsaking what we fear, what is wrong in our lives, and the self-sufficiency in our hearts.

The Israelites reached this place of surrender when they faced attackers. As they prepared for battle, King Jehoshaphat organized a choir to march out in advance of their enemy's army. The choir sang, "Praise the LORD, for His mercy endures forever" (2 Chronicles 20:21 NKJV). When the music started, Israel's enemies became confused and destroyed each other. As the prophet Jahaziel had predicted, Israel didn't need to fight at all (v. 17).

Whether we're facing a battle or feeling trapped, we can glorify God in our hearts—and with our lips. Truly, "Great is the LORD and most worthy of praise" (Psalm 96:4).   *Jennifer Benson Schuldt*

**Truly praising the Lord requires us to concentrate
on God's character while forsaking what we fear.**

EXTRA GRACE REQUIRED

Ephesians 2:1–10

For it is by grace you have been saved, through
faith . . . not by works. —Ephesians 2:8–9

While we decorated for a special event at church, the woman in charge griped about my inexperience. After she walked away, another woman approached me. "Don't worry about her. She's what we call an EGR—Extra Grace Required."

I laughed. Soon I started using that label every time I had a conflict with someone. Years later, I sat in that same church sanctuary listening to that EGR's obituary. The pastor shared how she had served God behind the scenes and given generously to others. I asked God to forgive me for judging and gossiping about her and anyone else I'd labeled as an EGR in the past. After all, I needed extra grace as much as any other believer in Jesus.

In Ephesians 2, the apostle Paul states that all believers were "by nature deserving of wrath" (v. 3). But God gave us the gift of salvation, a gift we did nothing to deserve—a gift we'd never be able to earn "so that no one can boast" (v. 9). No one.

As we submit to God moment by moment during this lifelong journey, the Holy Spirit will work to change our character so we can reflect the character of Christ. Every believer requires extra grace. But we can be grateful that God's grace is sufficient (2 Corinthians 12:9).

Xochitl Dixon

**God gave us the gift of salvation, a gift
which we did nothing to deserve.**

SONGS OF GRACE

MARCH

"Grace Greater Than Our Sin"

Julia H. Johnston and Daniel Towner

*Marvelous grace of our loving Lord, grace
that exceeds our sin and our guilt!*

More Than a Songwriter

After Julia Harriette Johnston died in March 1919, an *Associated Press* newspaper article about Johnston described her as "one of the most noted hymn writers of America." The list of gospel songs she wrote was long—more than five hundred in all. But it was a song she wrote in 1910 that most raised her profile as a songwriter.

The words to what would become the song we know as "Grace Greater Than Our Sin" were penned by someone who was more than a songwriter. Johnston, the daughter of a Presbyterian pastor

---

Sources: "Julia H. Johnston," Wikipedia, http://tinyurl.com/p5cp398r; "Gospel Songwriter Dies" (article clipped from *The Salina Evening Journal*), *Newspapers .com*, http://tinyurl.com/4dbphj52; "Grace Greater Than Our Sin," *Hymn Studies* (blog), http://tinyurl.com/yzkfd39m; T. Wes Moore. "Grace Greater Than Our Sin," Discipleship Ministries of The United Methodist Church, http://tinyurl.com /mr48pdck; all accessed November 6, 2023.

in Peoria, Illinois, was also a prolific producer of Sunday school curriculum for David C. Cook Publishing Company.

It is thought that her explanation of Romans 5 in the verses of this song was an attempt to do something women were not expected to do in her day: write biblical commentary. But she did that, both in song and in her curriculum.

Another of her songs that might be somewhat familiar to today's Christians is "He Ransomed Me." It can be found in many hymnals, including *Great Hymns of the Faith*.

Johnston also wrote numerous books, including notable books of missionary stories. Her love for missions led her to serve as president of the Presbyterian Mission Society of Peoria for twenty years. One of her books about Christians in overseas ministry, *Fifty Missionary Heroes Every Boy and Girl Should Know*, has been reprinted and can still be ordered online today.

The music for Johnston's verses for "Grace Greater than Our Sin" was composed by well-known musician and educator Dr. Daniel B. Towner in the same year Johnston wrote the words. Towner served for many years as the head of the music department at Moody Bible Institute. In addition to writing the music for "Grace Greater than Our Sin," Dr. Towner also composed the music for other standards such as "Trust and Obey" and "At Calvary."

The collaborative effort of Johnston and Towner resulting in "Grace That Is Greater" was first published in *Hymns Tried and True* in 1911.

Grace Greater Than Our Sin

Marvelous grace of our loving Lord,
Grace that exceeds our sin and our guilt!
Yonder on Calvary's mount out-poured—
There where the blood of the Lamb was spilt.

> *Chorus:*
> Grace, grace, God's grace,
> Grace that will pardon and cleanse within;
> Grace, grace, God's grace,
> Grace that is greater than all our sin!

PRINCIPLES OF GENEROSITY

Proverbs 11:24–34

A generous person will prosper; whoever refreshes
others will be refreshed. —Proverbs 11:25

Many years ago, two young men were working their way through
Stanford University. At one point, their money was almost
gone, so they decided to engage the great pianist Paderewski for a
concert and use the profits for board and tuition. Paderewski's manager asked for a guarantee of $2,000. The students worked hard to
promote the concert, but they came up $400 short. After the per-
formance, they went to the musician, gave him all the money they
had raised, and promised to pay the $400 as soon as they could. It
appeared that their college days were over. "No, boys, that won't do,"
said the pianist. "Take out of this $1,600 all your expenses, and keep
for each of you ten percent of the balance for your work. Let me have
the rest."

Years passed. Paderewski became premier of Poland following
World War I. Thousands of his countrymen were starving. Only
one man could help—the head of the US Food and Relief Bureau.
Paderewski's appeal to him brought thousands of tons of food.
Later, he met the American statesman to thank him. "That's all
right," replied Herbert Hoover. "Besides, you don't remember, but
you helped me once when I was a student in college."

The principle of generosity set forth in Proverbs 11:25 finds its
origin in God. He is overflowing in His goodness, lavish in His
mercy, and abounding in His grace. How inconceivable that we His
creatures, especially His redeemed children, could be greedy and selfish! Remember, generosity is part of God's way of taking care of us.

Dennis DeHaan

**God is overflowing in His goodness, lavish in
His mercy, and abounding in His grace.**

GROWING IN GOD'S GRACE

2 Peter 1:3–11

Make every effort to add to your faith goodness;
and to goodness, knowledge. —2 Peter 1:5

English preacher Charles H. Spurgeon lived life "full throttle." He became a pastor at age nineteen and soon was preaching to large crowds. He personally edited all his sermons, which eventually filled sixty-three volumes, and he wrote many commentaries, books on prayer, and other works. And he typically read six books a week! In one of his sermons, Spurgeon said, "The sin of doing nothing is about the biggest of all sins, for it involves most of the others. . . . Horrible idleness! God save us from it!"

Spurgeon lived with diligence, which meant he "[made] every effort" (2 Peter 1:5) to grow in God's grace and to live for Him. If we're Christ's followers, God can instill in us that same desire and capacity to grow more like Jesus, to "make every effort to add to [our] faith goodness; and to goodness, knowledge . . . self-control, perseverance . . . godliness" (vv. 5–7)

We each have different motivations, abilities, and energy levels—not all of us can, or should, live at Charles Spurgeon's pace! But when we understand all Jesus has done for us, we have the greatest motivation for diligent, faithful living. And we find our strength through the resources God has given us to live for and serve Him. God through His Spirit can empower us in our efforts—big and small—to do so.   *Alyson Kieda*

When we understand all Jesus has done for us, we have the greatest motivation for diligent, faithful living.

WITHIN A STONE'S THROW

John 7:53–8:11

Let any one of you who is without sin be the
first to throw a stone at her. —John 8:7

As a group of religious leaders herded an adulterous woman toward Jesus, they couldn't know they were carrying her within a stone's throw of grace. Their hope was to discredit Him. If He told them to let the woman go, they could claim He was breaking Mosaic law. But if He condemned her to death, the crowds following Him would have dismissed His words of mercy and grace.

But Jesus turned the tables on the accusers. Scripture says that rather than answering them directly, He started writing on the ground. When the leaders continued to question Him, He invited any of them who had never sinned to throw the first stone, and then He started writing on the ground again. The next time He looked up, all the accusers were gone.

Now the only person who could have thrown a stone—the only sinless one—looked at the woman and gave her mercy. "'Then neither do I condemn you,' Jesus declared. 'Go now and leave your life of sin'" (John 8:11).

Whether today finds you needing forgiveness for judging others or desiring assurance that no sin is beyond His grace, be encouraged by this: No one is throwing stones today; go and be changed by God's mercy. *Randy Kilgore*

The only sinless one looked at the woman and gave her mercy.

A TIME WITH GOD

Hebrews 4:14–16

But as for me, it is good to be near God. I have made
the Sovereign LORD my refuge. —Psalm 73:28

A woman desiring to pray grabbed an empty chair and knelt before it. In tears, she said, "My dear heavenly Father, please sit down here; you and I need to talk!" Then, looking directly at the vacant chair, she prayed. She demonstrated confidence in approaching the Lord; she imagined He was sitting on the chair, and she believed He was listening to her petition.

A time with God is an important moment when we engage the Almighty. God comes near to us as we draw near to Him in a mutual involvement (James 4:8). He has assured us, "I am with you always" (Matthew 28:20). Our heavenly Father is always waiting for us to come to Him, always ready to listen to us.

There are times when we struggle to pray because we feel tired, sleepy, sick, or weak. But Jesus sympathizes with us when we are weak or face temptations (Hebrews 4:15). Therefore, we can "approach God's throne of grace with confidence, so that we may receive mercy and find grace to help us in our time of need" (v. 16).

Lawrence Darmani

**Our heavenly Father is always waiting for us to
come to Him, always ready to listen to us.**

TERRIBLE AND BEAUTIFUL THINGS

Psalm 57

Awake, my soul! Awake, harp and lyre! I will
awaken the dawn. —Psalm 57:8

Fear can leave us frozen. We know all the reasons to be afraid—everything that's hurt us in the past and everything that could easily do so again. So sometimes we're stuck—unable to go back; too afraid to move forward. *I'm not smart enough, strong enough, or brave enough to handle being hurt like that again.*

I'm captivated by how author Frederick Buechner (1926–2022) described God's grace: like a gentle voice that says, "Here is the world. Terrible and beautiful things will happen. Don't be afraid. I am with you."

Terrible things will happen. In our world, hurting people hurt other people, often terribly. Like the psalmist David, we carry our own stories of when evil surrounded us, when, like "ravenous beasts," others wounded us (Psalm 57:4). And so, we grieve; we cry out (vv. 1–2).

But because of our faith in Jesus, God is with us, and beautiful things can happen too. As we run to Him with our hurts and fears, we find ourselves carried by a love far greater than anyone's power to harm us (vv. 1–3), a love so deep it fills the skies (v. 10). Even when disaster rages around us, His love is a solid refuge where our hearts find healing (vv. 1, 7). Then we can find ourselves awakening to renewed courage, ready to greet the day with a song of His faithfulness (vv. 8–10). *Monica La Rose*

God's love is a solid refuge where our hearts find healing.

UNEXPECTED KINDNESS

Ephesians 2:1–10

For we are God's handiwork, created in Christ
Jesus to do good works. —Ephesians 2:10

My friend was waiting to pay for her groceries when the man in front of her turned around and handed her a voucher for £10 ($14) off her bill. Short on sleep, she burst into tears because of his kind act; then she started laughing at herself for crying. This unexpected kindness touched her heart and gave her hope during a period of exhaustion. She gave thanks to the Lord for His goodness extended to her through another person.

The apostle Paul wrote about the theme of giving in his letter to gentile Christians in Ephesus. He called them to leave their old lives behind and embrace the new, reminding them that they were saved by grace (2:5). Out of this saving grace, he explained, flows our desire to "do good works," for we have been created in God's image and are His "handiwork" (v. 10). We, like the man at the supermarket, can spread God's love through our everyday actions.

Of course, we don't have to give material things to share God's grace; we can show His love through many other actions. We can take the time to listen to someone who speaks to us. We can ask someone who is serving us how he or she is doing. We can stop to help someone in need. As we give to others, we'll receive blessing in return (Acts 20:35). *Amy Boucher Pye*

We can spread God's love through our everyday actions.

WHEN GOD SAYS NO

Isaiah 25:1–5

In perfect faithfulness you have done wonderful
things, things planned long ago. —Isaiah 25:1

When I was conscripted into the military at age eighteen, as all young Singaporean men are, I prayed desperately for an easy posting. A clerk or driver, perhaps. Not being particularly strong, I hoped to be spared the rigors of combat training. But one evening as I read my Bible, one verse leaped off the page: "My grace is sufficient for you" (2 Corinthians 12:9).

My heart dropped—but it shouldn't have. God had answered my prayers. Even if I received a difficult assignment, He would provide for me.

So, I ended up as an armored infantryman, doing things I didn't always enjoy. Looking back, I'm grateful God didn't give me what I wanted. The training and experience toughened me physically and mentally, and it gave me confidence to enter adulthood.

In Isaiah 25:1–5, after prophesying Israel's punishment and subsequent deliverance from her enemies, the prophet praises God for His plans. All these "wonderful things," Isaiah notes, had been "planned long ago" (v. 1), yet they included some arduous times.

It can be hard to hear God saying no, and it's even harder to understand when we're praying for something good—like someone's deliverance from a crisis. This is when we need to hold on to the truth of God's good plans. We may not understand why, but we can keep trusting in His love, goodness, and faithfulness.   *Leslie Koh*

We need to hold on to the truth of God's good plans.

OUR GUILT IS GONE

Psalm 32:1–11

I said, "I will confess my transgressions to the LORD."
And you forgave the guilt of my sin. —Psalm 32:5

As a young girl, I invited a friend to browse with me through a gift shop near my home. She shocked me, though, by shoving a handful of colorful crayon-shaped barrettes into my pocket and yanking me out the door of the shop without paying for them. Guilt gnawed at me for a week before I approached my mom—my confession pouring out as quickly as my tears.

Grieved over my bad choice of not resisting my friend, I returned the stolen items, apologized, and vowed never to steal again. The owner told me never to come back. But because my mom forgave me and assured me that I had done my best to make things right, I slept peacefully that night.

King David also rested in forgiveness through confession (Psalm 32:1–2). He had hidden his sins against Bathsheba and Uriah (2 Samuel 11–12) until his "strength was sapped" (Psalm 32:3–4). But once David refused to "cover up" his wrongs, the Lord erased his guilt (v. 5). God protected him "from trouble" and wrapped him in "songs of deliverance" (v. 7). David rejoiced because the "LORD's unfailing love surrounds the one who trusts in him" (v. 10).

We can't choose the consequences of our sins or control people's responses when we confess and seek forgiveness. But the Lord can empower us to enjoy freedom from the bondage of sin and peace through confession, as He confirms that our guilt is gone—forever.

Xochitl Dixon

**The Lord can empower us to enjoy freedom from the
bondage of sin and peace through confession.**

I JUST CAN'T DO IT

1 Corinthians 1:26–31

The law was our tutor to bring us to Christ, that we
might be justified by faith. —Galatians 3:24 NKJV

"I just can't do it!" lamented the dejected student. On the page he
could see only small print, difficult ideas, and an unforgiving
deadline. He needed his teacher's help.

We might experience similar despair when we read Jesus's Sermon on the Mount. "Love your enemies" (Matthew 5:44). Anger
is as bad as murder (v. 22). Lust equals adultery (v. 28). And if we
dare think we can live up to these standards, we bump into this: "Be
perfect, therefore, as your heavenly Father is perfect" (v. 48).

"The Sermon on the Mount produces despair," says Oswald
Chambers. But he saw this as good, because at "the point of despair
we are willing to come to [Jesus] as paupers to receive from Him."

In the counterintuitive way God so often works, those who know
they can't do it on their own are the ones who receive God's grace. As
the apostle Paul put it, "Not many of you were wise by human standards. . . . But God chose the foolish things of the world to shame
the wise" (1 Corinthians 1:26–27).

In God's wisdom, the Teacher is also our Savior. When we come
to Him in faith, through His Spirit we enjoy His "righteousness,
holiness and redemption" (v. 30), and the grace and power to live
for Him. That's why He could say, "Blessed are the poor in spirit,
for theirs is the kingdom of heaven" (Matthew 5:3). *Tim Gustafson*

**Those who know they can't do it on their own
are the ones who receive God's grace.**

PLAYING WITH JOY

Galatians 5:22–26

The fruit of the Spirit is . . . joy. —Galatians 5:22

One of our sons, Brian, is a high school basketball coach. One year, as his team was dribbling its way through the Washington state basketball tournament, well-meaning folks around town asked, "Are you going to win it all this year?" Both players and coaches felt the pressure, so Brian adopted a motto: "Play with joy!"

I thought of the apostle Paul's last words to the elders of Ephesus: "That I may finish my race with joy" (Acts 20:24 NKJV). His aim was to complete the tasks Jesus had given him. I have made these words my motto and my prayer: "May I run and finish my race with joy." Or as Brian says, "May I play with joy!" And by the way, Brian's team did win the state championship that year.

We all have good reasons to get grouchy: world news, everyday stresses, health problems. Nevertheless, God can give us a joy that transcends these conditions if we ask Him. We can have what Jesus called "my joy" (John 15:11).

Joy is a fruit of the Spirit of Jesus (Galatians 5:22). So, we must remember each morning to ask Him to help us: "May I play with joy!" Author Richard Foster said, "To pray is to change. This is a great grace. How good of God to provide a path whereby our lives can be taken over by . . . joy."

David Roper

**God can give us a joy that transcends
everyday stresses if we ask Him.**

DYING WITH CERTAINTY

2 Timothy 4:6–18

The Spirit himself testifies with our spirit that
we are God's children. —Romans 8:16

Over a period of a few months, I visited two dying people—a man of eighty-two and a woman of fifty-two. Neither wanted to die. Both were greatly loved by their families. Each had many reasons for wanting to keep on living. Along with many others, I prayed earnestly for their healing, but God had other plans.

As soon as these two people realized God wasn't going to heal them, I saw an amazing transformation in them. They both displayed a calm acceptance of death. Their faces took on a new glow, and from their lips came words of testimony and praise. They knew they were God's children and had the assurance that they would soon be with Jesus in heaven. The peace and joy they radiated brought comfort to their loved ones and friends.

What was the source of such absolute certainty in the face of dying? It wasn't what any of those who ministered to them said or did. No, it was supernatural grace imparted by the indwelling Holy Spirit. Paul put it like this: "The Spirit himself testifies with our spirit that we are God's children" (Romans 8:16).

Praise God! No one who trusts Christ as Savior and walks in fellowship with Him needs to dread the hour of death.

Herb Vander Lugt

**The source of such absolute certainty is supernatural
grace imparted by the indwelling Holy Spirit.**

MERCY OVER JUDGMENT

James 2:1–13

Speak and act as those who are going to be judged
by the law that gives freedom. —James 2:12

When my children were squabbling and came to me to tattle on one another, I took each child aside separately to hear his or her account of the problem. Since both were guilty, at the end of our chat I asked them each what they felt would be an appropriate, fair consequence for their sibling's actions. Both suggested swift punishment for the other. To their surprise, I instead gave them each the consequence they had intended for their sibling. Suddenly, each child lamented how "unfair" the sentence seemed now that it was visited upon them—despite having deemed it appropriate when it was intended for the other.

My kids had shown the kind of "judgment without mercy" that Scripture warns against (James 2:13). James reminds us that instead of showing favoritism to the wealthy, or even to oneself, God desires that we love others as we love ourselves (v. 8). Instead of using others for selfish gain, or disregarding anyone whose position doesn't benefit us, according to James we should act as people who know how much we've been given and forgiven—and then extend that mercy to others.

God has given generously of His mercy. In all our dealings with others, let's remember the mercy He's shown us and extend it to others. *Kirsten Holmberg*

God desires that we love others as we love ourselves.

TELL YOUR STORY

1 Timothy 1:12–20

Your awe-inspiring deeds will be on every tongue; I
will proclaim your greatness. —Psalm 145:6 NLT

Michael Dinsmore, a former prisoner and relatively new Christian, was asked to give his testimony in a prison. After he spoke, some inmates came to him and said, "This is the most exciting meeting we've ever been to!" Michael was amazed that God could use his simple story.

In 1 Timothy, after Paul had charged Timothy to stay the course preaching the gospel (1:1–11), he shared his personal testimony to encourage the young man (vv. 12–16). He told about God's mercy in his own life. Paul said that he had mocked the Lord, but He changed him. In His mercy, God not only counted him faithful and gave him a job to do but also enabled him to do His work (v. 12). Paul considered himself the worst of sinners, but God saved him (v. 15).

The Lord is able! That is what Paul wanted Timothy to see, and it's what we need to see too. Through Paul's testimony, we recognize God's mercy. If God could use someone like Paul, He can use us. Since God could save the worst of sinners, then no one is beyond His reach.

Our story of God's work in our lives can encourage others. Let those around you know that the God of the Bible is still at work today! *Poh Fang Chia*

**Since God could save the worst of sinners,
no one is beyond His reach.**

LIVING WITH GRACE

1 Peter 5:5–11

Clothe yourselves with humility toward one
another, because, "God opposes the proud but
shows favor to the humble." —1 Peter 5:5

As one pastor tried to explain the grace of God, he likened it to an imaginary administrative assistant who compels him to treat other people as God does. The pastor explained: "Grace is my administrative assistant, but she won't let me obey my schedule book. She lets the strangest people into my workspace to interrupt me. Somehow, she lets calls get through that I would prefer to leave for a more convenient time. Doesn't Grace know that I have an agenda? Some days I wish Grace weren't here. But Grace has an amazing way of covering my mistakes and turning the office into a holy place. Grace finds good in everything, even failures."

By God's grace—His unmerited love and favor—we have been forgiven in Christ. God tells us that instead of relating to others from a position of superiority, we must put others ahead of ourselves. We should wear the clothes of humility because He "opposes the proud but shows favor to the humble" (1 Peter 5:5).

When "the God of all grace" (v. 10) controls our lives, He can transform interruptions into opportunities, mistakes into successes, pride into humility, and suffering into strength. That's the amazing power of God. That's the evidence of His grace!   *David McCasland*

God's grace enables us to treat others with humility and love.

FOOD FROM HEAVEN

Exodus 16:4–5, 13–18

The LORD said to Moses, "I will rain down bread
from heaven for you." —Exodus 16:4

In August 2020, residents of Olten, Switzerland, were startled to find that it was snowing chocolate! A malfunction in the ventilation system of the local chocolate factory had caused chocolate particles to be diffused into the air. As a result, a dusting of edible chocolate flakes covered cars and streets, making the whole town smell like a candy store.

When I think of delicious food "magically" falling from the heavens, I can't help but think of God's provision for the people of Israel in Exodus. Following their dramatic escape from Egypt, the people faced significant challenges in the desert, especially a scarcity of food and water. And God, moved by the plight of the people, promised to "rain down bread from heaven" (Exodus 16:4). The next morning, a layer of thin flakes appeared on the desert ground. This daily provision, known as manna, continued for the next forty years.

When Jesus came to earth, people began to believe He was sent from God when He miraculously provided bread for a large crowd (John 6:5–14). But Jesus taught that He himself was the "bread of life" (v. 35), sent to bring not just temporary nourishment but eternal life (v. 51).

For those of us hungry for spiritual nourishment, Jesus extends the offer of unending life with God. In response, let's believe and trust that He came to satisfy these deepest longings. *Lisa M. Samra*

**Jesus taught that He himself is the bread
of life, sent to bring eternal life.**

ALL OF GRACE

1 Corinthians 15:1–10

By the grace of God I am what I am. —1 Corinthians 15:10

A few years before John Newton, the penman of "Amazing Grace," died, a friend was having breakfast with him. Their custom was to read from the Bible after the meal. Because Newton's eyes were growing dim, his friend would read, then Newton would comment briefly on the passage.

That day the selection was from 1 Corinthians 15. When the words "by the grace of God I am what I am" were read, Newton was silent for several minutes. Then he said, "I am not what I ought to be. How imperfect and deficient I am! I am not what I wish to be, although I abhor that which is evil and would cleave to what is good. I am not what I hope to be, but soon I shall put off mortality, and with it all sin. . . . Though I am not what I ought to be, nor what I wish to be, nor yet what I hope to be, I can truly say I am not what I once was: a slave to sin and Satan. I can heartily join with the apostle and acknowledge that by the grace of God I am what I am!"

Newton's words apply to every Christian. Because of God's goodness, we are spared much bad that we deserve and are given much good that we do not deserve. Every good thing comes from His hand.

Does humble gratitude to God characterize your life? Do you acknowledge with Paul and with John Newton, "By the grace of God I am what I am"?   *Paul Van Gorder*

**God's grace is transforming me from what
I was to what I will become.**

IT'S NOT FAIR

Psalm 103:1–10

[God] does not treat us as our sins deserve or repay
us according to our iniquities. —Psalm 103:10

"Not fair!" Whether you've said it or at least thought it, you've got to admit, it's hard to see someone get away with something and not get what they deserve.

We learn this early in life. Just ask the parent of any teenager. Kids hate to see their siblings get off scot-free for the things they were punished for. Which is why they so readily tattle on each other. But then, we never really grow out of this. To our way of thinking, fairness means sinners deserve God's wrath and we, the good people, deserve His applause.

But if God were "fair," we would all be consumed by His judgment! We can be thankful for this: "[God] does not treat us as our sins deserve" (Psalm 103:10). We should be glad, not grumpy, that God chooses mercy over fairness and that He is willing to extend grace even to those who are undeserving and hopelessly lost. And while we are thinking about it, when was the last time we let mercy trump fairness with someone who offended us?

It's not God's fairness but His mercy that drives Him to pursue us so that heaven can have a party when we are found (Luke 15:7). Personally, I'm thankful God hasn't been "fair" with us! Aren't you?

Joe Stowell

**We should be glad, not grumpy, that God is willing to extend
grace even to those who are undeserving and hopelessly lost.**

JUST THE TICKET

Ephesians 1:1–10

In him we have . . . the forgiveness of sins, in accordance
with the riches of God's grace. —Ephesians 1:7

When a police officer stopped a woman because her young daughter was riding in the car without the required booster seat, he could have written her a ticket for a traffic violation. Instead, he asked the mother and daughter to meet him at a nearby store where he personally paid for the needed car seat. The mother was going through a difficult time and could not afford to buy a seat.

Although the woman should have received a fine for her misdemeanor, she walked away with a gift instead. Anyone who knows Christ as Savior has experienced something similar. All of us deserve a penalty for breaking God's laws (Ecclesiastes 7:20). Yet, because of Jesus, we experience undeserved favor from God. This favor excuses us from the ultimate consequence for our sin, which is death and eternal separation from God (Romans 6:23). "In [Jesus] we have . . . the forgiveness of sins, in accordance with the riches of God's grace" (Ephesians 1:7).

Some refer to grace as "love in action." When the young mother experienced this, she later remarked, "I will be forever grateful! . . . And as soon as I can afford it, I will be paying it forward." This grateful and big-hearted response to the officer's gift is an inspiring example for those of us who have received the gift of God's grace!

Jennifer Benson Schuldt

Because of Jesus, we experience undeserved favor from God.

DOESN'T GOD CARE?

Habakkuk 1:1–11

"For my thoughts are not your thoughts, neither are your
ways my ways," declares the LORD. —Isaiah 55:8

Why does the intoxicated driver escape an accident unharmed while his sober victim is seriously injured? Why do bad people prosper while good people suffer? How often have you been so confused by things going on in your life that you have cried out, "Doesn't God care?"

Habakkuk struggled with this question as he saw the distressing situation in Judah, where wickedness and injustice were running rampant (Habakkuk 1:1–4). His confusion drove him to ask God when He would act to fix the situation. God's reply was nothing short of perplexing.

God said He would use the Chaldeans as the means of Judah's correction. The Chaldeans were notorious for their cruelty (v. 7). They were bent on violence (v. 9) and worshiped nothing but their military prowess and false gods (vv. 10–11).

In moments when we don't understand God's ways, we need to trust His unchanging character. This is exactly what Habakkuk did. He believed that God is a God of justice, mercy, and truth (Psalm 89:14). In the process, he learned to look at his circumstances from the framework of God's character instead of looking at God's character from the context of his own circumstances. He concluded, "The Sovereign LORD is my strength; he makes my feet like the feet of a deer, he enables me to tread on the heights" (Habakkuk 3:19).

Poh Fang Chia

**When we don't understand God's ways, we
need to trust His unchanging character.**

RESCUED

Colossians 1:12–22

He has rescued us from the dominion of darkness and brought us into the kingdom of the Son he loves. —Colossians 1:13

A South African man surprised nine men robbing his home. Seven of the robbers ran away, but the homeowner managed to shove two into his backyard pool. After realizing that one of the robbers couldn't swim, the homeowner jumped in to save him. The *Cape Times* reports that once out of the pool, the wet thief called to his friends to come back. Then he pulled a knife and threatened the man who had just rescued him. The homeowner said, "We were still standing near the pool, and when I saw the knife, I just threw him back in. But he was gasping for air and was drowning. So, I rescued him again."

In his letter to the Colossians, the apostle Paul wrote of another rescue: God the Father had saved them from the domain of darkness. This rescue occurred at the death of Christ, but also at the Colossians' conversion. The imagery Paul used (1:12–13) suggests that believers have been rescued from the dark reign of Satan by being transferred as free people into the peaceable rule of Christ. By Jesus's death, believers become free citizens in the kingdom of light.

How should we respond to such amazing grace? By showing joyous gratitude and by worshiping God with reverence and awe (Hebrews 12:28). *Marvin Williams*

Show joyous gratitude by offering God acceptable service with reverence and awe.

A MOSAIC OF BEAUTY

Luke 1:46–55

My soul glorifies the Lord and my spirit rejoices
in God my Savior. —Luke 1:46–47

Sitting in the courtyard of the Church of the Visitation in Ein Karem, Israel, I was overwhelmed with the beautiful display of sixty-seven mosaics containing the words of Luke 1:46–55 in as many languages. Traditionally known as the Magnificat, from the Latin "to magnify," these verses are Mary's joyous response to the announcement that she would be the mother of the Messiah.

Each plaque contains Mary's words, including: "My soul glorifies the Lord and my spirit rejoices in God my Savior . . . for the Mighty One has done great things for me" (vv. 46–49). The biblical hymn etched in the tiles is a song of praise as Mary recounts the faithfulness of God to her and the nation of Israel.

A grateful recipient of God's grace, Mary rejoices in her salvation (v. 47). She acknowledges that God's mercy has extended to the Israelites for generations (v. 50). Looking back over God's care for the Israelites, Mary praises God for His powerful acts on behalf of His people (v. 51). She also thanks God, recognizing that her daily provision comes from His hand (v. 53).

Mary shows us that recounting the great things God has done for us is a way to express praise and can lead us to rejoice. Consider God's goodness as you reflect on what He has done for you. In doing so, you may create a mosaic of great beauty with your words of praise.

Lisa M. Samra

**Recounting the great things God has done for us is a
way to express praise and can lead us to rejoice.**

THE TRIUMPH OF FORGIVENESS

Psalm 32:1–7

Blessed is the one whose transgressions are forgiven,
whose sins are covered. —Psalm 32:1

Mack, having struggled with drug abuse and sexual sin, was desperate. Relationships he valued were in disarray, and his conscience was beating him up. In his misery, he found himself unannounced at a church asking to speak with a pastor. There he discovered relief in sharing his complicated story and in hearing about God's mercy and forgiveness.

Psalm 32 is believed to have been composed by David after his sexual sin. He compounded his wrongdoing by devising a sinister strategy that resulted in the death of the woman's husband (see 2 Samuel 11–12). While these ugly incidents were behind him, the effects of his actions remained. Psalm 32:3–4 describes the deep struggles he experienced before he acknowledged the ugliness of his deeds; the gnawing effects of unconfessed sin were undeniable. What brought relief? He confessed to God and accepted the forgiveness He offers (v. 5).

What a great place for us to start—at the place of God's mercy—when we say or do things that cause hurt and harm to ourselves and others. The guilt of our sin need not be permanent. There's One whose arms are open wide to receive us when we acknowledge our wrongs and seek His forgiveness. We can join the chorus of those who sing, "Blessed is the one whose transgressions are forgiven, whose sins are covered" (v. 1).   *Arthur Jackson*

**When we've caused hurt, what a great place for
us to start—at the place of God's mercy.**

GOD'S MOLDED INSTRUMENTS

Isaiah 64:5–9

We are the clay, you are the potter; we are all
the work of your hand. —Isaiah 64:8

Considered one of the greatest video games ever made, Nintendo's *The Legend of Zelda: Ocarina of Time* has sold more than seven million copies worldwide. It's also popularized the ocarina, a tiny, ancient, potato-shaped musical instrument made of clay.

The ocarina doesn't look like much of a musical instrument. However, when it's played—by blowing into its mouthpiece and covering various holes around its misshapen body—it produces a strikingly serene and hauntingly hopeful sound.

The ocarina's maker took a lump of clay, applied both pressure and heat, and transformed it into an amazing musical instrument.

I see a picture of God and us here. Isaiah 64:6, 8–9 tells us: "All of us have become like one who is unclean. . . . Yet you, LORD, are our Father. We are the clay, you are the potter. . . . Do not be angry beyond measure." In effect, the prophet was saying, "God, you're in charge. We're all sinful. Shape us into beautiful instruments for you."

This is exactly what God does! In His mercy, He sent His Son, Jesus, to die for our sin, and now He's shaping and transforming us as we walk in step with His Spirit every day. Just as the ocarina maker's breath flows through the instrument to produce beautiful music, God's Holy Spirit works through us—His molded instruments—to accomplish His beautiful will: to be more and more like Jesus (Romans 8:29).   *Ruth Wan-Lau*

**The Lord is shaping and transforming us as we
walk in step with His Spirit every day.**

YOU ARE HEARD

Psalm 116:1–7

He turned his ear to me. —Psalm 116:2

In the book *Physics*, Charles Riborg Mann and George Ransom Twiss ask: "When a tree falls in a lonely forest, and no animal is nearby to hear it, does it make a sound?" Over the years, this question has prompted philosophical and scientific discussions about sound, perception, and existence. A definitive answer, however, has yet to emerge.

One night, while feeling lonely and sad about a problem I hadn't shared with anyone, I recalled this question. *When no one hears my cry for help*, I thought, *does God hear?*

Facing the threat of death and overcome by distress, the writer of Psalm 116 may have felt abandoned. So, he called out to God—knowing He was listening and would help him. "He heard my voice," the psalmist wrote, "he heard my cry for mercy. . . . He turned his ear to me" (vv. 1–2). When no one knows our pain, God knows. When no one hears our cries, God hears.

Knowing that God will show us His love and protection (vv. 5–6), we can be at rest in difficult times (v. 7). The Hebrew word translated "rest" (*manoakh*) describes a place of quiet and safety. We can be at peace, strengthened by the assurance of God's presence and help.

The question posed by Mann and Twiss led to numerous answers. But the answer to the question, Does God hear? is simply yes.

Karen Huang

We can be at peace, strengthened by the assurance of God's presence and help.

MORE THAN A LITTLE PIECE

Matthew 16:21–28

Whoever wants to be my disciple must deny themselves
and take up their cross and follow me. —Matthew 16:24

We all leave a bit of ourselves behind when we move to a new place. But to become a long-term resident of Villa Las Estrellas, Antarctica, a cold and desolate place, leaving a piece of yourself behind is a literal thing. With the nearest full-service hospital 625 miles away, a person would be in serious trouble if their appendix bursts. So, every citizen must first undergo an appendectomy before moving there.

Drastic, right? But it's not as drastic as becoming a resident of the kingdom of God. Because people want to follow Jesus on their own terms and not His (Matthew 16:25–27), He redefines what it means to be a disciple. He said, "Whoever wants to be my disciple must deny themselves and take up their cross and follow me" (v. 24). This includes being prepared to let go of anything that competes with Him and His kingdom. And as we take up our cross, we declare a willingness to undergo social and political oppression and even death for the sake of devotion to Christ. Along with letting go and taking up, we're also to take on a willingness to truly follow Him. This is a moment-by-moment posture of following His lead as He guides us into service and sacrifice.

Following Jesus means so much more than leaving a little piece of our lives behind. As He helps us, it's about submitting and surrendering our whole lives—including our bodies—to Him alone.

Marvin Williams

**Devotion to Christ is a moment-by-moment posture of
following His lead as He guides us into service and sacrifice.**

SAFE IN HIS ARMS

Isaiah 40:9–11

He tends his flock like a shepherd: He gathers the lambs in
his arms and carries them close to his heart. —Isaiah 40:11

The weather outside was threatening, and the alert on my cell
phone warned about the possibility of flash floods. An unusual
number of cars was parked in my neighborhood as parents and others gathered to pick up children at the school bus drop-off point.
By the time the bus arrived, it had started to rain. That's when I observed a woman exit her car and retrieve an umbrella from the trunk.
She walked toward a little girl and made sure the child was shielded
from the rain until they returned to the vehicle. What a beautiful
"real-time" picture of parental, protective care that reminded me of
the care of our heavenly Father.

The prophet Isaiah forecast punishment for disobedience followed by brighter days for God's people (Isaiah 40:1–8). The heavenly dispatch from the mountain (v. 9) assured the Israelites of
God's mighty presence and tender care. The good news, then and
now, is that because of God's power and ruling authority, anxious
hearts need not fear (vv. 9–10). Included in the announcement
was news about the Lord's protection, the kind of protection shepherds provide (v. 11): vulnerable young sheep would find safety in
the Shepherd's arms; nursing ewes would be led gently.

In a world where circumstances aren't always easy, such images
of safety and care compel us to look confidently to the Lord. Those
who trust wholeheartedly in the Lord find security and renewed
strength in Him (v. 31). *Arthur Jackson*

**Because of God's power and ruling authority,
anxious hearts need not fear.**

NO HANDS BUT HIS

Ephesians 3:14–21

Now to him who is able to do immeasurably more
than all we ask or imagine, according to his power
that is at work within us. —Ephesians 3:20

Jennifer had just heard a disturbing report about an increase in cases of depression among women. The report cited a related up-swing in alcoholism and an increased reliance on prescription drugs.

"So, what are you doing about it, Lord?" Jennifer prayed. But the more she thought about it, the more she felt that God was asking her to do something. All she could see, however, were her own limitations.

To help her think it through, she listed reasons that were keeping her from action: shyness, fear of getting involved, lack of time, a cold heart, feelings of inadequacy, fear of failure—a daunting list!

As she finished her list, she saw that it was time to pick up her children from school. She put on her coat, then reached for her gloves. They were lying limp and useless—until she slipped her hands inside them. At that moment she realized that God didn't want her to think about her limitations. Rather, He wanted to put His power into her and work through her, just as her gloves became useful when she put her hands into them.

Why do we feel inadequate for the work God has given us? He wants to love others through us, "according to his power that is at work within us" (Ephesians 3:20). *Joanie Yoder*

God wants to love others through us.

GRACE, MERCY, AND PEACE

2 Timothy 1:1–10

Bless the LORD, . . . who crowns you with lovingkindness
and tender mercies. —Psalm 103:1, 4 NKJV

The words *grace* and *peace* are found in all of Paul's greetings in his New Testament letters to the churches. And in his letters to Timothy and Titus, he also includes *mercy*: "Grace, mercy and peace from God the Father and Christ Jesus our Lord" (2 Timothy 1:2). Let's examine each of these words.

Grace is what our holy God gives that we, as sinful people, don't deserve. In Acts 17:25, we learn that He "gives everyone life and breath and everything else." His gifts include our very next breath. Even in our darkest hour, God gives us strength so we can endure.

Mercy is what God withholds that we do deserve. In Lamentations 3:22, we read, "Through the LORD's mercies we are not consumed" (NKJV). Even when we're wayward, God gives time and help for us to turn back to Him.

Peace is what God brings to His people. Jesus said: "Peace I leave with you; my peace I give you. I do not give to you as the world gives" (John 14:27). Even in the worst of times, we have inner tranquility because our God is in control.

We can be encouraged that throughout our lives the Lord will give us the grace, mercy, and peace we need to live for Him.

Albert Lee

**Even in the worst of times, we have inner
tranquility because our God is in control.**

WHAT'S TRULY NEEDED

Mark 7:8–13

You have let go of the commands of God and are
holding on to human traditions. —Mark 7:8

While preparing a meal, a young mother cut a pot roast in half before she put it in a large pot. Her husband asked her why she cut the meat in half. She replied, "Because that's the way my mother does it."

Her husband's question, however, piqued the woman's curiosity. So, she asked her mother about the tradition. She was shocked to learn that her mother cut the meat so it would fit in the one small pot she used. Because her daughter had many large pots, cutting the meat was unnecessary.

Many traditions begin out of a necessity but are carried on without question—becoming "the way we do it." It's natural to want to hold on to human traditions—something the Pharisees were doing in Mark 7:1–2. They were distracted by what seemed like the breaking of one of their religious rules.

As Jesus said to the Pharisees, "You have let go of the commands of God and are holding on to human traditions" (v. 8). He revealed that traditions should never replace the wisdom of Scripture. A genuine desire to follow God (vv. 6–7) will focus on the attitude of our heart rather than outward actions.

It's a good idea to consistently evaluate traditions—anything we hold close to our heart and follow religiously. The things that God has revealed to be truly needed should always supersede traditions.

Katara Patton

**A genuine desire to follow God will focus on the
attitude of our heart rather than outward actions.**

COME HOME

Psalm 91:1–2, 14–16

He is my refuge and my fortress, my God,
in whom I trust. —Psalm 91:2

One early evening, while I was jogging near a construction site in our neighborhood, a skinny, dirty kitten meowed at me plaintively and followed me home. Today, Mickey is a healthy, handsome adult cat, enjoying a comfortable life in our household and deeply loved by my family. Whenever I jog on the road where I found him, I often think, "Thank you, God. Mickey was spared from living on the streets. He has a home now."

Psalm 91 speaks of "[dwelling] in the shelter of the Most High" (v. 1), making our home with God. The Hebrew word for *dwell* here means "to remain," to stay permanently. As we remain in Him, He helps us live according to His wisdom and to love Him above all (Psalm 91:14; John 15:10). God promises us the comfort of being with Him for eternity, as well as the security of His being with us through earthly hardship. Although trouble may come, we can rest in His sovereignty, wisdom, and love, and in His promises to protect and deliver us.

When we make God our refuge, we live "in the shadow of the Almighty" (Psalm 91:1). No trouble can touch us except that which His infinite wisdom and love allow. This is the safety of God as our home.   *Karen Huang*

God promises us the comfort of being with Him for eternity, as well as the security of His being with us through earthly hardship.

SHOW US

John 14:1–11

Anyone who has seen me has seen the Father. —John 14:9

At four months old, Leo had never seen his parents. He'd been born with a rare condition that left his vision blurred. For him, it was like living in dense fog. But then his eye doctors fit him with a special set of glasses.

Leo's father posted the video of Mom placing the new glasses over his eyes for the first time. We watch as Leo's eyes slowly focus. A smile spreads wide across his face as he truly sees his mom for the first time. Priceless. In that moment, little Leo could see.

John reports a conversation Jesus had with His disciples. Philip asked Him, "Show us the Father" (John 14:8). Even after all this time together, Jesus's disciples couldn't recognize who was right in front of them. He replied, "Don't you believe that I am in the Father, and that the Father is in me?" (v. 10). Earlier Jesus had said, "I am the way and the truth and the life" (v. 6). This is the sixth of Jesus's seven "I am" statements. He's telling us to look through these "I am" lenses and see who He truly is—God himself.

We are a lot like the disciples. In difficult times we struggle and develop blurred vision. We fail to focus on what God has done and can do. When little Leo put on the special glasses, he could see his parents clearly. Perhaps we need to put on our God-glasses so we can clearly see who Jesus really is. *Kenneth Petersen*

**Jesus tells us to look through the "I am" lenses
and see who He truly is—God himself.**

APRIL

"At the Cross"

Isaac Watts and Ralph Hudson

Amazing pity! Grace unknown!

A Cure for Boring Songs

Isaac Watts was not your average kid growing up in Southern England in the early eighteenth century. For instance, by the time he was thirteen years old, he had not only mastered the King's English but he also knew Latin, Greek, French, and Hebrew.

So, when he and his father had a discussion about church music, and young Isaac explained that he thought the music was both monotonous and less than inspiring, this wasn't the rant of a rebellious kid. It was a reasoned argument from an intelligent young man. Interestingly, Isaac's dad (also named Isaac) agreed with his young prodigy, telling him, "Write something better."

There was one catch to the plan. In most churches of the early

Sources: Angie Mosteller, "History of 'Alas! And Did My Savior Bleed (At the Cross),'" Celebrating Holidays, https://www.celebratingholidays.com/?page _id=11343; Clarence L. Haynes Jr. "Who Wrote 'Alas, and Did My Savior Bleed'?" *Christianity.com*, http://tinyurl.com/4tkhbay5; all accessed November 6, 2023.

1700s, it was customary and indeed expected that music sung in church had to be directly taken from Scripture.

Young Isaac set out to write a song for his congregation anyway, and when he presented it one Sunday, the congregation enthusiastically accepted it. This kicked off a two-year period in which he wrote several songs for his church.

The song "Alas! and Did My Savior Bleed" was probably written during this period, and it appeared in a 1707 hymnal by Watts called *Hymns and Spiritual Songs*. The song "Alas . . ." was popular on both sides of the Atlantic, and it has been said that Fanny Crosby was greatly influenced by this song.

Back in Britain, many critics still panned Watts's new songs because they were not limited to the exact words of Scripture. Fortunately, Watts was able to stay above that fray and continued to write, giving us such grand worship songs as "When I Survey the Wondrous Cross," "O God, Our Help in Ages Past," and, of course, what has become a Christmas standard, "Joy to the World."

Today, we often refer to the song "Alas! and Did My Savior Bleed" as "At the Cross." However, we need to acknowledge that this part of the song wasn't written by Watts. This is why some hymnals today contain two different songs with Watts's words—using both titles. In 1885, an American preacher and song writer named Ralph Hudson added a chorus to Watts's song. It says, "At the cross, at the cross where I first saw the light, and the burden of my heart rolled away—it was there by faith I received my sight, and now I am happy all the day!"

So, today's "At the Cross" is a collaboration by two Christian song writers who lived in two different centuries.

Alas! and Did My Savior Bleed

Alas! and did my Savior bleed,
And did my Sovereign die!
Would he devote that sacred head
For such a worm as I?

Was it for crimes that I have done,
He groaned upon the tree?

Amazing pity! Grace unknown!
And love beyond degree!

> *Chorus:*
> At the cross, at the cross
> Where I first saw the light,
> And the burden of my heart rolled way—
> It was there by faith
> I received my sight,
> And now I am happy all the day.

INTO OUR STORMS

Mark 4:35–41

[Jesus] got up, rebuked the wind and said to the
waves, "Quiet! Be still!" Then the wind died down
and it was completely calm. —Mark 4:39

Wind howled, lightning flashed, waves crashed, and I thought I was going to die.

My grandparents and I were fishing on a lake, but we'd stayed out too long. As the sun set, a fast-moving squall swept over our small boat. My grandfather instructed me to sit in front to keep it from capsizing. Terror flooded my heart. But then, somehow, I began to pray. I was fourteen.

I asked God for His reassurance and protection. The storm didn't weaken, but we made it to shore. To this day, I don't know if I've experienced a deeper certainty of God's presence than that night in the storm.

Jesus is no stranger to storms. In Mark 4:35–41, He told His disciples to head across a lake that would soon turn windy and wild. The storm that night tested and bested these rugged fishermen. They too thought they were going to die. But Jesus calmed the water and then led His disciples to deeper faith.

Likewise, Jesus invites us to trust Him in our storms. Sometimes He miraculously stills the winds and the waves. Sometimes He does something equally miraculous: He steadies our hearts and helps us to trust Him. He asks us to rest in the belief that He has the power to say to the waves, "Quiet! Be still!"   *Adam Holz*

Jesus invites us to trust Him in our storms.

TEARS OF A TEEN

Romans 9:1–5

*I have great sorrow and unceasing anguish
in my heart. —Romans 9:2*

As I sat with four teenagers and a twentysomething homeless man at a soup kitchen in Alaska, I was touched by the teens' compassion for him. They listened as he talked about what he believed, and then they gently presented the gospel to him—lovingly offering him hope in Jesus. Sadly, the man refused to seriously consider the gospel.

As we were leaving, one of the girls, Grace, expressed through her tears how much she didn't want the man to die without knowing Jesus. From the heart, she grieved for this young man who, at least at this point, was rejecting the love of the Savior.

The tears of this teen remind me of the apostle Paul, who served the Lord humbly and had great sorrow in his heart for his countrymen, desiring that they trust in Christ (Romans 9:1–5). Paul's compassion and concern must have brought him to tears on many occasions.

If we care enough for others who have not yet accepted God's gift of forgiveness through Christ, we will find ways to share with them. With the confidence of our own faith and with tears of compassion, let's take the good news to those who need to know the Savior. *Dave Branon*

**Let's take the good news to those who
need to know the Savior.**

WHO IS THAT?

2 Samuel 12:1–14

David said to Nathan, "I have sinned against
the LORD." Nathan replied, "The LORD has
taken away your sin." —2 Samuel 12:13

When a man installed a security camera outside his house, he
checked the video feature to ensure that the system was working. He was alarmed to see a broad-shouldered figure in dark clothing
wandering around his yard. He watched intently to see what the man
would do. The interloper seemed familiar, however. Finally, he realized he wasn't watching a stranger roam his property, but a recording
of himself in his own backyard!

What might we see if we could step out of our skin and observe
ourselves in certain situations? When David's heart was hardened
and he needed an outside perspective—a godly perspective—on
his involvement with Bathsheba, God sent Nathan to the rescue
(2 Samuel 12).

Nathan told David a story about a rich man who robbed a poor
man of his only lamb. Although the rich man owned herds of animals, he slaughtered the poor man's lone sheep and made it into a
meal. David "burned with anger" (v. 5). But when Nathan revealed
that the story illustrated David's actions, David realized how he had
harmed Uriah, Bathsheba's husband. Nathan explained the consequences, but more important, he assured David, "The LORD has
taken away your sin" (v. 13).

If God reveals sin in our lives, His ultimate purpose isn't to condemn us but to restore us and help us reconcile with those we've hurt.
Repentance clears the way for renewed closeness with God through
the power of His forgiveness and grace.   *Jennifer Benson Schuldt*

Repentance clears the way for renewed closeness with God.

WISDOM AND GRACE

James 1:1–8

If any of you lacks wisdom, you should ask God,
who gives generously to all without finding fault,
and it will be given to you. —James 1:5

On April 4, 1968, American civil rights leader Dr. Martin Luther King Jr. was assassinated, leaving millions angry and disillusioned. In Indianapolis, a predominately Black crowd of Americans had gathered to hear Robert F. Kennedy speak. Many had not yet heard of Dr. King's death, so Kennedy had to share the tragic news. He appealed for calm by acknowledging not only their pain but also his own abiding grief over the murder of his brother, President John F. Kennedy.

Kennedy then quoted a variation of an ancient poem by Aeschylus (526–456 BC): *Even in our sleep, pain which cannot forget falls drop by drop upon the heart until, in our own despair, against our will, comes wisdom through the awful grace of God.*

"Wisdom through the awful grace of God" is a remarkable statement. It means that God's grace fills us with awe and gives us the opportunity to grow in wisdom during life's most difficult moments.

James wrote, "If any of you lacks wisdom, you should ask God, who gives generously to all without finding fault, and it will be given to you" (James 1:5). He says this wisdom is grown in the soil of hardship (vv. 2–4), for there we not only learn *from* the wisdom of God but we also rest *in* the grace of God (2 Corinthians 12:9). In life's darkest times, we find what we need in Him.   *Bill Crowder*

**We not only learn from the wisdom of God
but we also rest in the grace of God.**

WORDS THAT WOUND

1 Samuel 1:1–8

The words of the reckless pierce like swords, but the tongue of the wise brings healing. —Proverbs 12:18

"Skinny bones, skinny bones," the boy taunted. "Stick," another chimed. In return, I could have chanted "sticks and stones may break my bones, but words will never hurt me." But even as a little girl, I knew the popular rhyme wasn't true. Unkind, thoughtless words did hurt—sometimes badly, leaving wounds that went deeper and lasted much longer than a welt from a stone or stick.

Hannah certainly knew the sting of thoughtless words. Her husband, Elkanah, loved her, but she had no children, while his second wife, Peninnah, had many. In a culture where a woman's worth was often based on having children, Peninnah made Hannah's pain worse when she "provoked her" for being childless. She kept it up until Hannah wept and couldn't eat (1 Samuel 1:6–7).

Elkanah probably meant well, but his thoughtless response, "Hannah, why are you weeping? . . . Don't I mean more to you than ten sons?" (v. 8) was still hurtful.

Like Hannah, many of us have been left reeling in the wake of hurtful words. And some of us have likely reacted to our wounds by lashing out and hurting others with our words. But all of us can run to our compassionate heavenly Father for strength and healing (Psalm 27:5, 12–14). He lovingly rejoices over us—speaking words of love and grace.   *Alyson Kieda*

We can run to our loving and compassionate God for strength and healing.

FINDING REST IN JESUS

Matthew 11:28–30

Come to me, all you who are weary and burdened,
and I will give you rest. —Matthew 11:28

The restless soul is never satisfied with wealth and success. A deceased country music icon could testify to this truth. He had nearly forty of his albums appear on *Billboard* magazine's country music top 10 charts and a dozen number one singles. But he also had multiple marriages and spent time in prison. Even with all his achievements, he once lamented: "There's a restlessness in my soul that I've never conquered, not with motion, marriages or meaning. . . . It's still there to a degree. And it will be till the day I die." He could have found rest in his soul before his life ended. And one could hope he did.

Jesus invites all those, like this musician, who have become weary from toiling in sin and its consequences to come to Him personally: "Come to me," He says. When we receive salvation in Jesus, He will take the burdens from us and "give [us] rest" (Matthew 11:28). The only requirements are to believe in Him and then learn from Him how to live the abundant life He provides (John 10:10). Taking on the yoke of Jesus's discipleship results in our finding "rest for [our] souls" (Matthew 11:29).

When we come to Jesus, He doesn't abbreviate our accountability to God. He gives peace to our restless souls by providing us a new and less burdensome way to live in Him. He gives us true rest.

Marvin Williams

**When we receive salvation in Jesus, He will
take the burdens from us and give us rest.**

KIND CORRECTION

James 5:19–20

He who turns a sinner from the error of his way
will save a soul from death. —James 5:20 NKJV

The early spring weather was refreshing and my traveling companion, my wife, couldn't have been better. But the beauty of those moments together could have quickly morphed into tragedy if it weren't for a red and white warning sign that informed me I was headed in the wrong direction. Because I hadn't turned wide enough, I momentarily saw a "Do Not Enter" sign staring me in the face. I quickly adjusted, but I shudder to think of the harm I could have brought to my wife, myself, and others if I'd ignored the sign that reminded me I was going the wrong way.

The closing words of James emphasize the importance of correction. Who among us hasn't needed to be "brought back" by those who care for us—brought back from paths or actions, decisions or desires that could have been hurtful? Who knows what harm we might have done to ourself or others had someone not courageously intervened at the right time.

James stresses the value of kind correction with these words, "He who turns a sinner from the error of his way will save a soul from death and cover a multitude of sins" (5:20 NKJV). Correction is an expression of God's mercy. May our love and concern for the well-being of others compel us to speak and act in ways that He can use to "bring that person back" (v. 19).   *Arthur Jackson*

Correction is an expression of God's mercy.

WHO WE ARE

Acts 9:13–16

This man is my chosen instrument to
proclaim my name. —Acts 9:15

I'll never forget the time I took my future wife to meet my family. With a twinkle in their eyes, my two elder siblings asked her, "What exactly do you see in this guy?" She smiled and assured them that by God's grace I had grown to be the man she loved.

I loved that clever reply because it also reflects how, in Christ, the Lord sees more than our past. In Acts 9, He directed Ananias to heal Saul, a known persecutor of the church whom God had blinded. Ananias was incredulous at receiving this mission, stating that Saul had been rounding up believers in Jesus for persecution and even execution. God told Ananias not to focus on who Saul had been but on who he had become: an evangelist who would bring the good news to all the known world, including to the gentiles (those who weren't Jews) and to kings (v. 15). Ananias saw Saul the Pharisee and persecutor, but God saw Paul the apostle and evangelist.

We can sometimes view ourselves only as we have been—with all our failures and shortcomings. But God sees us as new creations, not who we were but who we are in Jesus and who we're becoming through the power of the Holy Spirit. *O God, teach us to view ourselves and others in this way!*   *Peter Chin*

**God sees us as who we are in Jesus and who
we're becoming through the Holy Spirit.**

DON'T FEED THE TROLLS

Proverbs 26:4–12

Do not answer a fool according to his folly. —Proverbs 26:4

Ever heard the expression, "Don't feed the trolls"? "Trolls" refers to a new problem in today's digital world—online users who repeatedly post intentionally inflammatory and hurtful comments on news or social media discussion boards. But ignoring such comments—not "feeding" the trolls—makes it harder for them to derail a conversation.

Of course, it's nothing new to encounter people who aren't genuinely interested in productive conversation. "Don't feed the trolls" could almost be a modern equivalent of Proverbs 26:4, which warns that if we argue with an arrogant, unreceptive person, we risk stooping to their level.

And yet . . . even the most seemingly stubborn person is also a priceless image-bearer of God. If we're quick to dismiss others, we may be the ones in danger of being arrogant and becoming unreceptive to God's grace (see Matthew 5:22).

This might, in part, explain why Proverbs 26:5 offers the exact opposite guideline as verse 4 does. It takes humble, prayerful dependence on God to discern how best to show love in each situation (see Colossians 4:5–6). Sometimes we speak up; other times it's best to be silent.

But in every situation, we find peace in knowing that the same God who drew us near while we were still in hardened opposition to Him (Romans 5:6) is powerfully at work in each person's heart. Let's rest in His wisdom as we try to share Christ's love.   *Monica La Rose*

**It takes humble, prayerful dependence on God
to discern how best to show love to others.**

SHOWING GRACE

Colossians 4:2–6

Let your conversation be always full of grace,
seasoned with salt, so that you may know how
to answer everyone. —Colossians 4:6

The first Masters golf tournament was held in 1934, and since then only three players have won it two years in a row. On April 10, 2016, it appeared that twenty-two-year-old Jordan Spieth would become the fourth. But he faltered on the last nine holes and finished in a tie for second. Despite his disappointing loss, Spieth was gracious toward tournament champion Danny Willett, congratulating him on his victory and on the birth of his first child, something "more important than golf."

Writing in *The New York Times*, Karen Krouse said, "It takes grace to see the big picture so soon after having to sit through a trophy ceremony and watch someone else have his photograph taken." Krouse continued, "Spieth's ball-striking was off all week, but his character emerged unscathed."

Paul urged the followers of Jesus in Colossae to "be wise in the way you act toward outsiders; make the most of every opportunity. Let your conversation be always full of grace, seasoned with salt, so that you may know how to answer everyone" (Colossians 4:5–6).

As those who have freely received God's grace, it's our privilege and calling to demonstrate grace in every situation of life—win or lose.   *David McCasland*

Let your conversation be always full of grace.

FROM HOLEY TO HOLY

2 Timothy 1:6–10

He has saved us and called us to a holy life—not
because of anything we have done but because of
his own purpose and grace. —2 Timothy 1:9

As a child, my daughter loved playing with her Swiss cheese at
lunch. She'd place the pastel yellow square on her face like a
mask, saying, "Look, Mom," her sparkly green eyes peeking out
from two holes in the cheese. That Swiss-cheese mask summed up
my feelings about my efforts as a mom—genuinely offered, full of
love, but so very imperfect. Holey, not holy.

Oh, how we long to live a holy life—a life set apart for God and
characterized by being like Jesus. But day after day, holiness seems
out of reach. In its place, our "holeyness" remains.

In 2 Timothy 1:6–7, Paul writes to his protégé Timothy, urging
him to live up to his holy calling. The apostle then clarified that
"[God] has saved us and called us to a holy life—not because of
anything we have done but because of his own purpose and grace"
(v. 9). This life is possible not because of our character but because
of God's grace. Paul continues, "This grace was given us in Christ
Jesus before the beginning of time" (v. 9). Can we accept God's
grace and live from the platform of power it provides?

Whether in parenting, marriage, work, or loving our neighbor,
God calls us to a holy life—made possible not because of our efforts
to be perfect but because of His grace. *Elisa Morgan*

**A godly life is possible not because of our
character but because of God's grace.**

HOPE OF HEALING

John 5:1–9

At once the man was cured; he picked up
his mat and walked. —John 5:9

A new cause for hope has emerged for people paralyzed by spinal cord injuries. German researchers have discovered a way to stimulate nerve growth to reconnect the neural pathways between the muscles and the brain. The regrowth has enabled paralyzed mice to walk again, and testing will continue to determine whether the therapy is safe and effective for humans.

What science seeks to achieve on behalf of those who suffer paralysis, Jesus did through miracles. When he visited the pool at Bethesda, a place where many ailing people lingered in hopes of healing, Jesus sought out a man among them who "had been an invalid for thirty-eight years" (John 5:5). After confirming that the man did, indeed, wish to be healed, Christ instructed him to stand up and walk. "At once the man was cured; he picked up his mat and walked" (v. 9).

We're not promised that all our physical ailments will be healed by God—there were others at the pool who weren't healed by Jesus that day. But those who put their trust in Him can experience the life healing He brings—from despair to hope, from bitterness to grace, from hatred to love, from accusation to a willingness to forgive. No scientific discovery (or pool of water) can offer us such healing; it only comes by faith.   *Kirsten Holmberg*

**Those who put their trust in Him can experience
the life healing He brings—from despair to
hope, bitterness to grace, hatred to love.**

SHE DID WHAT SHE COULD

Mark 14:3–9

She did what she could. —Mark 14:8

When her friends say thoughtless or outrageous things on social media, Charlotte chimes in with gentle but firm dissent. She respects the dignity of everyone, and her words are unfailingly positive.

A few years ago, she became Facebook friends with a man who harbored anger toward Christians. He appreciated Charlotte's rare honesty and grace. Over time his hostility melted. Then Charlotte suffered a bad fall. Now housebound, she fretted over what she could do. About that time her Facebook friend died and then this message arrived from his sister: "[Because of your witness] I know he's now experiencing God's complete and abiding love for him."

During the week in which Christ would be killed, Mary of Bethany anointed Him with expensive perfume (John 12:3; Mark 14:3). Some of the other people present were appalled, but Jesus applauded her. "She has done a beautiful thing to me," He said. "She did what she could. She poured perfume on my body beforehand to prepare for my burial" (Mark 14:6–8).

"She did what she could." Christ's words take the pressure off. Our world is full of broken, hurting people. But we don't have to worry about what we can't do. Charlotte did what she could. So can we. The rest is in His capable hands.   *Tim Gustafson*

**"She has done a beautiful thing to me," Jesus said.
"She did what she could." —Mark 14:6, 8**

FINDING TREASURE

Matthew 13:44–46

The kingdom of heaven is like treasure
hidden in a field. —Matthew 13:44

John and Mary were walking their dog on their property when they stumbled on a rusty can partially unearthed by recent rains. They took the can home and opened it, discovering a cache of gold coins over a century old! The couple returned to the spot and located seven more cans, containing 1,427 coins in all. Then they protected their treasure by reburying it elsewhere until they could have it evaluated.

When they did, they found that the cache of coins was valued at $10 million. The Saddle Ridge Hoard, as it is called, is the largest find of its kind in US history. The story is strikingly reminiscent of a parable Jesus told: "The kingdom of heaven is like treasure hidden in a field. When a man found it, he hid it again, and then in his joy went and sold all he had and bought that field" (Matthew 13:44).

Tales of buried treasure have captured imaginations for centuries, though such discoveries rarely happen. But Jesus tells of a treasure accessible to all who confess their sins and receive and follow Him (John 1:12).

We'll never come to an end of that treasure. As we leave our old lives and pursue God and His purposes, we encounter His worth. Through "the incomparable riches of his grace, expressed in his kindness to us in Christ Jesus" (Ephesians 2:7), God offers us treasure beyond imagination—new life as His sons and daughters, new purpose on earth, and the incomprehensible joy of eternity with Him.

James Banks

God offers us treasure beyond imagination.

A NEW COMMAND

John 13:3–5, 12–15, 31–35

A new command I give you: Love one another. —John 13:34

In a tradition starting as early as the thirteenth century, members of the royal family in the United Kingdom give gifts to people in need on Maundy Thursday, the day before Good Friday. The practice is rooted in the meaning of the word *maundy*, which comes from the Latin *mandatum*, or "command." The command being commemorated is the new one that Jesus gave to His friends on the night before He died: "Love one another. As I have loved you, so you must love one another" (John 13:34).

Jesus was a leader who took on the role of a servant as He washed His friends' feet (v. 5). He then called them to do the same: "I have set you an example that you should do as I have done for you" (v. 15). And in an even greater act of sacrifice, He lay down His life, dying on the cross (19:30). Out of mercy and love He gave himself so we might enjoy the fullness of life.

The tradition of the British royal family serving people in need continues as a symbol of following Jesus's great example. We may not have been born into a place of privilege, but when we place our faith in Jesus, we become members of God's family. And we too can show our love by living out Jesus's new command. As we depend on God's Holy Spirit to change us from within, we can reach out to others with care, affirmation, and grace.   *Amy Boucher Pye*

Out of mercy and love Jesus gave himself that we might enjoy the fullness of life.

"NO GRACE"

1 Peter 4:1–11

A person's wisdom yields patience; it is to one's
glory to overlook an offense. —Proverbs 19:11

I have nicknamed our car "No Grace." Sunday mornings are the worst. I load the car with all the stuff I need for church, get myself in my seat, close the door, and Jay starts backing out of the garage. While I am still getting organized, the seat belt warning starts buzzing. "Please," I say to it, "all I need is another minute." The answer, apparently, is no, because it continues buzzing until I am buckled in.

This minor annoyance is a good reminder of what life would be like if indeed there were no grace. Each of us would immediately be called to account for every indiscretion. There would be no time for repentance or change of behavior. There would be no forgiveness. No mercy. No hope.

Living in this world sometimes feels like falling into a no-grace sinkhole. When minor flaws are blown up into major indiscretions or when people refuse to overlook the faults and offenses of others, we end up burdened by the weight of guilt that we were never meant to carry. God, in His grace, sent Jesus to carry the burden for us. Those who receive God's gift of grace have the privilege of offering it to others on Christ's behalf: "Above all, love each other deeply, because love covers over a multitude of sins" (1 Peter 4:8).

Julie Ackerman Link

God, in His grace, sent Jesus to carry the burden for us.

NOT MANY MIGHTY

1 Corinthians 1:26–31

Amos answered Amaziah, "I was neither a prophet nor the son of a prophet, but . . . the LORD . . . said to me, 'Go, prophesy to my people Israel.'" —Amos 7:14–15

Although God may choose prominent and well-known individuals for His glory, often He uses people who are considered least in the eyes of the world. This was true of Amos, a humble herdsman, who spoke the significant words of today's text. Through this obscure farmer, God gave amazing prophecies about Israel's dispersion and regathering. His background, natural gifts, and accomplishments hardly qualified Amos for the "Who's Who" of his day. But because of Amos's consecrated life, the Lord accomplished great things through him.

Amos is not alone in this. David was just a boy tending sheep when God commanded Samuel to anoint him king. And Abram belonged to an idolatrous family in Ur of the Chaldeans when he heard the divine call. Yet by submitting to the power of the Almighty, he became the father of a nation.

The marvel of God's sovereign grace is that He can work through any of us. Sometimes we say about a gifted person, "How God can use his tremendous talents!" But the heavenly Father is not limited by our superb abilities—or the lack thereof.

Rejoice in the grace of our Lord and realize that nothing in you—absolutely nothing—deserves His salvation. Then yield every talent you possess to Him. The God who used Amos can use you!

Paul Van Gorder

The heavenly Father does not save and call people because of their merits or superb abilities.

GRASPING THE CROSS

Philippians 3:7–12

Not that I have . . . already arrived at my goal, but
I press on to take hold of that for which Christ
Jesus took hold of me. —Philippians 3:12

In 1856, Charles Spurgeon, the great London preacher, founded the Pastors' College to train men for the Christian ministry. It was renamed Spurgeon's College in 1923.

Today's college crest shows a hand grasping a cross, along with the Latin words, *Et Teneo, Et Teneor*, which means, "I hold and am held." In his autobiography, Spurgeon wrote, "This is our College motto. We . . . hold forth the Cross of Christ with a bold hand . . . because that Cross holds us fast by its attractive power. Our desire is that every man may both hold the Truth, and be held by it; especially the truth of Christ crucified."

In Paul's letter to the Philippians, he expressed this truth as the bedrock of his life. "Not that I have . . . already arrived at my goal, but I press on to take hold of that for which Christ Jesus took hold of me" (Philippians 3:12). As followers of Jesus, we extend the message of the cross to others as Jesus holds us fast in His grace and power. "I have been crucified with Christ and I no longer live, but Christ lives in me" (Galatians 2:20).

Our Lord holds us in His grip of love each day—and we hold out His message of love to others.   *David McCasland*

**As followers of Jesus, we extend the message of the cross
to others as Jesus holds us fast in His grace and power.**

IT'S THE REAL DEAL

1 Peter 1:3–12

I have written to you briefly, encouraging you
and testifying that this is the true grace of
God. Stand fast in it. —1 Peter 5:12

One of the coolest things hanging on the wall in my home office is a Certificate of Authenticity.

It has on it the logo of US Space Shuttle Flight 110, which was launched in April 2002. Aboard the Atlantis on that flight was Mission Specialist Rex Walheim, who took into outer space an article from *Our Daily Bread* titled "Seeing God's Glory." Colonel Walheim sent me the certificate to prove that this devotional page actually left earth's atmosphere.

Sometimes we need these kinds of things—documents that verify truth. If I were to show that article to someone and say, "This flew on the space shuttle," I could be doubted because I would have no proof. But when Walheim sent me the Certificate of Authenticity, he gave me verification.

In 1 Peter, Simon Peter created a Certificate of Authenticity for his message about the grace of God. In chapter 5, he wrote, "I have written to you briefly, encouraging you and testifying that this [letter] is the true grace of God" (v. 12). Peter was assuring his readers that the many messages of 1 Peter—themes of hope and courage and even suffering—were all authentic and demonstrate the grace of God.

Looking for evidence of God's grace? Read 1 Peter and be confident that its teaching is the real deal.   *Dave Branon*

**The many messages of 1 Peter—themes of hope and
courage and even suffering—were all authentic.**

CHANGE IS POSSIBLE

Philippians 2:1–4

It is God who works in you to will and to act in order
to fulfill his good purpose. —Philippians 2:13

One Saturday afternoon, some youth group members from my church gathered to ask one another hard questions based on Philippians 2:3–4: "Do nothing out of selfish ambition or vain conceit. Rather, in humility value others above yourselves, not looking to your own interests but each of you to the interests of the others." Some of the difficult queries included: How often do you take an interest in others? Would someone describe you as humble or proud? Why?

As I listened, I was encouraged by their honest answers. The teenagers agreed that it's easy to acknowledge our shortcomings, but it's hard to change, or—for that matter—desire to change. As one teen lamented, "Selfishness is in my blood."

The desire to let go of our focus on self to serve others is only possible through Jesus's Spirit living in us. That's why Paul reminded the Philippian church to reflect on what God had done and made possible for them. He had graciously adopted them, comforted them with His love, and given His Spirit to help them (Philippians 2:1–2). How could they—and we—respond to such grace with anything less than humility?

Yes, God is the reason for us to change, and only He can change us. Because He gives us "the desire and the power to do what pleases him" (v.13 NLT), we can focus less on ourselves and humbly serve others.   *Poh Fang Chia*

**The desire to let go of our focus on self to serve others
is only possible through Jesus's Spirit living in us.**

A GOOD STRETCH

Romans 8:26–28

By faith Abraham, when called to go to a place he would
later receive as his inheritance, obeyed and went, even though
he did not know where he was going. —Hebrews 11:8

Physical therapy is a painful necessity after knee-replacement surgery. Part of my routine involved my therapist pulling my knee
back into a bent position and holding it taut. "Good stretch?" Mason
would ask encouragingly. "No," I winced, "not that good!"

I soon learned, however, how important it is to stretch one's muscles and joints—sometimes causing discomfort—to gain full range
of motion.

That wasn't the first time I've been "stretched" outside my comfort
zone. God has sometimes urged me to share my faith with someone I
didn't know very well, or to give an offering that was far beyond what
I usually give, or to confront someone about a situation.

Abraham's life illustrates the importance of faith when God asks
us to move beyond our comfort zone. "By faith Abraham, when
called to go to a place he would later receive as his inheritance,
obeyed and went, even though he did not know where he was going" (Hebrews 11:8).

While we stretch our spiritual muscles, we may feel discomfort.
But God assures us, "My grace is sufficient for you, for my power is
made perfect in weakness" (2 Corinthians 12:9). Our adequacy—
our sufficiency—is found in Him (3:5).

When you boldly step out in faith and obedience to God, you
may be surprised at how a "good stretch" can strengthen your spiritual life! *Cindy Hess Kasper*

Our adequacy—our sufficiency—is found in God.

GOD'S MERCY AT WORK

1 Samuel 24:1–10

May the LORD judge between you and me. —1 Samuel 24:12

My anger percolated when a woman mistreated me, blamed me, and gossiped about me. I wanted everyone to know what she'd done—wanted her to suffer as I'd suffered because of her behavior. I steamed with resentment until a headache pierced my temples.

But as I began praying for my pain to go away, the Holy Spirit convicted me. How could I plot revenge while begging God for relief? If I believed He would care for me, why wouldn't I trust Him to handle this situation? Knowing that people who are hurting often hurt other people, I asked God to help me forgive the woman and work toward reconciliation.

The psalmist David understood the difficulty of trusting God while enduring unfair treatment. Although David did his best to be a loving servant, King Saul succumbed to jealousy and wanted to murder him (1 Samuel 24:1–2). David suffered while God worked things out and prepared him to take the throne, but David still chose to honor God instead of seeking revenge (vv. 3–7). He did his part to reconcile with Saul and left the results in God's hands (vv. 8–22).

When it seems that others are getting away with wrongdoing, we struggle with the injustice. But with God's mercy at work in our hearts and the hearts of others, we can forgive as He's forgiven us and receive the blessings He's prepared for us. *Xochitl Dixon*

With God's mercy at work in our hearts and the hearts of others, we can forgive as He's forgiven us.

THE DOOR OF RECONCILIATION

2 Corinthians 5:14–21

All this is from God, who reconciled us to
himself through Christ and gave us the ministry
of reconciliation. —2 Corinthians 5:18

Inside St. Patrick's Cathedral in Dublin, Ireland, there's a door that tells a five-century-old tale.

In 1492 two families, the Butlers and the FitzGeralds, began fighting over a high-level position in the region. The fight escalated, and the Butlers took refuge in the cathedral. When the FitzGeralds came to ask for a truce, the Butlers were afraid to open the door. So, the FitzGeralds cut a hole in it, and their leader offered his hand in peace. The two families then reconciled, and adversaries became friends.

God has a door of reconciliation that the apostle Paul wrote passionately about in his letter to the church in Corinth. At God's initiative and because of His infinite love, He exchanged the broken relationship with humans for a restored relationship through Christ's death on the cross. We were far away from God, but in His mercy He didn't leave us there. He offers us restoration with himself—"not counting people's sins against them" (2 Corinthians 5:19). Justice was fulfilled when "God made [Jesus] who had no sin to be sin for us," so that in Him we "might become the righteousness of God" (v. 21) and be at peace with Him.

Once we accept God's hand in peace, we're given the important task of bringing that message to others. We represent the amazing, loving God who offers complete forgiveness and restoration to everyone who believes.

Estera Pirosca Escobar

**God exchanged the broken relationship with humans for a
restored relationship through Christ's death on the cross.**

RUNNING TO JESUS

John 20:1–10

Both were running, but the other disciple outran
Peter and reached the tomb first. —John 20:4

On a trip to Paris, Ben and his friends found themselves at one
of the renowned museums in the city. Although Ben wasn't a
student of art, he was in awe as he looked upon the painting titled
*The Disciples Peter and John Running to the Sepulchre on the Morning
of the Resurrection* by Eugène Burnand. Without words, the looks
on the faces of Peter and John and the position of their hands speak
volumes, inviting onlookers to step into their shoes and share their
adrenaline-charged emotions.

Based on John 20:1–10, the painting portrays the two running
in the direction of the empty tomb of Jesus (v. 4). The masterpiece
captures the intensity of the two emotionally conflicted disciples.
Although at that juncture their faith wasn't fully formed, they were
running in the right direction. Eventually the resurrected Jesus revealed himself to them (vv. 19–29).

Their search was not unlike that of Jesus seekers through the
centuries. Although we may be removed from the experiences of an
empty tomb or a brilliant piece of art, we can clearly see the good
news. Scripture compels us to hope and seek and run in the direction of Jesus and His love—even with doubts, questions, and uncertainties. Each year as we celebrate Jesus's resurrection, we remember
God's faithfulness: "You will seek me and find me when you seek me
with all your heart" (Jeremiah 29:13).   *Arthur Jackson*

**Scripture compels us to hope and seek and run
in the direction of Jesus and His love—even
with doubts, questions, and uncertainties.**

PROMPTED TO PRAY

1 Thessalonians 5:12–18

Rejoice always, pray continually. —1 Thessalonians 5:16–17

A coworker once told me that her prayer life had improved because of our manager. I was impressed, thinking that our difficult leader had shared some spiritual nuggets with her and influenced how she prays. I was wrong—sort of. My coworker and friend went on to explain: "Every time I see him coming, I start praying." Her time of prayer had improved because she prayed more before each conversation with him. She knew she needed God's help in her challenging work relationship with her manager, so she called out to Him more because of it.

My coworker's practice of praying during tough times and interactions is something I've adopted. It's also a biblical practice found in 1 Thessalonians when Paul reminds the believers in Jesus to "pray continually," and "give thanks in all circumstances" (5:17–18). No matter what we face, prayer is always the best practice. It keeps us connected with God and invites His Spirit to direct us (Galatians 5:16) rather than having us rely on our human inclinations. This helps us "live in peace with each other" (1 Thessalonians 5:13) even when we face conflicts.

As God helps us, we can rejoice in Him, pray about everything, and give thanks often. These practices will help us live in even greater harmony with everyone we encounter.   *Katara Patton*

No matter what we face, prayer is always the best practice.

THE POWER OF VOICE

Jeremiah 1:4–9

I have put my words in your mouth. —Jeremiah 1:9

The most powerful orators in history are often those leaders who have used their voices to bring about positive change. Consider Frederick Douglass, whose speeches on abolition and liberty spurred a movement that helped lead to the end of slavery in the United States. What if he'd chosen to be silent? We all possess the capacity to use our voice to inspire and help others, but the fear of speaking out can be paralyzing. In the moments when we feel overwhelmed by this fear, we can look to God, our source of divine wisdom and encouragement.

When God called Jeremiah to be a prophet to the nations, Jeremiah immediately began to doubt his own abilities. He cried out, "I do not know how to speak; I am too young" (Jeremiah 1:6). But God wouldn't allow Jeremiah's fear to get in the way of his divine calling to inspire a generation through his voice. Instead, He instructed the prophet to trust God by saying and doing whatever He commanded (v. 7). In addition to affirming Jeremiah, He also equipped him. "I have put my words in your mouth" (v. 9), He assured him.

When we ask God to show us how He wants to use us, He'll equip us to carry out our purpose. With His help, we can boldly use our voice to make a positive impact on those around us.

Kimya Loder

In the moments when we feel overwhelmed by fear, we can look to God, our source of encouragement.

GRACE AT THE END

Mark 5:5–34

Daughter, your faith has healed you. Go in peace
and be freed from your suffering. —Mark 5:34

Artist Doug Merkey's masterful sculpture *Ruthless Trust* features a bronze human figure clinging desperately to a cross made of walnut wood. He writes, "It's a very simple expression of our constant and appropriate posture for life—total, unfettered intimacy with and dependency upon Christ and the gospel."

This is the kind of trust we see expressed in the actions and words of the unnamed woman in Mark 5:25–34. For twelve years her life had been in shambles (v. 25). "She had suffered a great deal under the care of many doctors and had spent all she had, yet instead of getting better she grew worse" (v. 26). But having heard about Jesus, she made her way to Him, touched His cloak, and was "freed from her suffering" (vv. 27–29).

Have you come to the end of yourself? Have you depleted all your resources? Anxious, hopeless, lost, distressed people need not despair. The Lord Jesus still responds to desperate faith—the kind displayed by this suffering woman and depicted in Merkey's sculpture. This faith is expressed in the words of hymn writer Charles Wesley: "Father, I stretch my hands to Thee; no other help I know."

Don't have this kind of faith? Ask God to help you trust Him. Wesley's hymn concludes with this prayer: "Author of faith, to Thee I lift my weary, longing eyes; O may I now receive that gift! My soul, without it, dies."   *Arthur Jackson*

The Lord Jesus still responds to desperate faith.

A SIGN OF GREATNESS

Romans 12:9–16

Rejoice with those who rejoice; mourn with
those who mourn. —Romans 12:15

Forty thousand baseball fans were on hand in the Oakland Coliseum on April 28, 1991, when Rickey Henderson tied Lou Brock's Major League record for stolen bases. According to *USA Today*, Lou, who retired from baseball in 1979, had followed Henderson's career and was excited about his success. Realizing that Rickey would tie—and then break—his record, Brock said, "I'll be there. Do you think I'm going to miss it now? Rickey did in twelve years what took me nineteen. He's amazing."

The real success stories in life are with people who can rejoice in the successes of others. What Lou Brock did in cheering on Rickey Henderson should be a way of life in the family of God. Few circumstances give us a better opportunity to exhibit God's grace than when someone succeeds and surpasses us in an area of our own strength and reputation.

If we have not entrusted ourselves to the care and provision of God, this will be very difficult. If we're not drawing grace from our relationship with Jesus Christ, we will turn green with envy rather than be flushed with shared happiness.

What is a better test of our relationship with Christ? What is a better evidence of the goodness of God than when He enables us to be happy when others do well?

Let's "rejoice with those who rejoice."   *Mart DeHaan*

God enables us to be happy when others do well.

SMALL BUT GREAT

Zechariah 4:4–10

Who dares despise the day of small things? —Zechariah 4:10

Will I make the Olympics? The college swimmer worried that her speed was too slow. But when math professor Ken Ono studied her swim techniques, he saw how to improve her time by six full seconds—a substantial difference at that level of competition. Attaching sensors to the swimmer's back, he didn't identify major changes to improve her time. Instead, Ono identified tiny corrective actions that, if applied, could make the swimmer more efficient in the water, making the winning difference.

Small corrective actions in spiritual matters can make a big difference for us too. The prophet Zechariah taught a similar principle to a remnant of discouraged Jews who were struggling, along with their builder Zerubbabel, to rebuild God's temple after their exile. But "not by might nor by power, but by my Spirit," the Lord Almighty told Zerubbabel (Zechariah 4:6).

Zechariah declared, "Who dares despise the day of small things?" (v. 10). The exiles had worried that the temple wouldn't match the one built during King Solomon's reign. But just as Ono's swimmer made the Olympics—winning a medal after surrendering to small corrections—Zerubbabel's band of builders learned that even a small, right effort made with God's help can bring victorious joy if our small acts glorify Him. In God, small becomes great.

Patricia Raybon

Small corrective actions in spiritual matters can make a big difference.

TRUE SATISFACTION

Ecclesiastes 2:1–11

The eye never has enough of seeing, nor the
ear its fill of hearing. —Ecclesiastes 1:8

A man stopped at a travel agency and said he wanted to take an ocean voyage. "Where to?" the agent asked. "I don't know," the man replied. The travel agent suggested that he might find it helpful to look at a large globe in the room. The man studied it carefully. After quite some time, and with a look of frustration, he exclaimed, "Is this all you have to offer?"

The world in which we live has many things that appeal to us. Apart from what is sinful, we can and should enjoy its pleasures. A delicious meal graced with the good fellowship of friends warms our hearts. The beauties of nature inspire and fill us with wonder. Good music refreshes our souls. And work itself can be fulfilling.

Yes, even in a sin-cursed world we can find great enjoyment. And yet these pursuits do not bring full and lasting satisfaction. In fact, people who live only for self-gratification, no matter how lofty their achievements, long for more. It makes no difference how deeply they drink of the wells of this world's pleasures; their thirst is never satisfied. They must say in the words of Solomon that "all of it is meaningless, a chasing after the wind" (Ecclesiastes 2:17).

Richard DeHaan

**Only in the Christ-filled life do we
experience true satisfaction.**

MAY

"I Know Whom I Have Believed"

Daniel W. Whittle and James McGranahan

*I know not why God's wondrous grace
to me He had made known.*

What's in a Name?

Names. We treasure them because they represent who we are and sometimes where we came from. Former boxing champion George Foreman liked his name so much he gave it to each of his sons: George Jr., George III, George IV, and George V.

The writer of the great hymn "I Know Whom I Have Believed" has some interesting name connections as well. If you find this song in a hymnal and peek at the name attribution at the top left, you'll sometimes see the name El Nathan. Other times, the lyrics are attributed to Major Whittle. Some hymnals will give the name Daniel W. Whittle or D. W. Whittle in that spot.

Sources: Logan Herod, "History of Hymns: 'I Know Whom I Have Believed,'" Discipleship Ministries of The United Methodist Church, http://tinyurl.com /t6f97r59; "The Story Behind the Hymn—I Know Whom I Have Believed," *Faithful Stewardship* (blog), http://tinyurl.com/3apd3hct; all accessed November 6, 2023.

When Whittle was born, his parents gave him the name Daniel Webster. His dad had heard that famous statesman declare his lifelong dedication to the cause of American independence, and he wanted his boy to grow up as an advocate for freedom.

As the years passed, Daniel joined the Union Army to fight in the Civil War. He achieved the rank of major while serving, thus the name Major Whittle. And once he began writing songs that were published, he chose the pseudonym El Nathan.

But the name that counted the most to D. W. Whittle was the name of Jesus, the one he knew he believed in. Whittle came to faith in Christ while recovering from a serious injury in the war. One day he was asked to pray for another seriously injured soldier, but he felt inadequate because he wasn't sure he himself was a believer.

Yet Whittle went ahead and began to pray for the other soldier, realizing as he did that he also needed Jesus. So, he first confessed his own need for a Savior and asked Jesus to save him. Then he prayed for the other soldier, who died while Whittle was praying for both his body and his soul.

Whittle and his wife, May, had one daughter. She grew up to marry Dwight L. Moody's son. The close relationship between Whittle and Moody led the Major to become a part of Moody's evangelistic campaigns. He began writing songs during that time.

In 1883, Whittle took the words of the apostle Paul in 1 Timothy as the basis for one of his songs. Paul wrote, "I know whom I have believed, and am persuaded that he is able to keep that which I have committed unto him against that day." From this came the song we still sing today. The music for the words was written by James McGranahan, who also cowrote the song "There Shall Be Showers of Blessing" with Whittle.

I Know Whom I Have Believed

I know not why God's wondrous grace
To me He hath made known,
Nor why, unworthy, Christ in love
Redeemed me for His own.

Chorus:
But "I know whom I have believed,
And am persuaded that He is able
To keep that which I've committed
Unto Him against that day."

YOU FIRST!

Philippians 2:1–11

[Jesus] humbled himself. —Philippians 2:8

Tibetan-born Nawang Gombu Sherpa and American Jim Whittaker reached the top of Mount Everest on May 1, 1963. As they approached the peak, each considered the honor of being the first of the two to step to the summit. Whittaker motioned for Gombu to move ahead, but Gombu declined with a smile, saying, "You first, Big Jim!" Finally, they decided to step to the summit at the same time.

Paul encouraged the Philippian believers to demonstrate this kind of humility. He said, "Let each of you look out not only for his own interests, but also for the interests of others" (Philippians 2:4 NKJV). Selfishness and superiority can divide people, but humility unites us, since it is the quality of "being one in spirit and of one mind" (v. 2).

When quarrels and disagreements occur, we can often diffuse them by giving up our right to be right. Humility calls us to show grace and gentleness when we would rather insist on our own way. "In humility value others above yourselves" (v. 3).

Practicing humility helps us to become more like Jesus who, for our sake, "humbled himself by becoming obedient to death" (vv. 7–8). Following in Jesus's footsteps sometimes means backing away from what is best for us and doing what is best for others.

Jennifer Benson Schuldt

Humility calls us to show grace and gentleness when we would rather insist on our own way.

SURPRISED BY GRACE

Acts 9:1–19

I became a servant of this gospel by the gift of God's grace
given me through the working of his power. —Ephesians 3:7

A woman from Grand Rapids, Michigan, fell asleep on the
couch after her husband had gone to bed. An intruder sneaked
in through the sliding door, which the couple had forgotten to lock,
and crept through the house. He entered the bedroom where the
husband was sleeping and picked up the television set. The sleeping
man woke up, saw a figure standing there, and whispered, "Honey,
come to bed." The burglar panicked, put down the TV, grabbed a
stack of money from the dresser, and ran out.

The thief was in for a big surprise! The money turned out to be
a stack of Christian pamphlets with a likeness of a $20 bill on one
side and an explanation of the love and forgiveness God offers us on
the other side. Instead of the cash he expected, the intruder got the
gospel—the story of God's love for him.

I wonder what Saul expected when he realized it was Jesus ap-
pearing to him on the road to Damascus, since he had been per-
secuting and even killing Jesus's followers (Acts 9:1–9)? Saul, later
called Paul, must have been surprised by God's grace toward him,
which he called "a gift": "I became a servant of this gospel by the
gift of God's grace given me through the working of his power"
(Ephesians 3:7).

Have you been surprised by God's gift of grace in your life as He
shows you His love and forgiveness?   *Anne Cetas*

Have you been surprised by God's gift of grace?

A GLIMPSE OF GLORY

Acts 7:54–60

Stephen, full of the Holy Spirit, looked up to
heaven and saw the glory of God, and Jesus standing
at the right hand of God. —Acts 7:55

Death is the Christian's last great enemy. Dying is described as walking through the "valley of the shadow of death" (Psalm 23:4 NKJV). Jesus has removed its sting, which is sin (1 Corinthians 15:56), but it still creates apprehension, and God will give us special grace for that time.

This was illustrated in the life of Dwight L. Moody. When the great evangelist was on his deathbed, family and friends gathered to say goodbye. Thinking the end had come, they silently began to leave the room. Just then they heard a stirring. Turning, they found Moody's eyes open and his mind apparently clear. Someone began to pray, but Moody interrupted, "Do not pray that I may live. I have seen Dwight and Irene [two grandchildren who had died]. I have seen the face of Jesus and I am satisfied. Earth is receding, heaven is opening. God is calling me. This is my coronation day!"

Before being stoned to death, Stephen saw Jesus standing at the Father's right hand. How this must have strengthened him! I have heard of dying saints who voiced disappointment when, after lapsing into unconsciousness, they revived briefly and found that they were still on earth instead of in heaven.

God may take us to himself without warning. That would be instant glory! Or He may give us time to prepare. Whatever the circumstances, if we have trusted Christ as Savior, He will be with us when we pass from this world and catch our first glimpse of Glory.

Dennis DeHaan

When God calls us home, it will be our coronation day!

WALKING IN THE LIGHT

Hebrews 12:18–24

In him was life, and that life was the light
of all mankind. —John 1:4

Darkness descended on our forest village when the moon disappeared. Lightning slashed the skies, followed by a rainstorm and crackling thunder. As a child, awake and afraid, I imagined all kinds of grisly monsters about to pounce on me! By daybreak, however, the sounds vanished, the sun rose, and calm returned as birds jubilated in the sunshine. The contrast between the frightening darkness of the night and the joy of the daylight was remarkably sharp.

The author of Hebrews recalls the time when the Israelites had an experience at Mount Sinai so dark and stormy they hid in fear (Exodus 20:18–19). For them, God's presence, even in His loving gift of the law, felt dark and terrifying. This was because, as sinful people, the Israelites couldn't live up to God's standards. Their sin caused them to walk in darkness and fear (Hebrews 12:18–21).

But "God is light; in him there is no darkness at all" (1 John 1:5). In Hebrews 12:22–24, we read that Mount Sinai represents God's holiness and our old life of disobedience, while the beauty of Mount Zion represents God's grace and believers' new life in Jesus, "the mediator of a new covenant" (v. 24).

Whoever follows Jesus will "never walk in darkness, but will have the light of life" (John 8:12). Through Him, we can let go of the darkness of our old life and celebrate the joy of walking in the light and beauty of His kingdom.   *Lawrence Darmani*

"God is light; in him there is no darkness at all." —1 John 1:5

GREEDY BIRDS

2 Corinthians 9:6–15

God is able to bless you abundantly, so that in all
things at all times, having all that you need, you will
abound in every good work. —2 Corinthians 9:8

Every year when I put out the hummingbird feeder, the busy little birds start battling for position. Even though there are four
places at the "table," the birds fight for whatever place one of their
neighbors is using. The source of food at each place is the same—a
reservoir of syrup in the bottom of the feeder. Knowing that all the
feeding stations are equal, I shake my head at their greediness.

But then I wonder, *Why is it so much easier to see the birds' greed
than my own?* I often want the place at "God's table" that someone else has, even though I know all good things come from the
same source—God—and that His supply will never run out. Since
God can prepare a table for us even in the presence of our enemies
(Psalm 23:5), why be concerned that someone else might have the
station in life that we want?

The Lord is able to give us "all that [we] need" so that we will
"abound in every good work" (2 Corinthians 9:8). When we recognize the importance of our work as ministers of the grace of God
(1 Peter 4:10), we'll stop fighting to take over someone else's position and be grateful for the place God has given us to serve others
on His behalf.   *Julie Ackerman Link*

**Why are we concerned that someone else might
have the station in life that we want?**

USE ME

1 Corinthians 1:26–31

Let the one who boasts boast in the Lord. —1 Corinthians 1:31

James Morris was once described as "an illiterate but warmhearted layman," but God used him to draw Augustus Toplady to saving faith in Jesus Christ. Toplady, the eighteenth-century author of the timeless hymn "Rock of Ages," described hearing Morris preach: "Strange that I . . . should be brought nigh unto God . . . amidst a handful of God's people met together in a barn, and under the ministry of one who could hardly spell his name. Surely this is the Lord's doing, and it is marvelous."

Indeed, God does marvelous things in unlikely places and through those we may rank as "unqualified" or ordinary. In 1 Corinthians 1, Paul reminded believers in Jesus that they were an unimpressive lot. "Not many of you were wise by human standards; not many were influential; not many were of noble birth" (v. 26). Although the Corinthian believers were quite ordinary, by God's grace they weren't lacking in giftedness and usefulness (see v. 7). And God—who knows how to put boasters in their place (vv. 27–29)—was at work among them and through them.

Do you see yourself as "plain," "ordinary," or even "less than"? Don't fret. If you have Jesus and are willing to be used by Him, you have enough. Let your heart's prayer be, "God, use me!"

Arthur Jackson

God does marvelous things in unlikely places and through people we may consider unqualified or ordinary.

EXTENDING MERCY

Luke 17:1–5

If your brother or sister sins against you, rebuke them;
and if they repent, forgive them. —Luke 17:3

Reflecting on how she forgave Manasseh, the man who killed her husband and some of her children in the Rwandan genocide in 1994, Beata said, "My forgiving is based on what Jesus did. He took the punishment for every evil act throughout all time. His cross is the place we find victory—the only place!"

Manasseh had written to Beata from prison more than once, begging her—and God—for forgiveness as he detailed the regular nightmares that plagued him. At first, she could extend no mercy, saying she hated him for killing her family. But then "Jesus intruded into her thoughts," as she put it—and with God's help, some two years later, she forgave him.

In this, Beata followed Jesus's instruction to His disciples to forgive those who repent. He said that even if they "sin against you seven times in a day and seven times come back to you saying 'I repent,' you must forgive them" (Luke 17:4). But to forgive can be extremely difficult, as we see by the disciples' reaction: "Increase our faith!" (v. 5).

Beata's faith increased as she wrestled in prayer over her inability to forgive. If, like her, we're struggling to forgive, we can ask God through His Holy Spirit to help us to do so. As our faith increases, He helps us to forgive.   *Amy Boucher Pye*

**If we're struggling to forgive, we can
ask the Holy Spirit to help us.**

THE TEARS OF A CLOWN

Psalm 49:6–13

Surely the lowborn are but a breath, the highborn are
but a lie. If weighed on a balance, they are nothing;
together they are only a breath. —Psalm 62:9

In 1835 a man visited a doctor in Florence, Italy. He was filled
with anxiety and exhausted from lack of sleep. He couldn't eat,
and he avoided his friends. The doctor examined him and found
that he was in prime physical condition.

Concluding that his patient needed to have a good time, the phy-
sician told him about a circus in town and its star performer, a clown
named Grimaldi. Night after night he had the people rolling in the
aisles. "You must go and see him," the doctor advised. "Grimaldi
is the world's funniest clown. He'll make you laugh and cure your
sadness."

"No," replied the despairing man, "he can't help me. You see, I
am Grimaldi!"

Many people are like that clown—weak beneath the surface. The
psalmist refers to them as having riches and honor and as giving the
appearance of confidence and strength. Yet they lack spiritual understanding and will perish like the animals.

We see this even today. Let's not kid ourselves; we are all made of
the same flesh, and apart from the grace and power of God, we are
helpless and pathetic. Only by yielding to the Holy Spirit can we
find the inner resources we need.

Are you displaying His power, or are you wearing a mask that
covers weakness beneath the surface?   *Mart DeHaan*

Apart from the grace and power of God we are helpless.

TOO MUCH FOR ME

Matthew 26:36–46

My Father, if it is possible, may this cup be
taken from me. —Matthew 26:39

"God never gives us more than we can handle," someone said to a father whose five-year-old son had just lost his battle with cancer. These words, which were intended to encourage him, instead depressed him and caused him to wonder why he wasn't "handling" the loss of his boy at all. The pain was so much to bear that he could hardly even breathe. He knew his grief was too much for him and that he desperately needed God to hold him tight.

The verse that some use to support the statement "God never gives us more than we can handle" is 1 Corinthians 10:13, "When you are tempted, he will also provide a way out so that you can endure it." But the context of these words is temptation, not suffering. We can choose the way out of temptation that God provides, but we can't choose a way out of suffering.

Jesus himself wanted a way out of His upcoming suffering when He prayed, "My soul is overwhelmed with sorrow to the point of death. . . . My Father, if it is possible, may this cup be taken from me" (Matthew 26:38–39). Yet He willingly went through this for our salvation.

When life seems too much to bear, that's when we throw ourselves on God's mercy, and He holds on to us.   *Anne Cetas*

**Jesus himself wanted a way out of His upcoming suffering,
yet He willingly went through this for our salvation.**

SHOULD I FORGIVE?

Matthew 18:23–35

Forgive as the Lord forgave you. —Colossians 3:13

I arrived early at my church to help set up for an event. A woman stood crying at the opposite end of the sanctuary. She had been cruel and gossiped about me in the past, so I quickly drowned out her sobs with a vacuum cleaner. Why should I care about someone who didn't like me?

After the Holy Spirit reminded me how much God had forgiven me, I crossed the room. The woman shared that her baby had been in the hospital for months. We cried, embraced, and prayed for her daughter. After working through our differences, we're now good friends.

In Matthew 18, Jesus compares the kingdom of heaven to a king who decided to settle his accounts. A servant who owed a staggering amount of money pleaded for mercy. Soon after the king canceled his debt, that servant tracked down and condemned a man who owed him far less than what he had owed the king. When word got back to the king, the wicked servant was imprisoned because of his own unforgiving spirit (vv. 23–34).

Choosing to forgive doesn't condone sin, excuse the wrongs done to us, or minimize our hurts. Offering forgiveness simply frees us to enjoy God's undeserved gift of mercy as we invite Him to accomplish beautiful works of peace-restoring grace in our lives and our relationships. *Xochitl Dixon*

**Offering forgiveness frees us to enjoy
God's undeserved gift of mercy.**

GREAT NEWS!

Psalm 51:1–7

Have mercy on me, O God, according to
your unfailing love. —Psalm 51:1

The article in the local newspaper was short but heartwarming.
After attending a faith-based program on building stronger family ties, a group of prison inmates were given a rare treat of an open
visit with their families. Some hadn't seen their children in years.
Instead of talking through a glass panel, they could touch and hold
their loved ones. The tears flowed freely as families grew closer and
wounds began to heal.

For most readers, it was just a story. But for these families, holding one another was a life-changing event—and for some, the process of forgiveness and reconciliation was begun.

God's forgiveness of our sin and offer of reconciliation, made
possible through His Son, is more than a mere fact of the Christian
faith. The article's news of reconciliation reminds us that Jesus's sacrifice is great news not just for the world but also for you and me.

In times when we're overwhelmed by guilt for something we've
done, however, it's news we can cling to desperately. This is when
the fact of God's unending mercy becomes personal news: because
of Jesus's dying on our behalf, we can come to the Father washed
clean, "whiter than snow" (Psalm 51:7). In such times, when we
know we don't deserve His mercy, we can hold on to the only thing
we can depend on: God's unfailing love and compassion (v. 1).

Leslie Koh

**When we're overwhelmed by guilt for something we've
done, God's unending mercy becomes personal.**

JONAH ON BOARD

Jonah 1:1–2:2

This terrified them and they asked, "What have you done?" (They knew he was running away from the LORD, because he had already told them so.) —Jonah 1:10

The year is 1748. A trading ship departs from an island off Africa's west coast headed for England. Aboard is John Newton, a seaman with a reputation for profane language and ungodly living. As Newton later described it, the captain "would often tell me that to his grief he had a Jonah on board; that a curse attended me wherever I went, and that all the troubles he met with in the voyage were owing to his having taken me into the vessel."

The captain may have been right; Newton had earlier turned his back on God. But just as a storm had threatened to destroy the boat bearing Jonah, so too a fierce Atlantic wind rudely awakened John Newton. The vessel nearly broke apart. As the damaged ship drifted at sea, Newton prayed for God's mercy and put his faith in Jesus. It would take a few years of spiritual growth for Newton to be the man who could write "Amazing Grace," but he was now a new believer. With his sins forgiven, he could now grow in the faith and knowledge of his Savior.

If you, like Jonah, are a child of God who has deliberately run away from the Lord, turn to Jesus. Trust Him for salvation and begin to live for Him. Don't wait for one of life's storms to awaken you to your need. Turn to Jesus today. *Dave Branon*

If you have deliberately run away from the Lord, turn to Jesus.

PULL THE WEEDS

Matthew 13:11–23

The seed falling among the thorns refers to
someone who hears the word, but the worries of
this life . . . choke the word. —Matthew 13:22

After burying a few seeds in a planter in my backyard, I waited to
see the results. Having read that the seeds would sprout within
ten to fourteen days, I checked often as I watered the soil. Soon I
saw a few green leaves pushing their way out of the soil. But my
bubble burst quickly when my husband told me those were weeds.
He encouraged me to pull them quickly so they wouldn't choke the
plants I was trying to grow.

Similarly, Jesus told of the importance of dealing with intrud-
ers that can impede our spiritual growth. He explained a portion of
His parable this way: when a sower cast his seeds, some "fell among
thorns . . . and choked the plants" (Matthew 13:7). Thorns, or weeds,
will do that to plants—stop their growth (v. 22).

Worry is like this. It will surely stunt our spiritual growth. Reading Scripture and praying are great ways to grow our faith, but I've
found I need to watch out for the thorns of worry. They'll "choke"
the good word that has been planted in me, making me focus on
what could go wrong.

The fruit of the Spirit found in Scripture includes such things
as love, joy, and peace (Galatians 5:22). But in order for us to bear
that fruit, in God's strength we need to pull any weeds of doubt or
worry that may distract us and cause us to focus on anything other
than Him. *Katara Patton*

**To bear fruit in God's strength, we need to
pull out any weeds of doubt or worry.**

UNEXPECTED HELP

Joshua 2:1–14

The woman had taken the two men and
hidden them. —Joshua 2:4

In 1803, US President Thomas Jefferson commissioned Meriwether Lewis and William Clark to lead an expedition across an unexplored portion of America from St. Louis to the Pacific coast. The expedition was called the "Corps of Discovery Expedition"— and it lived up to its name. Lewis and Clark cataloged three hundred new species, identified nearly fifty Indian tribes, and traversed terrain that had never been seen by Europeans.

They were joined along the way by a French fur trader and his wife Sacajawea. They soon found her to be invaluable as an interpreter and guide.

During the trip, Sacajawea was reunited with her family. Her older brother had become one tribe's chief, and he helped them acquire horses and a map of the uncharted West. Without Sacajawea's and her brother's unexpected help, the expedition may not have succeeded.

The Bible tells of an expedition that also received unexpected help. The Israelites had sent spies into Jericho, a city in the land promised to them. Rahab agreed to ensure their escape in exchange for her family's protection when Jericho fell. In this way the sovereign God of grace used her to prepare the way for a victory in Israel's conquest and settlement of the promised land.

Are you in the middle of a challenge? Remember, God can provide help from unexpected sources.   *Dennis Fisher*

God can provide the help we need from unexpected sources.

REVEALED TO BE HEALED

Psalm 25:1–11

Show me your ways, LORD, teach me your paths. —Psalm 25:4

As a boy, I watched my father plow fields that had never been cultivated. On the first pass, the plowshare would turn up large rocks that he hauled away. Then he would plow the field again, and then a third time, to further break up the soil. With each pass, the plow turned up other, smaller rocks that he cast aside. The process continued, requiring many passes through the field.

Growth in grace can look like a similar process. When we first become believers, some "big" sins may be exposed. We confess them to God and accept His forgiveness. But as the years pass, and as God's Word works its way through us and sinks into our innermost being, the Holy Spirit brings other sins to the surface. Sins of the spirit once thought to be mere peccadilloes—small, seemingly unimportant offenses—are revealed as ugly, ruinous attitudes and actions. Sins like pride, self-pity, complaining, pettiness, prejudice, spite, self-serving indulgence.

God reveals each sin so He can cast it aside. He reveals to heal. When harmful hidden attitudes come to the surface, we can pray as the psalmist David did, "For the sake of your name, LORD, forgive my iniquity, though it is great" (Psalm 25:11).

Humbling exposure, though painful, is good for the soul. It's one of the ways in which He "instructs sinners in his ways" as He "guides the humble in what is right and teaches them his way" (vv. 8–9).

David Roper

God reveals each sin so He can cast it aside.

FINDING STRENGTH IN GOD

2 Corinthians 12:9–10

I will boast all the more gladly about my weaknesses, so that
Christ's power may rest on me. —2 Corinthians 12:9

Soccer player Christian Pulisic faced several injuries that influenced his career. After learning he wouldn't be in the starting lineup of the Champions League semifinals game, he was disappointed, but he described how God had revealed himself to him. "As always, I reach out to God, and He gives me strength," he said. "I feel like I always have Someone who's with me. I don't know how I would do any of this without that feeling."

Pulisic ultimately made a momentous impact when he was substituted later in the game. He initiated a clever play that led to the game-winning shot and secured his team's spot in the championship. These experiences taught him a valuable lesson: we can always view our weaknesses as opportunities for God to reveal His immeasurable power.

The world teaches us to rely on our own strength when encountering problems. However, biblical wisdom teaches us that God's grace and power give us strength in the most trying circumstances (2 Corinthians 12:9). Therefore, we can move in confidence, recognizing that we never face trials alone.

Our "weaknesses" become opportunities for God to reveal His power—strengthening and supporting us (vv. 9–10). We can then use our struggles to offer praise to God, giving thanks for His goodness and sharing these encounters with others so they can come to experience His love. *Kimya Loder*

**Biblical wisdom teaches us that God's grace and power
give us strength in the most trying circumstances.**

WHEN PLANS FALL THROUGH

1 Chronicles 28:2–12

I had it in my heart to build a house as a place of
rest for the ark of the covenant of the LORD, . . . and
I made plans to build it. —1 Chronicles 28:2

After raising money all year for a "trip of a lifetime," seniors from an Oklahoma high school arrived at the airport to learn that many of them had purchased tickets from a bogus company posing as an airline. "It's heartbreaking," one school administrator said. Yet, even though they had to change their plans, the students decided to "make the most of it." They enjoyed two days at nearby attractions, which donated the tickets.

Dealing with failed or changed plans can be disappointing or even heartbreaking. Especially when we've invested time, money, or emotion into the planning. King David "had it in [his] heart to build" a temple for God (1 Chronicles 28:2), but God told him: "You are not to build a house for my Name. . . . Solomon your son is the one who will build my house" (vv. 3, 6). David didn't despair. He praised God for choosing him to be king over Israel, and he gave the plans for the temple to Solomon to complete (vv. 11–13). As he did, he encouraged him: "Be strong and courageous, and do the work . . . for the LORD God . . . is with you" (v. 20).

When our plans fall through, no matter the reason, we can bring our disappointment to God who "cares for [us]" (1 Peter 5:7). He will help us handle our disappointment with grace.   *Alyson Kieda*

We can bring our disappointment to God, who cares for us.

BOLD PERSEVERANCE

Matthew 15:21–28

Jesus said to her, "Woman, you have great faith!
Your request is granted." —Matthew 15:28

In 1953, a fledgling business called Rocket Chemical Company and its staff of three set out to create a line of rust-prevention solvents and degreasers for use in the aerospace industry. It took them forty attempts to perfect their formula. That original secret formula for Water Displacement—fortieth attempt—is still in use today in most homes across North America. It's called WD-40. What a story of persistence!

The gospel of Matthew records another story of bold persistence. A Canaanite woman had a daughter who was possessed by a demon. She had no hope for her daughter—until she heard that Jesus was in the region.

This desperate woman came to Jesus with her need because she believed He could help her. She cried out to Him even though everything and everybody seemed to be against her—race, religious background, gender, the disciples, Satan, and seemingly even Jesus (Matthew 15:22–27). Despite all these obstacles, she did not give up. With bold persistence, she pushed her way through the dark corridors of difficulty, desperate need, and rejection. The result? Jesus commended her for her faith and healed her daughter (v. 28).

We too are invited to approach Jesus with bold persistence. As we keep asking, seeking, and knocking, we will find grace and mercy in our time of need.   *Marvin Williams*

We are invited to approach Jesus with bold persistence.

THE ULTIMATE HEALER

Numbers 21:4–9; 2 Kings 18:47

[Hezekiah] broke into pieces the bronze snake
Moses had made. —2 Kings 18:4

When a medical treatment began to provide relief for a family member's severe food allergies, I became so excited that I talked about it all the time. I described the intense process and extolled the doctor who had created the program. Finally, some friends commented, "We think God should always get the credit for healing." Their statement made me pause. Had I taken my eyes off the Ultimate Healer and made the healing treatment into an idol?

The nation of Israel fell into a similar trap when they began to burn incense to a bronze snake that God had used to heal them. They'd been performing this act of worship until Hezekiah identified it as idolatry and "broke into pieces the bronze snake Moses had made" (2 Kings 18:4).

Several centuries earlier, a group of venomous snakes had invaded the Israelite camp. The snakes bit the people, and many died (Numbers 21:6). Although spiritual rebellion had caused the problem, the people cried out to God for help. Showing mercy, He directed Moses to sculpt a bronze snake, fasten it to a pole, and hold it up for everyone to see. When the people looked at it, they were healed (vv. 4–9).

Think of God's gifts to you. Have any of them become objects of praise instead of evidence of His mercy and grace? Only our holy God—the source of every good gift (James 1:17)—is worthy of worship. *Jennifer Benson Schuldt*

Only our holy God is worthy of worship.

TEXTS, TROUBLES, AND TRIUMPHS

Hebrews 11:32, 35–39

We do not belong to those who shrink back . . . but to
those who have faith and are saved. —Hebrews 10:39

Jimmy hadn't allowed the reality of social unrest, danger, and discomfort to keep him from traveling to one of the poorest countries in the world to encourage ministry couples. The steady stream of text messages to our team back home revealed the challenges he encountered. "Okay, boys, activate the prayer line. We've gone ten miles in the last two hours. . . . Car has overheated a dozen times." Transportation setbacks meant that he arrived just before midnight to preach to those who'd waited for five hours. Later we received a text with a different tone. "Amazing, sweet time of fellowship. . . . About a dozen people came forward for prayer. It was a powerful night!"

Faithfully serving God can be challenging. The exemplars of faith listed in Hebrews 11 would agree. Compelled by their faith in God, ordinary men and women faced uncomfortable and unfathomable circumstances. "Some faced jeers and flogging, and even chains and imprisonment" (v. 36). Their faith compelled them to take risks and rely on God for the outcome.

The same is true for us. Living out our faith may not take us to risky places far away, but it may well take us across the street or across the campus or to an empty seat in a lunchroom or boardroom. Risky? Perhaps. But the rewards, now or later, will be well worth the risks as God helps us.   *Arthur Jackson*

**The faith of the Hebrews 11 heroes compelled them
to take risks and rely on God for the outcome.**

LIMITED BUT USEFUL

Matthew 25:24–28

I came to you in weakness with great fear
and trembling. —1 Corinthians 2:3

Suzanne Bloch, an immigrant from Germany, often played chamber music with Albert Einstein and other prominent scientists. She said that Einstein, though an accomplished violinist, irritated his fellow musicians by not coming in on the beat. "You see," Bloch explained, "he couldn't count." Einstein could project revolutionary theories about the cosmos, but he had difficulty with rhythmic counting. Despite his limitation, he remained an enthusiastic musician.

Do we sometimes lament our limitations? We all have abilities, but we are also afflicted with inabilities. We may be tempted to use our limitations as an excuse for not doing the things God has enabled us to do. Just because we may not be gifted to speak in public or to sing in a choir doesn't mean we can sit on the spiritual sidelines doing nothing.

When we realize that all of us have limitations, we can move forward by seeking God's guidance in using our gifts. We can pray. We can show kindness to others. We can visit the lonely, the sick, the elderly. We can tell with effective simplicity what Jesus means to us. Paul said, "We have different gifts, according to the grace given to each of us" (Romans 12:6). Let's use them.   *Vernon Grounds*

**When we realize that all of us have limitations, we can move
forward by seeking God's guidance in using our gifts.**

STRONG AND GOOD

Psalm 118:13–14, 22–29

The stone the builders rejected has become
the cornerstone. —Psalm 118:22

The young campus minister was troubled. But he looked conflicted when I dared to ask if he prays . . . for God's direction . . . for His help. To pray, as Paul urged, without ceasing. In reply, the young man confessed, "I'm not sure I believe anymore in prayer." He frowned. "Or believe that God is listening. Just look at the world." That young leader was "building" a ministry in his own strength and, sadly, he was failing. Why? He was rejecting God.

Jesus, as the cornerstone of the church, has always been rejected—starting, in fact, with His own people (John 1:11). Many still reject Him today, struggling to build their lives, work, even churches on lesser foundations—their own schemes, dreams, and other unreliable ground. Yet, our good Savior alone is our strength and defense (Psalm 118:14). Indeed, "the stone the builders rejected has become the cornerstone" (v. 22).

Set at the vital corner of our lives, He provides the only right alignment for anything His believers seek to accomplish for Him. To Him, therefore, we pray, "Lord, save us! Lord, grant us success!" (v. 25). The result? "Blessed is he who comes in the name of the Lord" (v. 26). May we give thanks to Him because He's strong and good.   *Patricia Raybon*

**Jesus provides the only right alignment for anything
His believers seek to accomplish for Him.**

SEIZE THE OPPORTUNITY

2 Timothy 4:1–5

Do the work of an evangelist. —2 Timothy 4:5

While waiting to enter the university, twenty-year-old Shin Yi decided to commit three months of her break to serving in a youth mission organization. It seemed like an odd time to do this, given the COVID-19 restrictions that prevented face-to-face meetings. But Shin Yi soon found a way. "We couldn't meet up with students on the streets, in shopping malls, or fast-food centers like we usually did," she shared. "But we continued to keep in touch with the Christian students via Zoom to pray for one another and with the nonbelievers via phone calls."

Shin Yi did what the apostle Paul encouraged Timothy to do: "Do the work of an evangelist" (2 Timothy 4:5). Paul warned that people would find teachers who would tell them what they wanted to hear and not what they needed to hear (vv. 3–4). Yet Timothy was called to take courage and "be prepared in season and out of season." He was to "correct, rebuke and encourage—with great patience and careful instruction" (v. 2).

Though not all of us are called to be evangelists or preachers, each of us can play a part in sharing our faith with those around us. Unbelievers are perishing without Christ. Believers need strengthening and encouragement. With God's help, let's proclaim His good news whenever and wherever we can. *Poh Fang Chia*

Each of us can play a part in sharing our faith with those around us.

BOASTING BOOMERANGS

Daniel 4:28–37

Do not boast about tomorrow, for you do not
know what a day may bring. —Proverbs 27:1

A young man received an award for an outstanding achieve-
ment. But he took too seriously the extravagant praise poured
out by the person who made the presentation. When the award-
winner got home, he repeated to his mother all that had been said.
Then he paused and asked, "How many great men do you suppose
there are in the world today?" Her wise reply? "One less than you
think, my son."

That young fellow had let success go to his head. If the foolish
expression of his inflated ego had not been squelched, he might
have later said something to others that would have brought him
public humiliation.

The story of Nebuchadnezzar also illustrates the folly of boasting.
Under his reign, Babylon had become the world's leading empire,
and its capital city was a marvel to all who saw it. But he made the
mistake of taking all the credit himself. Standing on the roof of the
palace, he surveyed the city and declared, "Is not this the great Babylon I have built . . . by my mighty power?" (Daniel 4 :30). Within
an hour this proud ruler was afflicted with a dreadful disease. Some
believe it was a condition called lycanthropy, the delusion of becoming a wolf.

If success comes your way, be careful. Don't be proud. Don't boast.
Whatever you have acquired or accomplished is by God's grace, and
you don't know when it may all be taken away. Your boasting could
come back at you like a boomerang.   *Herb Vander Lugt*

If success comes your way, be careful.

GOLD–MEDAL EFFORT

Philippians 2:4–11

Not looking to your own interests but each of you
to the interests of the others. —Philippians 2:4

At the Kansas high school state track championship one spring, an unusual thing happened. The team that won the girls 3,200-meter relay was disqualified. But what happened next was even more unusual. The team that was awarded the state championship by default turned right around and gave their medals to the team that had been disqualified.

The first school, St. Mary's Colgan, lost first place because judges ruled that a runner had stepped out of her lane as she handed off the baton. That meant the second team, Maranatha Academy, moved up to first. After receiving their medals, the girls from Maranatha saw the downtrodden looks on the faces of the St. Mary's girls, so they gave them their individual medals.

Why did they do this? As Maranatha's coach Bernie Zarda put it: "Our theme for the year was to run not for our glory, but for God's glory." As a result of the girls' action, their story was told throughout Kansas, and God's name was lifted up.

When we set aside our own interests and accomplishments to recognize that it's better to care for the interests of others (Philippians 2:4), we see God's name glorified. Acting with grace and kindness toward others is one of the best ways to point people to God.

Dave Branon

**"Run not for our glory, but for God's
glory." —Coach Bernie Zarda**

GOD UNDERSTANDS

Psalm 147:1–11

Great is our Lord and mighty in power; his
understanding has no limit. —Psalm 147:5

After a recent move, Mabel's seven-year-old son, Ryan, fussed as he prepared to attend a summer camp at his new school. Mabel encouraged him, assuring him that she understood change was hard. But one morning, Ryan's out-of-character grumpiness seemed excessive. With compassion, Mabel asked, "What's bothering you, Son?"

Staring out of the window, Ryan shrugged. "I don't know, Mom. I just have too many feelings."

Mabel's heart ached as she comforted him. Desperate for a way to help him, she shared that the move was hard for her too. She assured Ryan that God would stay close, that He knows everything, even when they couldn't understand or voice their frustrations. "Let's set up a visit with your friends before school starts," she said. They made plans, grateful that God understands even when His children have "too many feelings."

The writer of Psalm 147 experienced overwhelming emotions throughout his faith journey and recognized the benefits of praising the all-knowing Maker and Sustainer of all, the Healer of physical and emotional wounds (vv. 1–6). He praised God for the ways He provides and "delights in those who fear him, who put their hope in his unfailing love" (v. 11).

When we're struggling to make sense of our ever-changing emotions, we don't have to feel alone or discouraged. We can rest in the unconditional love and unlimited understanding of our unchanging God.   *Xochitl Dixon*

**We don't have to feel alone or discouraged. We
can rest in God's unconditional love.**

HELPING LOVE GROW

1 Corinthians 13

[Love] is not self-seeking. —1 Corinthians 13:5

A young man told his father, "Dad, I'm going to get married."
"How do you know you're ready to get married, Ron?" asked the father. "Are you in love?"

"I sure am," he replied.

The father then asked, "Ron, how do you know you're in love?"

"Last night as I was kissing my girlfriend goodnight, her dog bit me and I didn't feel the pain until I got home!"

Ron has that loving feeling, but he also has a lot of growing to do. Vernon Grounds, a former writer for *Our Daily Bread*, who was married for more than seventy years before his homegoing to heaven, shared these points about how to grow in love:

Ponder God's love in Christ. Take time to reflect on how He gave His life for you. Read about Him in the Gospels and thank Him.

Pray for the love of God. Ask Him to give you an understanding of His love and to teach you how to live that out in your relationships with your spouse and others (1 Corinthians 13).

Practice the love of God. Give of yourself. A newlywed told me he thinks love is practical. He said, "My responsibility is to make life easier for my spouse." The other, tougher side of love is to challenge each other to act in godly ways.

Love will grow when we ponder love, pray for love, and practice love.   *Anne Cetas*

Ponder God's love in Christ. Take time to reflect on how He gave His life for you.

THIS LOVE IS REAL

Romans 5:6–8

He is the atoning sacrifice for our sins, and not only for ours
but also for the sins of the whole world. —1 John 2:2

"I felt like the rug had been pulled from under me," my friend Jojie said. "The shock of the discovery was like a physical blow." She'd found out that her fiancé was seeing someone else. Jojie's previous relationship had ended similarly. So, when she later heard about God's love at a Bible study, she couldn't help wondering: *Is this another scam? Will I get hurt if I believe God when He says He loves me?*

Like Jojie, we may have experienced troubled relationships that left us feeling wary—or even afraid—of trusting someone's promise of love. We may even feel this way about God's love, wondering where the catch is. There is, however, no catch. "God demonstrates his own love for us in this: While we were still sinners, Christ died for us" (Romans 5:8).

"Eventually, I realized Jesus had already proven His love," Jojie says, "by dying for me." My friend discovered that since our sinful state separated us from God, He reached out to us by giving Jesus to die on our behalf (Romans 5:10; 1 John 2:2). Because of this, our sins are forgiven, and we can look forward to eternity with Him (John 3:16).

Whenever we wonder whether we can truly trust God's love, let's remember what Christ did for us on the cross. We can trust His promises of love, knowing that He's faithful.   *Karen Huang*

**Whenever we wonder whether we can truly trust God's
love, let's remember what Christ did for us on the cross.**

PRAYING IN DIFFICULT TIMES

Psalm 61:1–8

From the ends of the earth I call to you, I call as my heart grows
faint; lead me to the rock that is higher than I. —Psalm 61:2

Author and theologian Russell Moore described noticing the ee-
rie silence in the Russian orphanage where he adopted his boys.
Someone later explained that the babies there had stopped crying
because they learned that no one would respond to their cries.

When we face difficult times, we too can feel that no one hears.
And worst of all, we can feel that God himself doesn't listen to our
cries or see our tears. But He does! That's why we need the language
of petition and protest found in the Psalms. The psalmists are pe-
titioning for God's help and also protesting their situation to Him.
In Psalm 61, David brings his petitions and protests before his Creator, stating, "I call to you, I call as my heart grows faint; lead me to
the rock that is higher than I" (v. 2). David cries out to God because
he knows that He alone is his "refuge" and "strong tower" (v. 3).

Praying the petitions and protests of the Psalms is a way of affirming God's sovereignty and appealing to His goodness and faithfulness. They're proof of the intimate relationship we can experience
with God. In difficult moments, we can all be tempted to believe
the lie that He doesn't care. But He does. He hears us and is with us.

Glenn Packiam

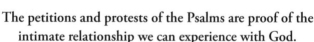

**The petitions and protests of the Psalms are proof of the
intimate relationship we can experience with God.**

PRAYER CARDS

Ephesians 6:10–20

Pray in the Spirit on all occasions with all kinds
of prayers and requests. —Ephesians 6:18

During a writing conference where I served as a faculty member, Tamy handed me a postcard with a handwritten prayer on the back. She explained that she read the faculty biographies, wrote specific prayers on each card, and prayed as she delivered them to us. In awe over the details in her personal message to me, I thanked God for encouraging me through Tamy's gesture. Then I prayed for her in return. When I struggled with pain and fatigue during the conference, I pulled out the postcard. The Lord refreshed my spirit as I reread Tamy's note.

The apostle Paul recognized the life-affirming impact of prayer for others. He urged believers to prepare for battle "against the spiritual forces of evil in the heavenly realms" (Ephesians 6:12). He encouraged ongoing and specific prayers, while emphasizing the need to intervene for one another in what we call intercessory prayer. Paul also requested bold prayers on his behalf. "Pray also for me, that whenever I speak, words may be given me so that I will fearlessly make known the mystery of the gospel, for which I am an ambassador in chains" (vv. 19–20).

As we pray for one another, the Holy Spirit comforts us and strengthens our resolve. He affirms that we need Him and one another, assuring us that He hears every prayer—silent, spoken, or scribbled on a prayer card—and He answers according to His perfect will.   *Xochitl Dixon*

**As we pray for one another, the Holy Spirit
comforts us and strengthens our resolve.**

SEEDS OF GRACE

Mark 4:26–29

The seed sprouts and grows, though he
does not know how. —Mark 4:27

For nearly four decades, a man in India has worked to bring a scorched, sandy wasteland back to life. Noticing how erosion and changing ecosystems had destroyed the river island he loved, he began to plant one tree at a time, bamboo then cotton. Now, lush forests and abundant wildlife fill more than 1,300 acres.

However, the man insists the rebirth was not something he made happen. Acknowledging the amazing way the natural world is designed, he marvels at how seeds are carried to fertile ground by the wind. Birds and animals participate in sowing them as well, and rivers also contribute in helping plants and trees flourish.

Creation works in ways we can't comprehend or control. According to Jesus, this same principle applies to the kingdom of God. "This is what the kingdom of God is like," Jesus said. "A man scatters seed on the ground . . . the seed sprouts and grows, though he does not know how" (Mark 4:26–27). God brings life and healing into the world as pure gifts, without our manipulation. We do whatever God asks of us, and then we watch life emerge. We know that everything flows from His grace.

It's tempting to believe we're responsible to change someone's heart or ensure results for our faithful efforts. However, we need not live under that exhausting pressure. God makes all our seeds grow. It's all grace.

Winn Collier

We know that everything flows from God's grace.

SONGS OF GRACE

JUNE

"The Solid Rock"

Edward Mote and William Bradbury

When darkness veils His lovely face,
I rest on His unchanging grace.

The Carpenter's Song

Have you ever headed to work and suddenly had a wild idea about something you'd like to do? Something that had nothing to do with your job. Maybe climb a mountain? Visit a tropical paradise? Write a book?

This happened one day to British carpenter Edward Mote (1797–1874). Edward was a relatively new believer in Jesus Christ, and he was enjoying the comfort and peace he had found in Jesus. At the age of thirty-seven, as he made his way to his cabinet shop one day in Southwark near London, he thought, *Maybe I should write a song about my faith.*

Sources: Michael Hawn, "History of Hymns: 'My Hope Is Built,'" Discipleship Ministries of The United Methodist Church, http://tinyurl.com/2esebrup; Lindsay Terry, "Story Behind the Song: 'The Solid Rock,'" *The St. Augustine Record*, September 10, 2015, http://tinyurl.com/y9brsa8f; "The Solid Rock," *Hymnstudiesblog* (blog), November 11, 2008, http://tinyurl.com/2ama26s6; all accessed November 6, 2023.

By the time he arrived and unlocked the front door to his shop, he'd already composed what would become the chorus to his new song: "On Christ, the solid rock I stand; all other ground is sinking sand."

During that workday, he composed four stanzas to accompany his chorus. The very next Sunday, Mote stopped by the home of a fellow churchgoer who was ill. When the lady's husband told Mote that each Sunday the family usually sang a hymn, read the Bible, and prayed together, Mote pulled his new song from his pocket—and "The Solid Rock" was sung for the first time.

Altogether, Mote wrote six stanzas, but music editors trimmed it to four. Over the years, the song has been edited extensively to help the flow of ideas. The current tune was composed in 1863 by William Bradbury.

Mote eventually gave up his cabinet shop to go into the ministry. He became the pastor of a Baptist church where he preached for the next twenty-one years. It has been reported that Mote never missed a Sunday of preaching the entire time he served as the church's pastor.

Throughout his life, Mote penned more than one hundred songs, many of which he included in a hymnbook he produced in 1836, *Hymns of Praise: A New Selection of Gospel Hymns*.

The Solid Rock

My hope is built on nothing less
Than Jesus's blood and righteousness;
I dare not trust the sweetest frame,
But wholly lean on Jesus's name.

When darkness veils His lovely face,
I rest on His unchanging grace;
In every high and stormy gale
My anchor holds within the veil.

> *Chorus:*
> On Christ the solid Rock I stand—
> All other ground is sinking sand,
> All other ground is sinking sand.

NOT AFRAID TO DIE

1 Corinthians 15:12–22

Peace I leave with you; my peace I give you. —John 14:27

Ole was ninety-nine years old—the oldest man in our church. He was of Norwegian descent and had a strong body and a determined will. But for several months, Ole had been bedridden.

When I first visited him during his illness, he would lead his family and me in singing "Amazing Grace," but on my last visit he was too tired to sing. I said, "Ole, you're going to see Jesus soon. You won't be disappointed. He's waiting for you."

Earlier he and his family had been sharing together their confidence that he would soon be absent from his body and present with the Lord. I wanted to hear from his own lips the confidence God had given him, so I asked, "Ole, are you afraid?" He opened his eyes wide—as wide as he could—and looked straight into mine. Although his voice was nearly gone, it seemed as if he focused ninety-nine years of strength into his answer. Lifting his head, he said firmly, "Nooooo!"

God does give strength throughout our lives, but He also helps us face the end. Jesus Christ conquered death when He rose from the grave, and He is alive forevermore. Now all who trust Him as their Savior will live with Him throughout eternity. This is why Ole could say he wasn't afraid to die.

Do you have that confidence?   *Dave Burnham*

Jesus Christ conquered death.

PROMISE KEEPER

Hebrews 6:13–20

After waiting patiently, Abraham received
what was promised. —Hebrews 6:15

Gripped by the gravity of the promises he was making to
LaShonne, Jonathan found himself stumbling as he repeated
his wedding vows. He thought, *How can I make these promises and
not believe they're possible to keep?* He made it through the ceremony,
but the weight of his commitments remained. After the reception,
Jonathan led his wife to the chapel where he prayed—for more than
two hours—that God would help him keep his promise to love and
care for LaShonne.

Jonathan's wedding-day fears were based on the recognition of his
human frailties. But God, who promised to bless the nations through
Abraham's offspring (Galatians 3:16), has no such limitations.

To challenge his Jewish Christian audience to perseverance and
patience to continue in their faith in Jesus, the writer of Hebrews
recalled God's promises to Abraham, the patriarch's patient waiting,
and the fulfillment of what had been promised (Hebrews 6:13–15).
Abraham's and Sarah's status as senior citizens was no barrier to the
fulfillment of God's promise to give Abraham "many descendants"
(v. 14).

Are you challenged to trust God despite being weak, frail, and
human? Are you struggling to keep your commitments, to fulfill
your pledges and vows? In 2 Corinthians 12:9, God promises to
help us: "My grace is sufficient for you, for my power is made perfect in weakness." For more than thirty-six years God has helped
Jonathan and LaShonne to remain committed to their vows. Why
not trust Him to help you?   *Arthur Jackson*

**Despite our weakness, frailty, and
humanity, we can trust God.**

RINGS AND GRACE

Hebrews 8:6–13

[I] will remember their sins no more. —Hebrews 8:12

When I look at my hands, I am reminded that I lost my wedding and engagement rings. I was multitasking as I packed for a trip, and suddenly they were gone. I still have no idea where they ended up.

I dreaded telling my husband about my careless mistake—worried how the news would affect him. But he responded with more compassion and care for me than concern over the rings. However, there are times when I still want to do something to earn his grace! He, on the contrary, doesn't hold this episode against me.

So many times we remember our sins and feel we must do something to earn God's forgiveness. But God has said it is by grace, not by works, that we are saved (Ephesians 2:8–9). Speaking of a new covenant, God promised Israel, "I will forgive their wickedness and will remember their sins no more" (Jeremiah 31:34). We have a God who forgives and no longer calls to mind the wrongs we have done.

We may still feel sad about our past, but we need to trust His promise and believe His grace and forgiveness is real through faith in Jesus Christ. This news should lead us to thankfulness and the assurance faith brings. When God forgives, He forgets. *Keila Ochoa*

We have a God who forgives and no longer calls to mind the wrongs we have done.

WEEDING OUT SINS

1 John 1:5–2:2

If we confess our sins, he is faithful and just and
will forgive us our sins. —1 John 1:9

When I noticed a sprig budding next to the garden hose by our porch, I ignored the seemingly harmless eyesore. How could a little weed possibly hurt our lawn? But as the weeks passed, that nuisance grew to be the size of a small bush and began taking over our yard. Its stray stalks arched over a portion of our walkway and sprouted up in other areas. Admitting its destructive existence, I asked my husband to help me dig out the wild weed by the roots and then protect our yard with weed killer.

When we ignore or deny its presence, sin can invade our lives like unwanted overgrowth and darken our personal space. Our sinless God has no darkness in Him . . . at all. As His children, we're equipped and charged to face sins head-on so we can "walk in the light, as he is in the light" (1 John 1:7). Through confession and repentance, we experience forgiveness and freedom from sin (vv. 8–10) because we have a great advocate—Jesus (2:1). He willingly paid the ultimate price for our sins—His lifeblood— and "not only for ours but also for the sins of the whole world" (v. 2).

When God brings our sin to our attention, we can deny, avoid, or deflect responsibility. But when we confess and repent, He weeds out sin that harms our relationships with Him and others.

Xochitl Dixon

**Through confession and repentance, we experience
forgiveness and freedom from sin.**

MOVED BY LOVE

Philippians 1:1–11

Grace and peace to you from God our Father and
the Lord Jesus Christ. —Philippians 1:2

After a godless faction overtook an Asian country in 1949, tens of thousands of refugees flooded into a nearby territory, bringing with them poverty, misery, and despair. A Christian man who worked there recalled feeling great pity for the little children in rags he saw playing in the streets.

He came to know and love a few of them very dearly, however, and what a difference that made! One child he had known for several years showed him her shoes. Both had holes in their soles, exposing her bare feet. Without hesitation the man gave her new shoes and bought her a pretty, new dress. "When I gave them to her," he recalls, "she climbed on my knee, buried her head on my shoulder, her heart too full for words." That man's deed was grace in action, but grace moved by love.

So too, it was love that moved the heavenly Father to extend His undeserved favor to guilty, condemned sinners. This is what is meant by the grace of God. It's a theme that was close to the heart of the apostle Paul and appears over and over in his epistles.

God's grace to you and me comes from His great love—a love that led Him to send His Son Jesus to die on the cross for our sins. Let's praise Him every day for His infinite, matchless grace!

Paul Van Gorder

God's grace to you and me comes from His great love.

WHAT SIN DOES

Romans 7:14–25

Let us run with perseverance the race
marked out for us. —Hebrews 12:1

I was having lunch with a pastor-friend when the discussion sadly turned to a mutual friend in ministry who had failed morally. As we grieved together over this fallen comrade, now out of ministry, I wondered aloud, "I know anyone can be tempted and anyone can stumble, but he's a smart guy. How could he think he could get away with it?" Without blinking, my friend responded, "Sin makes us stupid." It was an abrupt statement intended to get my attention, and it worked.

I have often thought of that statement in the ensuing years, and I continue to affirm the wisdom of those words. How else can you explain the actions of King David, the man after God's own heart turned adulterer and murderer? Or the reckless choices of Samson? Or the public denials of Christ by Peter, the most public of Jesus's disciples? We are flawed people who are vulnerable to temptation and to the foolishness of mind that can rationalize and justify almost any course of action if we try hard enough.

If we are to have a measure of victory over the power of sin, it will come only as we lean on the strength and wisdom of Christ (Romans 7:24–25). As His grace strengthens our hearts and minds, we can overcome our own worst inclination to make foolish choices.

Bill Crowder

**Victory over the power of sin will come only as we
lean on the strength and wisdom of Christ.**

REFLECTING HIS LIGHT

John 1:4–9

The true light that gives light to everyone was
coming into the world. —John 1:9

To capture the beauty of reflective light in his landscape oil paintings, artist Armand Cabrera works with a key artistic principle: "Reflected light is never as strong as its source light." He observes that novice painters tend to exaggerate reflected light. He says, "Reflected light belongs to the shadow and as such it must support, not compete with the lighted areas" of a painting.

We hear similar insight in the Bible concerning Jesus as "the light of all mankind" (John 1:4). John the Baptist "came as a witness to testify concerning that light, so that through him all might believe" (v. 7). The gospel writer tells us, "He himself [John] was not the light; he came only as a witness to the light" (v. 8).

As with John, we're chosen by God to reflect Christ's light to those living in the shadows of an unbelieving world. This is our role, as one source says, "perhaps because unbelievers are not able to bear the full blazing glory of His light firsthand."

Cabrera teaches his art students that "anything that has direct light falling on it . . . becomes a source of light itself." Similarly, with Jesus as "the true light that gives light to everyone" (v. 9), we can shine as witnesses. As we reflect Him, may the world be amazed to see His glory shine through us.   *Patricia Raybon*

**We're chosen by God to reflect Christ's light to those
living in the shadows of an unbelieving world.**

WHEN HARD-PRESSED

Psalm 118:5–14

The LORD is with me; I will not be afraid. —Psalm 118:6

Many years ago, a friend told me how intimidated she was while trying to cross a street where several roads intersected. "I'd never seen anything like this; the rules I'd been taught for crossing the street seemed ineffective. I was so frightened that I'd stand on the corner, wait for the bus, and ask the bus driver if he'd please allow me to ride to the other side of the street. It took a long time before I successfully learned to navigate this intersection both as a pedestrian and later as a driver."

As complicated as a dangerous traffic intersection can be, navigating life's complexities can be even more menacing. Although the psalmist's specific situation in Psalm 118 is uncertain, we know it was difficult and just right for prayer: "When hard pressed, I cried to the LORD" (v. 5), the psalmist exclaimed. And his confidence in God was unmistakable: "The LORD is with me; I will not be afraid. . . . The LORD is with me; he is my helper" (vv. 6–7).

It's not unusual to be fearful when we need to change jobs or schools or housing—or even sides of the street. Anxieties arise when health declines, relationships change, or dollars disappear. But these challenges needn't be interpreted as abandonment by God. When we're hard-pressed, may we find ourselves prayerfully pressing into His presence. *Arthur Jackson*

Our confidence in God is unmistakable:
"The LORD is with me; I will not be afraid."
—Psalm 118:6

RUNNING ON EMPTY

Isaiah 40:28–31

They will run and not grow weary, they will
walk and not be faint. —Isaiah 40:31

"I just don't think I can do this anymore," my friend said through her tears as she discussed the overwhelming sense of hopelessness she faced as a nurse in a global health crisis. "I know that God has called me to nursing, but I'm overwhelmed and emotionally drained," she confessed. Seeing that a cloud of exhaustion had come over her, I responded, "I know you feel helpless right now, but ask God to give you the direction you're seeking and the strength to persevere." At that moment, she decided to intentionally seek God through prayer. Soon after, my friend was invigorated with a new sense of purpose. Not only was she emboldened to continue nursing but she also felt that God gave her the strength to serve even more people by traveling to hospitals around the country.

As believers in Jesus, we can always look to God for help and encouragement when we feel overburdened, because "He will not grow tired or weary" (Isaiah 40:28). The prophet Isaiah states that our Father in heaven "gives strength to the weary and increases the power of the weak" (v. 29). Although God's strength is everlasting, He knows we'll inevitably have days when we're physically and emotionally consumed (v. 30). But when we look to God for our strength instead of trying to sprint through life's challenges alone, we'll never have to run on empty. He'll renew us and give us the resolve to press on in faith.

Kimya Loder

**As believers in Jesus, we can always look to God for help
and encouragement when we feel overburdened.**

ARRIVING LATE

Matthew 20:1–16

The last will be first, and the first will be last. —Matthew 20:16

Eddie, an outspoken agnostic, spent his entire life of fifty years denying the existence of God. Then he contracted a debilitating disease, and his health slowly deteriorated. As he lay in a hospice house awaiting death, Christian friends he'd known in high school visited him almost every day. They told him again of Christ's love. But the closer Eddie came to dying, the more it appeared he was not interested in God.

One Sunday, a pastor stopped by to visit. To everyone's surprise, Eddie prayed with him and asked Jesus for forgiveness and salvation. Two weeks later, he died.

Eddie denied Christ for fifty years and spent only two weeks loving and trusting Him. But because of his faith, he will experience forever God's presence, glory, love, majesty, and perfection. Some may argue that this isn't fair. But according to Jesus's parable in Matthew 20, it's not about fairness. It's about God's goodness and grace (vv. 11–15).

Have you waited such a long time to trust Jesus for salvation that you think it might be too late? Consider the thief on the cross, who put his faith in Jesus just before he died (Luke 23:39–43). Trust Jesus now and receive His gift of eternal life. If you're reading this, it's not too late!

Dave Branon

Salvation is about God's goodness and grace.

JOIN THE CHOIR

Psalm 89:1–8

I will sing of mercies of the LORD forever; with
my mouth will I make known Your faithfulness
to all generations. —Psalm 89:1 NKJV

I'll never forget the first time I saw the Brooklyn Tabernacle Choir in concert. Nearly two hundred people who had been redeemed out of the bowels of Brooklyn—former crack addicts and prostitutes included—sang their hearts out to God. Their faces glistened with tears running down their cheeks as they sang about God's work of redemption and forgiveness in their lives.

As I watched them, I felt somewhat shortchanged. Since I was saved when I was six, I didn't feel the same depth of gratefulness they displayed as they sang about the dramatic rescue God had provided for them. I was saved from things like biting my sister—not exactly a significant testimony!

Then the Spirit reminded me that if He had not rescued me when I was young, who knows where my life would be today? What destructive paths would I have stumbled down if He had not been teaching me qualities like servanthood and self-control?

It became clear that I too am a great debtor to His grace. It's not only what we are saved "out of" but also what we have been saved "from" that makes our hearts worthy of a spot in the chorus of the redeemed. Anyone who receives Jesus as Savior is welcome to join in the choir of praise. Start now, because we "will sing of the mercies of the LORD forever" (Psalm 89:1 NKJV).   *Joe Stowell*

**It's not only what we are saved "out of" but also what
we have been saved "from" that makes our hearts
worthy of a spot in the chorus of the redeemed.**

FIGHTING "FLASHY" THINGS

Proverbs 22:1–6

Start children off on the way they should go, and even when
they are old they will not turn from it. —Proverbs 22:6

In the 1960s-era TV series *The Andy Griffith Show*, a man tells Andy
he should let his son Opie decide how he wants to live. Andy dis-
agrees: "You can't let a young'un decide for himself. He'll grab at the
first flashy thing with shiny ribbons on it. Then, when he finds out
there's a hook in it, it's too late. Wrong ideas come packaged with so
much glitter that it's hard to convince them that other things might
be better in the long run." He concludes that it's important for parents to model right behavior and help "keep temptation away."

Andy's words are related to the wisdom found in Proverbs: "Start
children off on the way they should go, and even when they are
old they will not turn from it" (22:6). Although many may read
these words as a promise, they're really a guide. All of us are called
to make our own decision to believe in Jesus. But we can help lay
a biblical foundation through our love for God and Scripture. And
we can pray that as the little ones under our care mature, they will
choose to trust Christ as Savior and walk in His ways—avoiding
"the paths of the wicked" (v. 5).

Our own victory over "flashy things" through the Holy Spirit's
enabling is also a powerful testimony. Jesus's Spirit helps us to withstand temptation and molds our lives into examples worth imitating.

Alyson Kieda

**We can help lay a biblical foundation for our children
through our love for God and Scripture.**

FOR THE SAKE OF THE GOSPEL

Titus 2:1–10

In every way they will make the teaching about
God our Savior attractive. —Titus 2:10

The year was 1916, and Nelson graduated from medical school in his home state of Virginia. Within six months of graduation, he had married Virginia Leftwich and had moved to China to become a surgeon at Love and Mercy Hospital in Jiangsu Province. It was the only hospital in an area of at least two million Chinese residents.

Nelson, together with his family, lived in the area for twenty-four more years, running the hospital, performing surgeries, and sharing the gospel with thousands of people. From once being called "foreign devil" by those who distrusted foreigners, Nelson Bell later became known as "The Bell Who Is Lover of the Chinese People." The Bells' daughter Ruth later married evangelist Billy Graham.

Although Nelson was a brilliant surgeon and Bible teacher, it wasn't his skills that drew many to Jesus; it was his character and the way he lived out the gospel.

In Paul's letter to Titus, the young gentile leader who was taking care of the church in Crete, the apostle said that living like Christ is crucial because it can make the gospel "attractive" (Titus 2:10). Yet we don't do this in our own strength. God's grace helps us live "self-controlled, upright and godly lives" (v. 12), reflecting the truths of our faith (v. 1).

Many people around us still don't know the good news of Christ, but they know us. Let's ask Him to help us reflect and reveal His message in attractive ways.   *Karen Huang*

**Living like Christ is crucial because it
can make the gospel attractive.**

JUST ENOUGH?

Proverbs 30:7–9

Give me neither poverty nor riches, but give me
only my daily bread. —Proverbs 30:8

In the movie *Fiddler on the Roof*, the character Tevye talks honestly
with God about His economics: "You made many, many poor
people. I realize, of course, that it's no shame to be poor. But it's no
great honor either! So, what would have been so terrible if I had a
small fortune! . . . Would it have spoiled some vast, eternal plan—if
I were a wealthy man?"

Many centuries before author Sholem Aleichem placed these honest words on Tevye's tongue, Agur lifted an equally honest but somewhat different prayer to God in the book of Proverbs. Agur asked
God to give him neither poverty nor wealth—just his "daily bread"
(Proverbs 30:8). He knew that having "too much" could make him
proud and transform him into a practical atheist—denying the character of God. In addition, he asked God to not let him "become poor"
because it might cause him to dishonor God's name by stealing from
others (v. 9). Agur recognized God as his sole provider, and he asked
Him for "just enough" to satisfy his daily needs. His prayer revealed a
pursuit of God and the contentment that's found in Him alone.

Let's seek to adopt Agur's attitude, recognizing God as the provider of all we have. And as we pursue financial stewardship that
honors His name, let's live in contentment before Him—the One
who provides not "just enough," but more than enough.

Marvin Williams

**Let's live in contentment before God, the
One who provides more than enough.**

LITTLE THINGS

James 3:1–12

Consider what a great forest is set on fire by a small
spark. The tongue also is a fire. —James 3:5–6

A mosquito is a tiny insect—but its potential for devastation is huge. When I was in the fifth grade, I was bitten by mosquitoes on both knees. The bites became infected and deteriorated into a threatening case of blood poisoning. For over a month, I was pricked repeatedly with penicillin shots, and my knees had to be lanced and drained twice daily to remove the infection. It was excruciatingly painful, and quite terrifying for a ten-year-old kid. To this day, I carry scars on my knees from the numerous lancings. All because of something as tiny as a mosquito.

James, the half brother of Jesus, warns us of another little thing that can also be very destructive. He says that even though the tongue is little, it boasts great things. It's like a small spark that sets a great forest on fire (3:5). Although the tongue is small, there is nothing small about the damage it can do. Words carry with them the power of healing or the capacity for destruction far greater than the poison of any mosquito bite.

It is essential that we use our words with great wisdom and care, wisely considering the words we choose. Will they be seasoned with the touch of grace or with the poison of anger?　　*Bill Crowder*

**Words carry with them the power of
healing or a destructive capacity.**

THANKFUL FOR MONDAY

Ecclesiastes 2:17–25

[People] can do nothing better than to . . . find
satisfaction in their own toil. —Ecclesiastes 2:24

I used to dread Mondays.

Sometimes, when I got off the train to head to a previous job, I'd sit at the station for a while, trying to delay reaching the building, if only for a few minutes. My heart would beat fast as I worried over meeting the deadlines and managing the moods of a temperamental boss.

For some of us, it can be especially difficult to start another dreary workweek. We may feel overwhelmed or underappreciated in our job. King Solomon described the toil of work when he wrote: "What do people get for all the toil and anxious striving with which they labor under the sun? All their days their work is grief and pain" (Ecclesiastes 2:22–23).

While the wise king didn't give us a cure-all for making work less stressful or more rewarding, he did offer us a change in perspective. No matter how difficult our work is, he encourages us to "find satisfaction" in it with God's help (v. 24). Perhaps it will come as the Holy Spirit enables us to display Christlike character. Or as we hear from someone who's been blessed through our service. Or as we remember the wisdom God provided to deal with a difficult situation. Although our work may be difficult, our faithful God is there with us. His presence and power can light up even gloomy days. With His help, we can be thankful for Monday.   *Poh Fang Chia*

**Though our work may be difficult, our
faithful God is there with us.**

STRONGER THAN HATE

Luke 23:32–34, 44–46

Father, forgive them, for they do not know
what they are doing. —Luke 23:34

Within twenty-four hours of his mother Sharonda's tragic death, Chris found himself uttering these powerful, grace-filled words: "Love is stronger than hate." His mother, along with eight others, had been killed at a Wednesday night Bible study in Charleston, South Carolina. What was it that had so shaped this teenager's life that these words could flow from his lips and his heart? Chris, a believer in Jesus, had a mother who "loved everybody with all her heart."

In Luke 23:26–49 we get a front-row seat to an execution scene that included two criminals and the innocent Jesus (v. 32). All three were crucified (v. 33). Amid the gasps and sighs and groans from those hanging on the crosses, the following words of Jesus could be heard: "Father, forgive them, for they do not know what they are doing" (v. 34). The hate-filled initiative of the religious leaders had resulted in the crucifixion of the very One who championed love. Although He was in intense agony, Jesus's love continued to triumph.

How have you or someone you love been the target of hate, ill-will, bitterness, or ugliness? Allow your pain to prompt your prayers as you allow the example of Jesus and people like Chris to encourage you by the power of the Spirit to choose love over hate.

Arthur Jackson

**Amid the gasps and sighs and groans from those hanging
on the crosses, Jesus could be heard: "Father, forgive
them, for they do not know what they are doing."**

HEARING CHRIST, NOT CHAOS

John 10:1–6, 27

My sheep listen to my voice. —John 10:27

After watching TV news for hours each day, the elderly man grew agitated and anxious—worried the world was falling apart and taking him with it. "Please turn it off," his grown daughter begged him. "Just stop listening." But the man continued to spend an excessive amount of time on social media and other news sources.

What we listen to matters deeply. We see this in Jesus's encounter with Pontius Pilate. Responding to criminal charges brought against Jesus by religious leaders, Pilate summoned Him and asked, "Are you the king of the Jews?" (John 18:33). Jesus replied with a stunning question: "Is that your own idea . . . or did others talk to you about me?" (v. 34).

The same question tests us. In a world of panic, are we listening to chaos or to Christ? Indeed, "My sheep listen to my voice," He said. "I know them, and they follow me" (10:27). Jesus "used this figure of speech" (v. 6) to explain himself to doubting religious leaders. As with a good shepherd, He said that "his sheep follow him because they know his voice. But they will never follow a stranger; in fact, they will run away from him because they do not recognize a stranger's voice" (vv. 4–5).

As our Good Shepherd, Jesus bids us to hear Him above all. May we listen well by studying His Word and find His peace.

Patricia Raybon

Jesus bids us to hear Him above all.

THE MARRIAGE METAPHOR

Ephesians 4:2–13

Each one of you also must love his wife as he loves himself,
and the wife must respect her husband. —Ephesians 5:33

After more than twenty years together, I sometimes wonder how my marriage to Merryn works. I'm a writer; Merryn is a statistician. I work with words; she works with numbers. I want beauty; she wants function. We come from different worlds.

Merryn arrives to appointments early; I'm occasionally late. I try new things on the menu; she orders the same. After twenty minutes at an art gallery, I'm just getting started, while Merryn is already in the cafe downstairs wondering how much longer I'll be. We give each other many opportunities to learn patience!

We do have things in common—a shared sense of humor, a love of travel, and a common faith that helps us pray through options and compromise as needed. With this shared base, our differences even work to our advantage. Merryn has helped me learn to relax, while I've helped her grow in discipline. Working with our differences has made us better people.

Paul uses marriage as a metaphor for the church (Ephesians 5:21–33), and with good reason. Like marriage, church brings very different people together, requiring them to develop humility and patience and to "[bear] with one another in love" (4:2). And, as in marriage, a shared base of faith and mutual service helps a church become unified and mature (vv. 11–13).

Differences in relationships can cause great frustration—in the church and in marriage. But managed well, they can help us become more Christlike.   *Sheridan Voysey*

As in marriage, a shared base of faith and mutual service helps a church become unified and mature.

THE BEST FIND

2 Chronicles 34:14–21

Hilkiah said to Shaphan the secretary, "I have found the Book of the Law in the temple of the LORD." —2 Chronicles 34:15

In 1987, a West Michigan couple, the Zartmans, bought four books at an estate sale. They were excited to find that the books contained two collections of letters and sermons by hymn writer John Newton, who wrote the beloved hymn "Amazing Grace." Also included was a two-volume set of his sermons based on Handel's *Messiah*.

Newton's family had preserved these writings by passing them down through the years. Then in the 1840s his heirs brought the books to the United States. The books were used in 2007 as part of a commemoration of the 200th year since Newton's death. The books were then donated to a museum in England.

An even greater literary find is recorded in 2 Chronicles 34:15. During Josiah's reign as king of Judah, he ordered the repair of the temple. In the temple, Hilkiah, the high priest, found the Book of the Law that had been given to Moses by the Lord. When Josiah "heard the words of the Law" (v. 19), he felt convicted and later stood before his people to make a covenant to keep all that was written in the book (v. 31).

The Bible is still the best book we can discover. In it we learn what God wants us to do to please Him.   *Anne Cetas*

The Bible is the best book we can discover.

MONSTRO THE GOLDFISH

Luke 10:27–37

Love your neighbor as yourself. —Luke 10:27

Lacey Scott was at her local pet store when a sad fish at the bottom of the tank caught her eye. His scales had turned black, and lesions had formed on his body. Lacey rescued the ten-year-old fish, named him "Monstro" after the whale in the fairytale *Pinocchio*, and placed him in a "hospital" tank, changing his water daily. Slowly, Monstro improved, began to swim, and grew. His black scales transformed to gold. Through Lacey's committed care, Monstro was made new!

In Luke 10, Jesus tells the story of a traveler who was beaten, robbed, and left for dead. Both a priest and a Levite passed by, ignoring the man's suffering. But a Samaritan—a member of a despised people group—took care of him, even paying for his needs (Luke 10:33–35). Pronouncing the Samaritan as the true "neighbor" in the story, Jesus encouraged His listeners to do the same.

What Lacey did for a dying goldfish we can do for people in need around us. Homeless, unemployed, disabled, and lonely "neighbors" lie in our path. Let us allow their sadness to catch our eyes and draw us to respond with neighborly care. A kind greeting. A shared meal. A few dollars slipped from palm to palm. How might God use us to offer His love to others, a love that can make all things new?

Elisa Morgan

**Let us allow the sadness of others to catch our eyes
and draw us to respond with neighborly care.**

GOD'S MOVES

Exodus 12:24–28

It is the Passover sacrifice to the LORD, who
passed over the houses of the Israelites in Egypt
and spared our homes. —Exodus 12:27

I love a good game of *Scrabble*. After one particular game, my friends named a move after me—calling it a "Katara." I'd been trailing the entire game, but at the end of it—with no tiles left in the bag—I made a seven-letter word. This meant the game was over, and I received fifty bonus points as well as all the points from all my opponents' leftover tiles, moving me from last place to first. Now whenever we play and someone is trailing, they remember what happened and hold out hope for a "Katara."

Remembering what has happened in the past has the power to lift our spirits and give us hope. And that's exactly what the Israelites did when they celebrated Passover. The Passover commemorates what God did for the Israelites when they were in Egypt, oppressed by Pharaoh and his crew (Exodus 1:6–14). After they cried out to God, He delivered the people in a mighty way. He told them to put blood on their doorposts so the death angel would "pass over" their firstborn people and animals (12:12–13). Then they would be kept safe from death.

Centuries later, believers in Jesus regularly take communion as we remember His sacrifice on the cross—providing what we needed to be delivered from sin and death (1 Corinthians 11:23–26). Remembering God's loving acts in the past gives us hope for today.

Katara Patton

**Remembering what has happened in the past has
the power to lift our spirits and give us hope.**

THE RIGHT INFORMATION

1 Thessalonians 4:13–18

Brothers and sisters, we do not want you to be
uninformed about those who sleep in death, so
that you do not grieve like the rest of mankind,
who have no hope. —1 Thessalonians 4:13

Our flight had been airborne about fifteen minutes when the pilot
announced that the aircraft had a serious problem the crew was
trying to analyze. A few minutes later, he announced that it was a
vibration and we would have to return to the airport. Then the flight
attendants made a series of step-by-step announcements explaining
what was going on and what would happen once we were on the
ground. In an event that could have been terrifying, the crew relieved
our fears by giving us the right information.

In the first century, a group of believers in Thessalonica were
afraid that their believing loved ones who had died were gone forever
and would miss out on the second coming of Christ. For that reason,
Paul wrote, "we do not want you to be uninformed about those who
sleep in death, so that you do not grieve like the rest of mankind,
who have no hope" (1 Thessalonians 4:13). Paul's words of comfort
were intended to soften their fears by giving them the right information, which made all the difference in the world. While grieving
their loss, they could still have hope of a coming reunion with those
who were in Christ.

In seasons of loss, we too can find comfort and hope because the
Bible has given us the right information. *Bill Crowder*

**While grieving a loss, we can still have hope of a
coming reunion with those who were in Christ.**

BECOMING WHOLE

Romans 7:13–25

Therefore, my dear friends, as you have always obeyed—
not only in my presence, but now much more in
my absence—continue to work out your salvation
with fear and trembling. —Philippians 2:12–13

When a friend fell off her bike and suffered a severe brain injury, doctors weren't sure she would survive. For several days she remained suspended between life and death.

The first good news came when she opened her eyes. Then she responded to simple voice commands. But with every small improvement, anxiety remained. How far would she progress?

After one difficult day of therapy, her husband was discouraged. But the very next morning he shared these welcome words: "Sandy's back!" Physically, emotionally, psychologically, and mentally, Sandy was becoming the "self" we knew and loved.

Sandy's fall reminds me of what theologians refer to as "the fall" of mankind (Genesis 3). And her struggle to recover parallels our struggle to overcome the brokenness of sin (Romans 7:18). If only her body healed, recovery would be incomplete. The same would be true if her brain worked but her body didn't. Wholeness means that all parts work together for one purpose.

God is the one healing Sandy, but she must work hard in therapy to improve. The same is true of us spiritually. After God saves us through Christ, we must "work out" our salvation (Philippians 2:12)—not to earn it but to bring our thoughts and actions into agreement with His purpose. *Julie Ackerman Link*

After God saves us through Christ, we must "work out" our salvation . . . to bring our thoughts and actions into agreement with His purpose.

QUESTIONABLE QUOTES

Acts 17:10–15

The Berean Jews . . . received the message with great
eagerness and examined the Scriptures every day to
see if what Paul said was true. —Acts 17:11

Many people don't know what the Bible really says. It's good to
check up on our knowledge. For example, which of the following are biblical quotations?

- Cleanliness is next to godliness.
- God helps those who help themselves.
- An honest confession is good for the soul.
- We are as prone to sin as sparks fly upward.
- Money is the root of all evil.
- Honesty is the best policy.

The answer? While some of these statements are truisms, none
of them as quoted are found in the Bible!

One pastor called another pastor one Saturday night and said,
"I have my sermon prepared from a certain text, but I can't find
the reference in the Bible." The second pastor asked, "What is the
verse?" His friend replied, "Give me liberty or give me death." This
is a noble statement by the American Revolutionary leader Patrick
Henry, but it's not in the Bible.

A thorough knowledge of God's Word comes by diligent study.
If we are to grow in grace and in the knowledge of the Lord, we
must "let the word of Christ dwell in [us] richly in all wisdom"
(Colossians 3:16 NKJV).

Let's search and study the Scriptures with diligence. Questionable
quotes are no substitute for God's sure Word.   *Paul Van Gorder*

A thorough knowledge of God's Word comes by diligent study.

ABOVE ALL ELSE

Matthew 6:25–34

Seek the Kingdom of God above all else, and live righteously,
and he will give you everything you need. —Matthew 6:33 NLT

In Manila, Lando drives a jeepney (a form of public transport in the Philippines). One day he gulped down coffee at a roadside stall. Daily commuters were back again after the COVID-19 lockdowns. *And the sports event today means more passengers. I'll get back lost income. Finally, I can stop worrying*, Lando thought.

He was about to start driving when he spotted Ronnie on a bench nearby. The street sweeper looked troubled, like he needed to talk. *But every minute counts*, Lando thought. *The more passengers, the more income. I can't linger.* But he sensed that God wanted him to approach Ronnie, so he did.

Jesus understands how difficult it is not to worry when we're unsure of how our needs will be met (Matthew 6:25–27). So He assures us that our heavenly Father knows exactly what we need (v. 32). He reminds us not to be anxious, but to trust Him and devote ourselves to doing what He wants us to do (vv. 31–33). As we embrace and obey His purposes, we can have confidence that our Father who "clothes the grass of the field, which is here today and tomorrow is thrown into the fire" will provide for us according to His will—just as He provides for all creation (v. 30).

Because of Lando's conversation with Ronnie, the street sweeper eventually prayed to become a believer in Christ. "And God still provided enough passengers that day," Lando shared. "He reminded me my needs were His concern; mine was simply to follow Him."

Karen Huang

**We can have confidence that our Father will
provide for us according to His will.**

FIVE GOOD THINGS

Psalm 107:1–9

Give thanks to the LORD, for he is good; his
love endures forever. —Psalm 107:1

According to research, people who are intentionally grateful for what they have report better sleep, fewer symptoms of illness, and more happiness. These are impressive benefits. Psychologists even suggest that we keep a "gratitude journal" to improve our well-being, writing down five things we're grateful for each week.

Scripture has long promoted the practice of gratitude. From meals and marriage (1 Timothy 4:3–5), to the beauties of creation (Psalm 104), the Bible has called us to see such things as gifts and to thank the Giver for them. Psalm 107 lists five things Israel could be especially grateful for: their rescue from the desert (vv. 4–9), their release from captivity (vv. 10–16), healing from disease (vv. 18–22), safety at sea (vv. 23–32), and their flourishing in a barren land (vv. 33–42). "Give thanks to the LORD," the psalm repeats, for these are all signs of God's "unfailing love" (vv. 8, 15, 21, 31).

Do you have a notepad handy? Why not write down five good things you're grateful for now? It might be the meal you just enjoyed, your marriage, or like Israel, God's rescue points in your life. Give thanks for the birds' singing outside, the smells from your kitchen, the comfort of your chair, the voice of loved ones. Each is a gift and a sign of God's unfailing love.   *Sheridan Voysey*

Write down five good things you're grateful for.

SIMPLY HELPING

Isaiah 58:6–12

Help those in trouble. Then your light will shine
out from the darkness. —Isaiah 58:10 NLT

Ole Kassow of Copenhagen loved bicycling. One morning, when
he saw an elderly man sitting alone with his walker in a park,
Ole felt inspired by a simple idea: why not offer elderly people the joy
and freedom of a bike ride. So, one sunny day he stopped at a nursing home with a rented trishaw (a three-wheeled bike) and offered a
ride to anyone there. He was delighted when a staff member and an
elderly resident became the first riders of Cycling Without Age.

Now, more than twenty years later, Ole's dream to help those
who missed cycling has blessed some 575,000 elderly people with
2.5 million rides. Where? To see a friend, enjoy an ice-cream cone,
and "feel the wind in their hair." Participants say they sleep better,
eat better, and feel less lonely.

Such a gift brings to life God's beautiful words to His people in
Isaiah 58:10–11. "Help those in trouble," He told them. "Then your
light will shine out from the darkness, and the darkness around you
will be as bright as noon" (NLT). God promised, "The LORD will guide
you continually, giving you water when you are dry and restoring your
strength. You will be like a well-watered garden, like an ever-flowing
spring."

God told His people, "Some of you will rebuild the deserted ruins of your cities" (v. 12 NLT). What might He do through us? As He
helps us, may we always be ready to help others.   *Patricia Raybon*

May we always be ready to help others.

GIVE THANKS!

Psalm 92

It is good to praise the LORD and make music to
your name, O Most High. —Psalm 92:1

Psalm 92 is "A song. For the Sabbath day," a resting place for
those who are troubled.

The song begins with a commendation of praise: "It is good to
praise the LORD." It does us good to turn from our unsettling and
anxious thoughts to declare God's "love in the morning and [His]
faithfulness at night" (v. 2). God loves us and is always faithful! He
makes us glad (v. 4).

Praise not only makes us glad but it also makes us wise. We begin to understand something of God's greatness and creative design
in all He does (vv. 5–9). We gain a wisdom that is hidden from
those who don't know God. The wicked may "flourish" and "spring
up like grass" for a moment (v. 7), but ultimately, they will wither
away.

The righteous, however, are joined to the One who dwells in eternity (v. 8). They "flourish like a palm tree" and "like a cedar in Leba-
non" (v. 12), symbols of graceful beauty and unbending strength.
For they have been "planted in the house of the LORD" (v. 13). Their
roots go down into the soil of God's faithfulness; they draw on His
unquenchable love.

Give thanks and praise to the Lord today!   *David Roper*

**It does us good to turn from our unsettling and
anxious thoughts to declare God's lovingkindness.**

GOD KNOWS

Joshua 22:21–27

The Mighty One, God, the Lord! He knows! —Joshua 22:22

A couple who stopped to admire a large abstract painting noticed open paint cans and brushes underneath it. Assuming it was a "work in progress" that anyone could help create, they stroked in some color and left. The artist, though, had purposefully left the supplies there as part of the finished work's display. After reviewing video footage of the incident, the gallery acknowledged the misunderstanding and didn't press charges.

The Israelites who lived east of the Jordan created a misunderstanding when they built a massive altar next to the river. The western tribes viewed this as rebellion against God—everyone knew that the tabernacle was the only God-approved place for worship (Joshua 22:16).

Tensions mounted until the eastern tribes explained that they only meant to make a replica of God's altar. They wanted their descendants to see it and recognize their spiritual and ancestral connection with the rest of Israel (vv. 28–29). They exclaimed: "The Mighty One, God, the Lord! He knows!" (v. 22). Thankfully, the others listened. They saw what was going on, praised God, and returned home.

Because God "searches every heart and understands every desire and every thought" (1 Chronicles 28:9), everyone's motives are clear to Him. If we ask Him to help us sort out confusing situations, He may give us the chance to explain ourselves or the grace we need to forgive offenses. We can turn to Him when we're striving for unity with others. *Jennifer Benson Schuldt*

"[God] searches every heart and understands every desire and every thought." —1 Chronicles 28:9

JULY

"All the Way My Savior Leads Me"

Fanny Crosby and Robert Lowry

[God] gives me grace for every trial,
feeds me with the living bread.

Fanny Finds a Five

The number of songs attributed to Fanny Crosby (1829–1915) is astounding. It is generally accepted that she penned more than eight thousand hymns during her ninety-five years of life. We don't have a record of the origin story for every song, but we do know what led her to write one of her most famous and most helpful hymns, "All the Way My Savior Leads Me."

According to her autobiography, Crosby needed a small sum of money—"needed it very badly," she recalled. So, having no idea how to get the five dollars, she prayed God would meet that need. "Not long after I prayed for the money," she wrote, "a gentleman

---

Sources: "Hymn History: All the Way My Savior Leads Me," *Enjoying the Journey* (blog), Jan. 26, 2022, http://tinyurl.com/yck6hvhb; Tammy Kennington, "10 Things You Need to Know about Fanny Crosby," Christianity.com, updated April 14, 2022, http://tinyurl.com/4kaz45et; all accessed November 6, 2023.

came into the house, passed the time of day, shook hands with me, and went out immediately."

As he left, she closed her right hand and discovered it had a bill in it. Later, she asked a friend what it was, because, of course, Fanny could not see. When her friend said it was a five-dollar bill, Fanny's first thought was, *What a wonderful way the Lord helps me! All the way my Savior leads me.*

"I have no way of accounting for this except to believe that God put it into the heart of this good man to bring the money," she commented in her autobiography.

Fanny Crosby then did what Fanny Crosby did better than almost anyone else who ever lived: She wrote a song. It began "All the way my Savior leads me—what have I to ask beside?" When she finished writing the words, she turned them over to Dr. Robert Lowry, who set these beautiful words to music. For a hundred and fifty years, this song, based on a God-given gift of five dollars, has encouraged and strengthened Christians around the world.

During her long life, Fanny never regretted the incident that caused her to lose her vision as an infant. She trusted Jesus as Savior as an adult and spent the last sixty-four years spreading Jesus, the Light of the world, to whomever would listen.

As she thought about her disability, she proclaimed a perspective that helps us understand how she could say, "All the way my Savior leads me." She said, "If I had a choice, I would still choose to remain blind. . . . For when I die, the first face I will ever see will be the face of my blessed Savior."

All the Way My Savior Leads Me

All the way my Savior leads me—
What have I to ask beside?
Can I doubt His tender mercy,
Who thru life has been my Guide?
Heavenly Peace, divinest comfort.
Here by faith in Him to dwell!
For I know, whate'er befall me,
Jesus doeth all things well.

All the way my Savior leads me—
Cheers each winding path I tread,
Gives me grace for ev'ry trial,
Feeds me with the living bread.
Tho my weary steps may falter,
And my soul athirst may be,
Gushing from the Rock before me,
Lo! A spring of joy I see.

PRESSING ON IN JESUS

Philippians 3:12–16

Forgetting what is behind and straining toward what
is ahead, I press on. —Philippians 3:13–14

On a run in the forest, I tried to find a shortcut and went down an unfamiliar path. Wondering if I was lost, I asked a runner coming the other way if I was on the right track.

"Yup," he replied confidently. Seeing my doubtful look, he quickly added: "Don't worry, I've tried all the wrong routes! But that's okay, it's all part of the run."

What an apt description of my spiritual journey! How many times have I strayed from God, given in to temptation, and been distracted by the things of life? Yet God has forgiven me each time and helped me to move on—knowing I will certainly stumble again. God knows our tendency to go down the wrong path. But He's always ready to forgive, again and again, if we confess our sins and allow His Spirit to transform us.

The apostle Paul knew this was all part of the faith journey. Fully aware of his sinful past and current weaknesses, he knew he had yet to obtain the Christlike perfection he desired (Philippians 3:12). "But one thing I do," he added, "forgetting what is behind and straining toward what is ahead, I press on" (vv. 13–14). Stumbling is part of our walk with God: it's through our mistakes that He refines us. His grace enables us to press on, as His forgiven children.

Leslie Koh

God is always ready to forgive, again and again, if we confess our sins and allow His Spirit to transform us.

A KNIGHTLY SOLDIER

2 Timothy 2:1–4, 24–25

The Lord's servant must not be quarrelsome but must be
kind to everyone, able to teach, not resentful. Opponents
must be gently instructed. —2 Timothy 2:24–25

Before he enlisted in the Union Army to fight during the US Civil
War, Joshua Chamberlain was a quiet and unassuming college
professor. In the crucible of military combat, he distinguished himself for his heroism in holding the line at Little Round Top on July
2, 1863, during the Battle of Gettysburg. He was later awarded the
Congressional Medal of Honor.

To recognize Chamberlain's contribution to the Union victory,
General Ulysses S. Grant designated him to receive the first flag of
surrender at Appomattox Courthouse. The defeated troops of the
South expected to be ridiculed and humiliated. Instead, Chamberlain showed them kindness and respect. For this, the Confederate
commanding officer wrote in his memoirs that Chamberlain was
"one of the knightliest soldiers of the Federal Army."

As a committed Christian, Chamberlain reflected the grace of
Christ. We too need to stand for what we believe but also to be
kind to those with whom we disagree. Paul exhorted Timothy, "like
a good soldier of Christ Jesus . . . be kind to everyone, able to teach,
not resentful. Opponents must be gently instructed" (2 Timothy
2:3, 24–25).

In conflict and in reconciliation, our response should reflect the
gracious heart of a knightly soldier of Christ.   *Dennis Fisher*

**We need to stand for what we believe but also to
be kind to those with whom we disagree.**

GRACE OR GRASS

Genesis 13:1–18

Lot chose for himself the whole plain of
the Jordan. —Genesis 13:11

My friend Archie came home from vacation to find that his neighbor had erected a wooden fence five feet inside Archie's property line. Several weeks went by during which Archie tried to work with his neighbor to remove the fence. He offered to help and to split the cost of the work, but to no avail. Archie could have appealed to civil authorities, but he chose to forgo that right in this instance and allow the fence to stand—to show his neighbor something of the grace of God.

"Archie is a wimp!" you may say. No, he was a man of towering strength, but he chose grace over a patch of grass.

I think of Abraham and Lot, who fell into conflict because their flocks and herds overwhelmed the land. "Quarreling arose between Abram's herders and Lot's. The Canaanites and Perizzites [the unbelieving community] were also living in the land at that time" (Genesis 13:7). Lot chose the best of the land and lost everything in the end. Abraham took what was left over and gained the promised land (vv. 12–17).

We *do* have rights and we *can* claim them, especially when others' rights are involved. And sometimes we *should* insist on them. Paul did when the Sanhedrin acted unlawfully (see Acts 23:1–3). But we can choose to set them aside to show the world a better way. This is what the Bible calls "meekness"—not weakness. Strength under God's control.   *David Roper*

**Sometimes we can choose to set our rights
aside to show the world a better way.**

HUMILITY IS THE TRUTH

James 4:1–11

Humble yourselves before the Lord, and
he will lift you up. —James 4:10

Reflecting one day on why God values humility so highly, sixteenth-century believer Teresa of Avila suddenly realized the answer: "It is because God is the supreme Truth, and humility is the truth. . . . Nothing good in us springs from ourselves. Rather, it comes from the waters of grace, near which the soul remains, like a tree planted by a river, and from that Sun which gives life to our works." Teresa concluded that it's by prayer that we anchor ourselves in that reality, for "the whole foundation of prayer is humility. The more we humble ourselves in prayer, the more will God lift us up."

Teresa's words about humility echo the language of Scripture in James 4, where James warned of the self-destructive nature of pride and selfish ambition—the opposite of a life lived in dependence on God's grace (vv. 1–6). The only solution to a life of greed, despair, and constant conflict, he emphasized, is to repent of our pride in exchange for God's grace. Or, in other words, to "humble yourselves before the Lord," with the assurance that "he will lift you up" (v. 10).

Only when we're rooted in the waters of grace can we find ourselves nourished by the "wisdom that comes from heaven" (3:17). Only in Him can we find ourselves lifted up by the truth.

Monica La Rose

**The only solution to a life of greed, despair, and constant
conflict is to repent of our pride in exchange for God's grace.**

PRICELESS WORSHIP

Mark 12:38–44

She, out of her poverty, put in everything—
all she had to live on. —Mark 12:44

I use writing to worship and serve God, even more so now that health issues often limit my mobility. So, when an acquaintance said he found no value in what I wrote, I became discouraged. I doubted the significance of my small offerings to God.

Through prayer, study of Scripture, and encouragement from my husband, family, and friends, the Lord affirmed that only He—not the opinions of other people—could determine our motives as a worshiper and the worth of our offerings to Him. I asked the Giver of all gifts to continue helping me develop skills and provide opportunities to share the resources He gives me.

Jesus contradicted our standards of merit regarding our giving (Mark 12:41–44). While the rich tossed large amounts of money into the temple treasury, a poor widow put in coins "worth only a few cents" (v. 42). The Lord declared her gift greater than the rest (v. 43), although her contribution seemed insignificant to those around her (v. 44).

While the widow's story focuses on financial offerings, every act of giving can be an expression of worship and loving obedience. Like the widow, we honor God with intentional, generous, and sacrificial gifts given from whatever He's already given us. When we present God the best of our time, talents, or treasure with hearts motivated by love, we are lavishing Him with offerings of priceless worship.   *Xochitl Dixon*

**Every act of giving can be an expression
of worship and loving obedience.**

SAYING GRACE

Colossians 3:12–17

Whatever you do, whether in word or deed, do it
all in the name of the Lord Jesus, giving thanks to
God the Father through him. —Colossians 3:17

For many years, I've enjoyed the writings of British author G. K. Chesterton (1874–1936). His humor and insight often cause me to chuckle and then pause for more serious contemplation. For example, he wrote, "You say grace before meals. All right. But I say grace before the play and the opera, and grace before the concert and pantomime, and grace before I open a book, and grace before sketching, painting, swimming, fencing, boxing, walking, playing, dancing; and grace before I dip the pen in the ink."

It's good for us to thank the Lord before every meal, but we shouldn't stop there. The apostle Paul saw every activity, every endeavor as something for which we should thank God and that we should do for His glory. "Whatever you do, whether in word or deed, do it all in the name of the Lord Jesus, giving thanks to God the Father through him" (Colossians 3:17). Recreation, occupation, and education are all avenues through which we can honor the Lord and express our gratefulness to Him.

Paul also encouraged the believers in Colossae to "let the peace of Christ rule in your hearts, since as members of one body you were called to peace. And be thankful" (v. 15).

The best place to "say grace" is anywhere and anytime we want to give thanks to the Lord and honor Him.   *David McCasland*

**The apostle Paul saw every activity, every endeavor
as something for which we should thank God.**

STRENGTHENED THROUGH TRIALS

Romans 5:1–5

We know that suffering produces perseverance; perseverance,
character; and character, hope. —Romans 5:3–4

The memories flooded back when I rustled through some enve-
lopes and glimpsed a sticker that said, "I've had an eye test." In
my mind I saw my four-year-old son proudly wearing the sticker
after enduring stinging eyedrops. Because of weak eye muscles, he
had to wear a patch for hours each day over his strong eye—thereby
forcing the weaker eye to develop. He also needed surgery. He met
these challenges one by one, looking to us as his parents for comfort
and depending on God with childlike faith. Through these challenges he developed resilience.

People who endure trials and suffering are often changed by the
experience. But the apostle Paul went further and said to "glory in
our sufferings" (Romans 5:3) because through them we develop
perseverance. With perseverance comes character; and with character, hope (vv. 3–4). Paul certainly knew trials—not only ship-
wrecks but also imprisonment for his faith. Yet he wrote to the
believers in Rome that "hope does not put us to shame, because
God's love has been poured out into our hearts through the Holy
Spirit" (v. 5). He recognized that God's Spirit keeps our hope in
Jesus alive when we put our trust in Him.

Whatever hardships you face, remember that God will pour out
His grace and mercy on you. He loves you.   *Amy Boucher Pye*

**God's Spirit keeps our hope in Jesus alive
when we put our trust in Him.**

WALKING ON WATER

Matthew 14:25–33

Jesus immediately said to them: "Take courage!
It is I. Don't be afraid." —Matthew 14:27

During an especially cold winter, I ventured out to Lake Michigan, the fifth largest lake in the world, to see it frozen over. Bundled up on the beach where I usually enjoy soaking up the sun, the view was breathtaking. The water was frozen in waves creating an icy masterpiece.

Because the water was frozen solid next to the shore, I had the opportunity to "walk on water." Even with the knowledge that the ice was thick enough to support me, I took the first few steps tentatively. I was fearful the ice wouldn't continue to hold me. As I cautiously explored this unfamiliar terrain, I couldn't help but think of Jesus calling Peter out of the boat onto the Sea of Galilee.

When the disciples saw Jesus walking on the water, their response was also fear. But Jesus responded, "Take courage! It is I. Don't be afraid" (Matthew 14:27). Peter was able to overcome his fear and step out onto the water because he knew Jesus was present. When his courageous steps faltered because of the wind and waves, Peter cried out to Jesus. Jesus was still there, near enough to simply reach out His hand to rescue him.

If you are facing a situation today where Jesus is calling you to do something that may seem as impossible as walking on water, take courage. The One who calls you will be present with you.

Lisa M. Samra

**Peter was able to overcome his fear and step out onto
the water because he knew Jesus was present.**

A DISTINCT CRY

Isaiah 30:15–26

People of Zion, who live in Jerusalem, you will
weep no more. How gracious [God] will be
when you cry for help! —Isaiah 30:19

When a baby cries, it's a signal that she's tired and hungry, right? Well, according to doctors at Brown University, subtle differences in a newborn's cries can also provide important clues for other problems. Doctors have devised a computer program that measures cry factors like pitch, volume, and how clear the cry sound is to determine if something's wrong with the baby's central nervous system.

Isaiah prophesied that God would hear the distinct cries of His people, determine their hearts' condition, and respond with grace. Judah, rather than consulting God, had ignored His prophet and sought help in an alliance with Egypt (30:1–7). God told them that if they chose to continue in their rebellion, He would bring about their defeat and humiliation. However, He also longed "to be gracious to [them]; . . . to show [them] compassion" (v. 18). Rescue would come, but only through their cries of repentance and faith. If God's people did cry out to Him, He would forgive their sins and renew their spiritual strength and vitality (vv. 8–26).

The same holds true for believers in Jesus today. When our distinct cries of repentance and trust reach the ears of our heavenly Father, He hears them, forgives us, and renews our joy and hope in Him.

Marvin Williams

**God would hear the distinct cries of His people, determine
their hearts' condition, and respond with grace.**

PUTTING UP HAY

Luke 15:11–24

Blessed are those whose transgressions
are forgiven. —Romans 4:7

When I was in college, I worked a summer on a ranch in Colorado. One evening, tired and hungry after a long day of mowing hay, I drove the tractor into the yard. Acting like the hot shot I thought I was, I cranked the steering wheel hard left, stamped on the left brake, and spun the tractor around.

The sickle was still down, and it swept the legs out from under a 500-gallon gasoline tank standing nearby. The tank hit the ground with a resounding boom, the seams split, and all the gasoline spewed out.

The rancher stood nearby surveying the scene.

I got off the tractor, stammered an apology, and—because it was the first thing that popped into my mind—offered to work the rest of the summer without pay.

The old rancher stared at the wreckage for a moment and turned toward the house. "Let's go have dinner," he drawled.

A scrap of a story Jesus told passed through my mind—a story about a young man who had done a terrible thing: "Father, I have sinned against heaven and against you," he cried. He intended to add, "Make me like one of your hired servants," but before he could get all the words out of his mouth his father interrupted him. In essence, he said, "Let's go have dinner" (Luke 15:17–24).

Such is God's amazing grace. *David Roper*

The prodigal's father said, in essence, "Let's go have dinner."

TRAIN TO FINISH STRONG

1 Corinthians 9:19–27

I discipline my body and bring it into subjection,
lest, when I have preached to others, I myself should
become disqualified. —1 Corinthians 9:27 NKJV

In 1924, Eric Liddell electrified the sports world by capturing an Olympic gold medal in the 400 meters—a race he was not expected to win. Liddell was the favorite at 100 meters, but he had earlier withdrawn from that race after learning the qualifying heats would be held on Sunday, a day he observed as one of worship and rest. Instead of lamenting his lost chance in the 100, he spent the next six months training for the 400—and set a new Olympic record.

The apostle Paul used a sports metaphor to emphasize the Christian's need for spiritual discipline. "Everyone who competes in the games goes into strict training" (1 Corinthians 9:25). "They do it to get a crown that will not last, but we do it to get a crown that will last forever." Paul desired to remain faithful to Christ because he wanted to bring the message of salvation to others (vv. 19, 27).

Throughout Liddell's life, he disciplined himself spiritually each day by spending time in God's Word and in prayer. He remained faithful until he died of a brain tumor in a Japanese internment camp during World War II.

Strengthened by the grace and power of God, Eric Liddell ran well and finished strong in the race of life. And so can we.

David McCasland

**Eric Liddell disciplined himself spiritually each day
by spending time in God's Word and in prayer.**

THE ADVENTURE

Ephesians 1:3–14

In him we were also chosen . . . that we . . . might be
for the praise of his glory. —Ephesians 1:11–12

"Christianity is not for me. It's boring. One of my values I hold on to is adventure. That's life to me," a young woman told me. It saddened me that she hadn't yet learned the incredible joy and excitement that comes with following Jesus—an adventure like no other. I excitedly shared with her about Jesus and how real life is found in Him.

Mere words are inadequate to describe the adventure of knowing and walking with Jesus, God's Son. But in Ephesians 1, the apostle Paul gives us a small but powerful glimpse of life with Him. God gives us spiritual blessings directly from heaven (v. 3), holiness and blamelessness in God's eyes (v. 4), and adoption as His own into the King's royal family (v. 5). He blesses us with the lavish gift of His forgiveness and grace (vv. 7–8), understanding of the mystery of His will (v. 9), and a new purpose of living "for the praise of his glory" (v. 12). The Holy Spirit comes to live in us to empower and lead us (v. 13), and He guarantees eternity in God's presence forever (v. 14).

When Jesus Christ enters our life, we discover that getting to know Him more and following Him closely are the greatest of adventures. Seek Him now and every day for real life.   *Anne Cetas*

**Mere words are inadequate to describe the adventure
of knowing and walking with Jesus, God's Son.**

GOD'S RESCUE

Psalm 40:1–4

He lifted me out of the slimy pit, out of the
mud and mire; he set my feet on a rock and gave
me a firm place to stand. —Psalm 40:2

A compassionate volunteer was called a "guardian angel" for his heroic efforts. Jake Manna was installing solar panels at a job site when he joined an urgent search to find a missing five-year-old girl. While neighbors searched their garages and yards, Manna took a path that led him into a nearby wooded area where he spotted the girl waist-deep in a marsh. He waded carefully into the sticky mud to pull her out of her predicament and return her, damp but unharmed, to her grateful mother.

Like that little girl, David also experienced deliverance. The singer "waited patiently" for God to respond to his heartfelt cries for mercy (Psalm 40:1). And He responded. God leaned in, paid close attention to his cry for help, and rescued him from the "mud and mire" of his circumstances (v. 2)—providing sure footing for David's life. The past rescues from the muddy marsh of life reinforced his desire to sing songs of praise, to make God his trust in future circumstances, and to share his story with others (vv. 3–4).

When we find ourselves in life challenges such as financial difficulties, marital turmoil, and feelings of inadequacy, let's cry out to God and patiently wait for Him to respond (v. 1). He's there, ready to help us in our time of need and give us a firm place to stand.

Marvin Williams

Cry out to God and patiently wait for Him to respond.

THE FINAL OUTCOME

Psalm 145

When I tried to understand all this, it troubled me
deeply till I entered the sanctuary of God; then I
understood their final destiny. —Psalm 73:16–17

The young woman's face was twisted in agony. "It just isn't fair!" she cried. "My father robbed me of my childhood. He destroyed my teenage years. He almost deprived me of any chance of marital happiness. How could God let it happen?"

She was right. It wasn't fair. Her father had humiliated and abused her from the time she was a little girl. He had mocked her and called her ugly and stupid. She was the victim of a depraved cruelty that had crippled her emotionally for years. How could God let that happen? Why didn't He step in and rescue her?

The Lord may not give us the answers we want. Instead, He may want us to conclude, as did suffering Job (Job 42:3) and David (Psalm 145:17), that God can be trusted to do what is right.

Part of God's righteousness is letting a fallen world suffer the consequences of its sinful depravity. Another part is that God offers grace to all who suffer. And when His final judgment comes (2 Peter 2:9), abusers and oppressors will get what they deserve.

Are you suffering because of cruel or thoughtless abuse? Don't let it crush your spirit or make you doubt God. Because He is righteous, you still haven't seen the final outcome. And He will give mercy and grace to help you through your difficulties.

David Egner

God will give mercy and grace to help you.

TRUE RELIGION

James 1:19–27

Religion that God our Father accepts as pure and faultless is this: to look after orphans and widows in their distress and to keep oneself from being polluted by the world. —James 1:27

The summer after my sophomore year of college, a classmate died unexpectedly. I'd seen him just a few days prior and he looked fine. We and our classmates were young and in what we thought was the prime of our lives, having just become sisters and brothers after pledging our respective sorority and fraternity.

What I remember most about my classmate's death was witnessing my fraternity friends live out what James calls true religion. The men in his fraternity became like brothers to the sister of the deceased. They attended her wedding and traveled to her baby shower years after her brother's death. One even gave her a cell phone to contact him whenever she needed to call.

The "brothers" remind me of what James calls "genuine religion" (James 1:27 NLT): "to look after orphans and widows in their distress" (v. 27). While my friend's sister wasn't an orphan in the literal sense, she no longer had her brother. Her new "brothers" filled in the gap.

This is what all of us who want to practice true and pure life in Jesus can do—"do what [Scripture] says" (v. 22), including caring for those in need (2:14–17). Our faith in Him prompts us to look after the vulnerable as we keep ourselves from the negative influences of the world. After all, it's the only true religion God accepts.

Katara Patton

Our faith in Jesus prompts us to look after the vulnerable.

TENNIS AND PARENTING

Ephesians 6:1–9

Fathers, do not exasperate your children; instead, bring them
up in the training and instruction of the Lord. —Ephesians 6:4

What do tennis and parenting have in common? At first glance, not much. One is a game; the other is anything but a game. But there are certain similarities in the way the two tasks are carried out.

Tennis can be played two ways: with sportsmanship and graciousness; or with temper tantrums, "bashing" the officials, and bitter excuses.

Parents have similar options. They can concentrate on developing grace, self-control, and skill. Or they can make excuses by saying, "Sometimes I think I'm losing my mind. These kids are bringing out the worst in me. I know I shouldn't yell and scream, but I can't help it." Sound familiar?

Like successful tennis players, parents need a good coach—one who understands parenting's fine points and is experienced in self-control and unconditional love. We need Christ, the master teacher. Success is possible only when we seek His help and rely on Him. He said, "I am the vine, you are the branches. If you remain in me and I in you, you will bear much fruit; apart from me you can do nothing" (John 15:5).

No, parenting isn't easy. Some tough shots may be fired at us. We may not win in straight sets. But Christ will help us respond to our children with love and grace.   *Mart DeHaan*

**Success is possible only when we seek
His help and rely on Him.**

TRUSTING GOD

Psalm 20

Some trust in chariots and some in horses, but we trust
in the name of the LORD our God. —Psalm 20:7

I needed two medications urgently. One was for my mom's allergies and the other for my niece's eczema. Their discomfort was worsening, but the medicines were no longer available in pharmacies. Desperate and helpless, I prayed repeatedly, *Lord, please help them.*

Weeks later, their conditions became manageable. God seemed to be reminding me: "There are times when I use medicines to heal. But medicines don't have the final say; I do. Don't place your trust in them, but in Me."

In Psalm 20, King David took comfort in God's trustworthiness. The Israelites had a powerful army, but they knew that their biggest strength came from "the name of the LORD" (v. 7). They placed their trust in God's name—in who He is, His unchanging character, and His unfailing promises. They held on to the truth that He who is sovereign and powerful over all situations would hear their prayers and deliver them from their enemies (v. 6).

While God may use the resources of this world to help us, ultimately, victory over our problems comes from Him. Whether He gives us a resolution or the grace to endure, we can trust that He'll be to us everything He says He is. We don't have to be overwhelmed by our troubles, but we can face them with His hope and peace.

Karen Huang

God may use the resources of this world to help us, but ultimately the victory over our problems comes from Him.

GIVING OUT OF LOVE

Matthew 6:1–4

Your Father, who sees what is done in secret,
will reward you. —Matthew 6:4

Every day, Glen purchases his morning coffee at a nearby drive-through. And every day he also pays for the order of the person in the car behind him, asking the cashier to wish that person a good day. Glen has no connection to them. He's not aware of their reactions; he simply believes this small gesture is "the least he can do." On one occasion, however, he learned of the impact of his actions when he read an anonymous letter to the editor of his local newspaper. He discovered that the kindness of his gift on July 18, 2017, caused the person in the car behind him to reconsider their plans to take their own life later that day.

Glen gives daily to the people in the car behind him without receiving credit for it. Only on this single occasion did he get a glimpse of the impact of his small gift. When Jesus says we should "not let [our] left hand know what [our] right hand is doing" (Matthew 6:3), He's urging us to give—as Glen does—without need for recognition.

When we give out of our love for God, without concern for receiving the praise of others, we can trust that our gifts—large or small—will be used by Him to help meet the needs of those receiving them.

Kirsten Holmberg

Jesus urges us to give without need for recognition.

GRACELAND

Romans 5:15–21

How much more did God's grace and the gift that
came by the grace of the one man, Jesus Christ,
overflow to the many! —Romans 5:15

The Graceland Mansion in Memphis, Tennessee, is one of the most visited homes in the United States. It was built in the 1930s and named after the original owner's great aunt, Grace. It later became famous as the home of music legend Elvis Presley.

I love the name Graceland because it describes the amazing territory into which God placed me when He forgave me of my sin and made me His own. He took me out of the darkness and brought me into His own "graceland."

The apostle Paul says that "God's grace and the gift that came by the grace of the one man, Jesus Christ, overflow[s] to the many" (Romans 5:15). I'll be forever thankful that the "many" includes me and that God's love has transferred me into the territory of His marvelous, infinite, matchless grace!

Think of the blessing of being in God's graceland. It is a realm where He has given us entrance into His presence and where that same grace continues to overflow into our lives every day. Paul tells us that even in times of despair God showers us with sufficient grace to see us through (see 2 Corinthians 12:9).

No matter what life may bring, nothing can remove us from the realm of God's grace. *Joe Stowell*

Even in times of despair God showers us with sufficient grace.

CELESTIAL COMMUNION

1 Corinthians 11:23–26

Whenever you eat this bread and drink this cup, you proclaim
the Lord's death until he comes. —1 Corinthians 11:26

When Apollo 11's *Eagle* lunar module landed on the moon's
Sea of Tranquility on July 20, 1969, the space travelers took
time to recover from their flight before stepping onto the moon's surface. Astronaut Buzz Aldrin had received permission to bring bread
and wine so he could take communion. After reading Scripture, he
tasted the first foods ever consumed on the moon. Later, he wrote:
"I poured the wine into the chalice our church had given me. In the
one-sixth gravity of the moon the wine curled slowly and gracefully
up the side of the cup." As Aldrin enjoyed this celestial communion,
his actions proclaimed his belief in Christ's sacrifice on the cross and
the guarantee of His second coming.

The apostle Paul encourages us to remember how Jesus sat with
His disciples "on the night he was betrayed" (1 Corinthians 11:23).
Christ compared His soon-to-be-sacrificed body to the bread (v. 24).
He declared the wine as a symbol of "the new covenant" that secured
our forgiveness and salvation through His blood shed on the cross
(v. 25). Whenever and wherever we take communion, we're pro-
claiming our trust in the reality of Jesus's sacrifice and our hope in
His promised second coming (v. 26).

No matter where we are, we can celebrate our faith in the one and
only risen and returning Savior—Jesus Christ—with confidence.

Xochitl Dixon

**Whenever and wherever we take communion, we're
proclaiming our trust in the reality of Jesus's sacrifice
and our hope in His promised second coming.**

"LOVE YOU—WHOLE WORLD"

1 John 4:7–19

God is love. Whoever lives in love lives in
God, and God in them. —1 John 4:16

When she was three years old, my niece, Jenna, had an expression that never failed to melt my heart. When she loved something (*really* loved it), be it banana cream pie, jumping on the trampoline, or playing Frisbee, she'd proclaim, "I love it—whole world!" ("whole world" accompanied with a dramatic sweep of her arms).

Sometimes I wonder, *When's the last time I've dared to love like that? With nothing held back, completely unafraid?*

"God is love," John wrote, repeatedly (1 John 4:8, 16), perhaps because the truth that God's love—not our anger, fear, or shame—is the deepest foundation of reality, is hard for us grown-ups to "get." The world divides us into camps based on what we're most afraid of—and all too often we join in, ignoring or villainizing the voices that challenge our preferred vision of reality.

Yet amid the deception and power struggles (vv. 5–6), the truth of God's love remains, a light that shines in the darkness, inviting us to learn the path of humility, trust, and love (1:7–9; 3:18). For no matter what painful truths the light uncovers, we can know that we'll still be loved (4:10, 18; Romans 8:1).

When Jenna would lean over and whisper to me, "I love you—whole world!" I would whisper back, "I love you—whole world!" I'm grateful for a gentle reminder that every moment I'm held in God's limitless love and grace.

Monica La Rose

**The truth of God's love remains, a light
that shines in the darkness.**

A HEART OF COMPASSION

Colossians 3:12–17

Clothe yourselves with compassion, kindness, humility,
gentleness and patience. —Colossians 3:12

Seven of us were attending a musical production at a crowded amusement park.

Wanting to sit together, we tried to squeeze into one row. But as we did, a woman rushed between us. My wife mentioned to her that we wanted to stay together, but the woman quickly said, "Too bad," as she and her two companions pushed on into the row.

As three of us sat one row behind the other four, my wife, Sue, noticed that the woman had an adult with her who appeared to have special needs. She had been trying to keep her little group together so she could take care of her friend. Suddenly, our irritation faded. Sue said, "Imagine how tough things are for her in a crowded place like this." Yes, perhaps the woman did respond rudely. But we could respond with compassion rather than anger.

Wherever we go, we will encounter people who need compassion. Perhaps these words from the apostle Paul can help us view everyone around us in a different light—as people who need the gentle touch of grace. "As God's chosen people, holy and dearly loved, clothe yourselves with compassion, kindness, humility, gentleness and patience" (Colossians 3:12). He also suggests that we "bear with each other and forgive one another" (v. 13).

As we show compassion, we will be pointing others to the One who poured out His heart of grace and compassion on us.

Dave Branon

Let's view everyone around us as people
who need the gentle touch of grace.

PROMISE FULFILLED

Luke 1:26–45

Blessed is she who has believed that the Lord would
fulfill his promises to her! —Luke 1:45

Each summer when I was a child, I would travel two hundred miles to enjoy a week with my grandparents. I wasn't aware until later how much wisdom I soaked up from those two people I loved. Their life experiences and walk with God had given them perspectives that my young mind couldn't yet imagine. Conversations with them about the faithfulness of God assured me that God is trustworthy and fulfills every promise He makes.

Mary, the mother of Jesus, was a teenager when an angel visited her. The incredible news Gabriel brought must have been overwhelming, yet she willingly accepted the task with grace (Luke 1:38). Perhaps her visit with her elderly relative Elizabeth—who was also in the midst of a miraculous pregnancy (some scholars believe she may have been sixty years old)—brought her comfort as Elizabeth enthusiastically confirmed Gabriel's words that she was the mother of the promised Messiah (vv. 39–45).

As we grow and mature in Christ, as my grandparents did, we learn that He keeps His promises. He kept His promise of a child for Elizabeth and her husband Zechariah (vv. 57–58). And that son, John the Baptist, became the harbinger of a promise made hundreds of years before—one that would change the course of humanity's future. The promised Messiah—the Savior of the world—was coming (Matthew 1:21–23). *Cindy Hess Kasper*

**As we grow and mature in Christ, we
learn that He keeps His promises.**

SWEET GRACE

Proverbs 16:1–2, 21–24

Gracious words are a honeycomb, sweet to the soul
and healing to the bones. —Proverbs 16:24

The speaker's topic was racial tension. Yet he remained calm and collected. Standing on stage before a large audience, he spoke boldly—but with grace, humility, kindness, and even humor. Soon the tense audience visibly relaxed, laughing along with the speaker about the dilemma they all faced: how to resolve their hot issue, but cool down their feelings and words. Yes, how to tackle a sour topic with sweet grace.

King Solomon advised this same approach for all of us: "Gracious words are a honeycomb, sweet to the soul and healing to the bones" (Proverbs 16:24). In this way, "The hearts of the wise make . . . their lips promote instruction" (v. 23).

Why would a powerful king like Solomon devote time to addressing how we speak? Because words can destroy. During Solomon's time, kings relied on messengers for information about their nations, and calm and reliable messengers were highly valued. They used prudent words and reasoned tongues, not overreacting or speaking harshly, no matter the issue.

We all can benefit by gracing our opinions and thoughts with godly and prudent sweetness. In Solomon's words, "To humans belong the plans of the heart, but from the LORD comes the proper answer of the tongue" (v. 1). *Patricia Raybon*

We all can benefit by gracing our opinions and thoughts with godly and prudent sweetness.

CONSIDER THE CLOUDS

Job 37:1–16

Do you know how the clouds hang poised? —Job 37:16

One day many years ago, my boys and I were lying on our backs in the yard watching the clouds drift by. "Dad," one asked, "why do clouds float?" "Well, son," I began, intending to give him the benefit of my vast knowledge, but then I lapsed into silence. "I don't know," I admitted, "but I'll find out for you."

The answer, I discovered, is that condensed moisture, descending by gravity, meets warmer temperatures rising from the land. That moisture then changes into vapor and ascends back into the air. This is a natural explanation for the phenomenon.

But natural explanations are not final answers. Clouds float because God in His wisdom has ordered the natural laws in such a way that they reveal the "wonders of him who has perfect knowledge" (Job 37:16). Clouds then can be thought of as a symbol—an outward and visible sign of God's goodness and grace in creation.

So someday, when you're taking a few calm minutes to see what pictures you can imagine in the clouds, remember this: The One who made all things beautiful makes the clouds float through the air. He does so to call us to wonder and adoration. The heavens—even the cumulus, stratus, and cirrus clouds—declare the glory of God.

David Roper

Clouds can be thought of as a symbol—an outward and visible sign of God's goodness and grace in creation.

NO FISHING ALLOWED

Psalm 130

[God will] hurl all our iniquities into the
depths of the sea. —Micah 7:19

Holocaust survivor Corrie ten Boom knew the importance of forgiveness. In her book *Tramp for the Lord*, she says her favorite mental picture was of forgiven sins thrown into the sea. "When we confess our sins, God casts them into the deepest ocean, gone forever. . . . I believe God then places a sign out there that says, 'No Fishing Allowed.'"

She points to an important truth that believers in Jesus can sometimes fail to grasp—when God forgives our wrongdoing, we're forgiven fully! We don't have to keep dredging up our shameful deeds, wallowing in any mucky feelings. Rather, we can accept His grace and forgiveness, following Him in freedom.

We see this idea of "no fishing allowed" in Psalm 130. The psalmist proclaims that although God is just, He forgives the sin of those who repent: "But with you there is forgiveness" (v. 4). As the psalmist waits for God, putting his trust in Him (v. 5), he states in faith that He "himself will redeem Israel from all their sins" (v. 8). Those who believe will find "full redemption" (v. 7).

When we're caught in feelings of shame and unworthiness, we can't serve God with our whole hearts. Instead, we're restricted by our past. If you feel stymied by the wrong you've done, ask God to help you fully believe in His gift of forgiveness and new life. He has cast your sins into the ocean! *Amy Boucher Pye*

When God forgives our wrongdoing, we're forgiven fully.

WITHIN GOD'S REACH

Psalm 139:1–12

Where can I go from your Spirit? Where can I
flee from your presence? —Psalm 139:7

After an officer searched me, I stepped into the county jail, signed the visitor's log, and sat in the crowded lobby. I prayed silently, watching adults fidgeting and sighing while young children complained about the wait. Over an hour later, an armed guard called a list of names including mine. He led my group into a room and motioned us to our assigned chairs. When my stepson sat in the chair on the other side of the thick glass window and picked up the telephone receiver, the depth of my helplessness overwhelmed me. But as I wept, God assured me that my stepson was still within His reach.

In Psalm 139, David said to the Lord, "You know me . . . you are familiar with all my ways" (vv. 1–3). His proclamation of an all-knowing God led to a celebration of His intimate care and protection (v. 5). Overwhelmed by the vastness of God's knowledge and the depth of His personal touch, David asked two rhetorical questions: "Where can I go from your Spirit? Where can I flee from your presence?" (v. 7).

When we or our loved ones are stuck in situations that leave us feeling hopeless and helpless, God's hand remains strong and steady. Even when we believe we've strayed too far for God's loving redemption, we're always within His reach.   *Xochitl Dixon*

**When we or our loved ones are stuck in hopeless, helpless
situations, God's hand remains strong and steady.**

COME AND WORSHIP

Deuteronomy 31:9–13

Assemble the people—men, women and children, and the foreigners residing in your towns. —Deuteronomy 31:12

As they sang praise songs together in the multigenerational worship service, many experienced joy and peace. But not one frazzled young mother. As she jiggled her baby, who was on the verge of crying, she held the songbook for her five-year-old, while trying to stop her toddler from running off. Then an older gentleman sitting behind her offered to walk the toddler around the church, and a young woman motioned that she could hold the songbook for the eldest child. Within two minutes, the mother's experience was transformed; she could exhale, close her eyes, and worship God.

God has always intended that all His people worship Him—men and women, old and young, longtime believers and newcomers. As Moses blessed the tribes of Israel before they entered the promised land, he urged them all to meet together, "men, women and children, and the foreigners residing in your towns," so they could "listen and learn to fear the LORD your God" and follow His commands (Deuteronomy 31:12). It honors God when we make it possible for His people to worship Him together, no matter our stage of life.

That morning in church, the mother, the older gentleman, and the young woman each experienced God's love through giving and receiving. Perhaps the next time you're at church, you too could extend God's love through an offer of help or you could be the one accepting the act of grace. *Amy Boucher Pye*

It honors God when we make it possible for His people to worship Him together, no matter our stage of life.

FINISH STRONG

Acts 20:17–24

I consider my life worth nothing to me; my only
aim is to finish the race and complete the task the
Lord Jesus has given me—the task of testifying to
the good news of God's grace. —Acts 20:24

As I enter the final few minutes of my forty-minute workout, I
can almost guarantee that my instructor will yell out, "Finish
strong!" Every personal trainer or group fitness leader I've known
uses the phrase a few minutes before cool down. They know that
the end of the workout is just as important as showing up for it.
And they know the human body has a tendency to want to slow
down or slack off when it's been in motion for a while.

The same is true in our journey with Jesus. Paul told the elders of
the church at Ephesus that he needed to finish strong as he headed
to Jerusalem, where he was certain to face more persecution as an
apostle of Christ (Acts 20:17–24). Paul, however, was undeterred.
He had a mission—to finish the journey he'd begun and to do what
God called him to do. He had one job—to tell "the good news of
God's grace" (v. 24). And he wanted to finish strong. Even if hardship awaited him (v. 23), he continued to run toward his finish line,
focused and determined to remain steadfast in his journey.

Whether we're exercising our physical muscles or working out
our God-given abilities through actions, words, and deeds, we too
can be encouraged by the reminder to finish strong. Don't "become
weary" (Galatians 6:9). Don't give up. God will provide what you
need to finish strong.   *Katara Patton*

**Paul had a mission—to finish the journey he'd
begun and to do what God called him to do.**

COURAGE TO STAND FOR JESUS

John 13:36–38; 21:18–19

Whoever does not take up their cross and follow
me is not worthy of me. —Matthew 10:38

In AD 155, the early church father Polycarp was threatened with death by fire for his faith in Christ. He replied, "For eighty and six years I have been his servant, and he has done me no wrong. And how can I now blaspheme my king who saved me?" Polycarp's response can be an inspiration for us when we face extreme trial because of our faith in Jesus, our King.

Just hours before Jesus's death, Peter boldly pledged his allegiance to Christ: "I will lay down my life for you" (John 13:37). Jesus, who knew Peter better than Peter knew himself, replied, "Very truly I tell you, before the rooster crows, you will disown me three times!" (v. 38). However, after Jesus's resurrection, the same one who'd denied Him began to serve Him courageously and would eventually glorify Him through his own death (see 21:16–19).

Are you a Polycarp or a Peter? Most of us, if we're honest, are more of a Peter with a "courage outage"—a failure to speak or act honorably as a believer in Jesus. Such occasions—whether in a classroom, boardroom, or break room—needn't indelibly define us. When these failures occur, we must prayerfully dust ourselves off and turn to Jesus, the One who died for us and lives for us. He'll help us to be faithful and to courageously live for Him daily in difficult places.   *Arthur Jackson*

**"How can I now blaspheme my king
who saved me?" —Polycarp**

MADE TO SOAR

Romans 6:1–14

For sin shall no longer be your master, because you are
not under the law, but under grace. —Romans 6:14

When I visit the zoo, I skip the eagles' cage. I can't stand the pain of seeing those majestic birds sit there on their perches day after day, their burnished brown wings draped over them like an ill-fitting old coat. They were created for the heights, to dance among the clouds, not to be prisoners in a cage. Those birds were made to fly.

Many people who profess they are Christ's men and women are like those caged eagles. They are made to live as free citizens of heaven, but they are imprisoned by their own sin. Their condition must break God's heart. He knows what they could become, but they have put themselves in a cage. And the irony is that it is a cage with open doors.

The apostle Paul said that we who have put our trust in Christ have died with Him to the sin that confined us in our old life. And we are now alive in Him. We are not the person we used to be. Therefore, we must stop facing life as we used to face it.

Think long about these truths. Remind yourself of them often. Through Christ, you have been set free! You were never meant to be imprisoned in a cage. Confess your sin and trust God anew. You were made to soar. *Haddon Robinson*

**We who have put our trust in Christ have died with
Him to the sin that confined us in our old life.**

AUGUST

"O Worship the King"

Robert Grant and Johann Michael Haydn

O tell of His might, O sing of His grace.

The Governor and the King

We seldom hear of classic Christian song writers who were political figures. So it may surprise you to discover the career of Robert Grant, the man who wrote "O Worship the King."

Grant was born in Bengal, India, in 1780. His British family lived there because his father served as an official of the East India Company, a company that facilitated trade between England and India. Eventually, the East India Company gained political control of parts of India.

When Grant was six years old, the family returned to England,

Sources: "O Worship the King," Hymnary.org., http://tinyurl.com/ywpwbzf4; "History/Historical Background," Grant Government Medical College and Sir J. J Group of Hospitals, Mumbai, http://tinyurl.com/4n4jh8zv; "History of Hymns: 'O Worship the King,'" Discipleship Ministries of the United Methodist Church, http://tinyurl.com/48rkv4zs; "Robert Grant," *The Canterbury Dictionary of Hymnology*, http://tinyurl.com/yr4tezhw; Dan Graves MSL I. "Sir Robert Grant Penned 'O Worship the King,'" *Christianity.com*, updated July 1, 2011, http://tinyurl.com/y2sbwjjk; all accessed November 6, 2023.

where Robert later went to law school. He served in Parliament and in several other political positions. In 1834, Grant was appointed the governor of Bombay, India, which was still under British rule. His leadership was respected in India, and a medical school he envisioned for Bombay is still in operation, Grant Government Medical College.

Before his appointment as India's governor, Grant was involved in antislavery activities alongside William Wilberforce and worked to keep the door open for the gospel to be proclaimed in India.

Politically active and concerned for the betterment of the people he served, Robert Grant stayed true to his long-held faith in Jesus Christ. As he was reading a book about the psalms, he was touched by William Kethe's translation of Psalm 104 and felt compelled to write his own interpretation of that psalm in verse form.

Thus was formed the poem that would become the great hymn of the faith: "O Worship the King." Knowing the origin of Grant's composition helps us see more clearly the essence of Psalm 104. The tune, attributed to Johann Michael Haydn, helps carry along the message.

The governor wrote about the King of kings, and we still benefit from this collaboration today.

O Worship the King

O worship the King all-glorious above,
O gratefully sing His power and His love:
Our shield and defender, the Ancient of Days,
Pavilioned in splendor and girded with praise.

O tell of His might and sing of His grace,
Whose robe is the light, whose canopy space.
His chariots of wrath the deep thunderclouds form,
And dark is His path on the wings of the storm.

THE ADDICTION OF US ALL

John 8:21–36

If the Son sets you free, you will be free indeed. —John 8:36

"There, but for the grace of God, go I." How often I've said that—especially when observing the drug-addicted people I worked with. I think I say it humbly—but am I really sincere?

In John 8, Jesus told His listeners that His truth could make them free (v. 32). But weren't they free already, they protested? So, Jesus tightened the screws a bit more: "Very truly I tell you, everyone who sins is a slave of sin" (v. 34). In other words, sin is addictive. And because we're all sinners, it's the addiction of us all.

At the heart of every person's sin problem is a "self" habit that can be kicked only through Christ's intervention. Many recovered drug addicts have found that their "self" habit is a deeper problem than their drug habit. This certainly is Ken's story. After years of running from his problems through drugs and alcohol, he finally yielded his life to Christ. "Since then," Ken testifies, "things haven't always been smooth, but Christ has been transforming my selfish way of life. I was shocked to find that I was completely addicted to me!"

We all battle this same addiction. Instead of flippantly saying, "There, but for the grace of God, go I," we should say, "There go I." No one is an exception. We all need the same grace.

Joanie Yoder

At the heart of every person's sin problem is a "self" habit that can be kicked only through Christ's intervention.

THREE SISTERS

Romans 4:1–11

To Timothy my true son in the faith: Grace,
mercy and peace from God the Father and
Christ Jesus our Lord. —1 Timothy 1:2

Grace, mercy, and peace are the three sisters of salvation. In these three words we have the gospel in capsule form. They sum up our complete salvation in Jesus Christ.

Grace is the foundation of our redemption, *mercy* is the manifestation of our redemption, and *peace* is the consummation.

Grace points to the past—our salvation goes back "before the creation of the world" (Ephesians 1:4). *Mercy* speaks of the present—it is manifested to us day by day. And *peace* is the consummation because it makes our future secure.

Grace is receiving what we do not deserve. *Mercy* is not receiving what we do deserve. We do not deserve to go to heaven, but by grace we'll spend eternity there. We deserve to go to hell, but through God's mercy we will never go there. Grace justifies. Mercy pardons. Grace admits us to heaven. Mercy saves us from hell. The death of Christ was enough to pardon us in mercy, but it took the resurrection to accomplish our justification. He "was delivered over to death for our sins and was raised to life for our justification" (Romans 4:25).

And now, by faith, we have "*peace* with God through our Lord Jesus Christ" (Romans 5:1).   *M. R. DeHaan*

Grace is receiving what we do not deserve.

THANKFUL HEARTS

Luke 17:11–19

Has no one returned to give praise to God
except this foreigner? —Luke 17:18

Hansle Parchment was in a predicament. He caught the bus to the wrong place for his semifinal in the Tokyo Olympics and was left stranded with little hope of getting to the stadium on time. Thankfully, he met Trijana Stojkovic, a volunteer helping at the games. She gave him some money to take a taxi. Parchment made it to the semifinal on time and eventually captured the gold medal in the 110-meter hurdle. Later, he went back to find Stojkovic, showed her his medal, and thanked her for her kindness.

In Luke 17, we read of the Samaritan leper who came back to thank Jesus for healing him (vv. 15–16). Jesus had entered a village where He met ten lepers. All of them asked Jesus for healing, and all of them experienced His grace and power. Ten were happy they'd been healed, but only one returned to express his gratitude. He "came back, praising God in a loud voice. He threw himself at Jesus' feet and thanked him" (vv. 15–16).

Every day we experience God's blessings in multiple ways. It could be as dramatic as an answered prayer after an extended time of suffering or receiving timely help from a stranger. Sometimes, His blessings can come in ordinary ways, such as good weather to accomplish an outdoor task. Like the Samaritan leper, let's remember to thank God for His kindness toward us.   *Poh Fang Chia*

**Every day we experience God's blessings in
multiple ways. Let's remember to thank Him.**

MAKING FACES AT A BULLDOG

1 Peter 3:8–12

Do not repay anyone evil for evil. —Romans 12:17

A little girl was making angry faces at a bulldog. When her mother noticed what she was doing, she asked her daughter to stop. The girl replied, "But Mom, he started it!"

In one sense, the girl was right. A bulldog naturally looks tough and mean. But the girl gained nothing by competing with him in making faces.

So too, the person who thinks he must return every angry look he sees or repay any hurtful deed directed toward him will have a never-ending and profitless job. In the end, he is the one who will suffer the most.

As heirs of the grace of God, we should be gracious in our attitude toward others. The spirit of the world says, "Get even with those who mistreat you." The Spirit of Christ says, "Love your enemies, bless those who curse you, do good to those who hate you, and pray for those who spitefully use you" (Matthew 5:44 NKJV).

If you want to know how spiritual you are, ask yourself, "What is my attitude toward those who mistreat me? Am I kind, considerate, and loving in my words and actions toward them?"

To live like Christ is not natural; it's supernatural. Only as we yield to the Holy Spirit can we ever hope to exhibit the life of Christ.

Henry Bosch

To live like Christ is not natural; it's supernatural.

GRACE AMID THE CHAOS

Psalm 107:23–32

They were glad when it grew calm, and he guided
them to their desired haven. —Psalm 107:30

I was drifting off into an impromptu nap when competing sounds hit me. From the basement, my son ripped a chord on his electric guitar. The walls reverberated. No peace. No quiet. No nap. Moments later, far different music greeted my ears: my daughter playing "Amazing Grace" on the piano.

Normally, I love my son's guitar playing. But in that moment, it jarred and unsettled me. Just as quickly, the familiar notes of John Newton's hymn reminded me that grace thrives amid the chaos. No matter how loud, unwanted, or disorienting the storms of life might be, God's notes of grace ring clear and true, reminding us of His watchful care over us.

We see this reality in Scripture. In Psalm 107:23–32, sailors struggle mightily against a maelstrom that could easily devour them. "In their peril their courage melted away" (v. 26). Still, they didn't despair but "cried out to the Lord in their trouble, and he brought them out of their distress" (v. 28). Finally, we read: "They were glad when it grew calm, and he guided them to their desired haven" (v. 30).

In chaotic moments, whether they're life-threatening or merely sleep-threatening, the barrage of noise and fear can storm our souls. But as we trust God and pray to Him, we experience the grace of His presence and provision—the haven of His steadfast love.

Adam Holz

**As we trust God and pray to Him, we experience
the grace of His presence and provision.**

GOD REMEMBERS NAMES

Isaiah 43:1–7

Do not fear, for I have redeemed you; I have summoned
you by name; you are mine. —Isaiah 43:1

The Sunday after I'd started working as a youth leader at a church and had met several of the young people, I spoke to a teen seated next to her mom. As I greeted the shy girl with a smile, I said her name and asked how she was doing. She lifted her head and her beautiful brown eyes widened. She too smiled and said in a small voice: "You remembered my name." By simply calling that young girl by name—a girl who may have felt insignificant in a church filled with adults—I began a relationship of trust. She felt seen and valued.

In Isaiah 43, God is using the prophet Isaiah to convey a similar message to the Israelites: they were seen and valued. Even through captivity and time in the wilderness, God saw them and knew them "by name" (v. 1). They were not strangers; they belonged to Him. Even though they may have felt abandoned, they were "precious," and His "love" was with them (v. 4). Along with the reminder that God knew them by name, He shared all that He would do for them, especially during trying times. When they went through trials, He would be with them (v. 2). They didn't need to be afraid or worried, since God remembered their names.

God knows each of His children's names—and this is good news, especially as we pass through the deep, difficult waters in life.

Katara Patton

**God knows each of His children's
names—and this is good news.**

TIRED TENTS

2 Corinthians 4:16–5:5

While we are in this tent, we groan and are
burdened. —2 Corinthians 5:4

"The tent is tired!" Those were the words of my friend Paul, who pastors a church in Nairobi, Kenya. For several years, the congregation had worshiped in a tentlike structure. Then Paul wrote this note to me: "Our tent is worn out and it is leaking when it rains."

My friend's words about their tent's structural weaknesses remind us of the apostle Paul's words regarding the frailty of our human existence. "Outwardly we are wasting away. . . . While we are in this tent, we groan and are burdened" (2 Corinthians 4:16; 5:4).

Although we become aware of our fragile human existence relatively early in life, we become more conscious of it as we age. Indeed, time picks our pockets. The vitality of youth surrenders reluctantly to the reality of aging (see Ecclesiastes 12:1–7). Our bodies—our tents—get tired.

But tired tents need not equate to tired trust. Hope and heart needn't fade as we age. "Therefore we do not lose heart," the apostle says (2 Corinthians 4:16). The One who has made our bodies has made himself at home there through His Spirit. And when this body can no longer serve us, we'll have a dwelling not subject to breaks and aches—we'll "have a building from God, an eternal house in heaven" (5:1).   *Arthur Jackson*

Hope and heart need not fade as we age.

ALWAYS TRUSTWORTHY

Psalm 145:9–13

The LORD is trustworthy in all he promises. —Psalm 145:13

I'm a worrier. Early mornings are the worst because I'm alone with my thoughts. So, I taped this quote from British-born missionary Hudson Taylor (1832–1905) on my bathroom mirror, where I can see it when I'm feeling vulnerable: "There is a living God. He has spoken in the Bible. He means what He says and will do all He has promised."

Taylor's words came from years of walking with God, and they remind us of who He is and all He can do through our times of illness, poverty, loneliness, and grief. Taylor didn't merely know God is trustworthy—he'd experienced His trustworthiness. And because he'd trusted God's promises and obeyed Him, thousands of Chinese people gave their lives to Jesus.

Experiencing God and His ways helped King David know He's trustworthy. He wrote Psalm 145, a song of praise to the God he'd discovered to be good, compassionate, and faithful to all His promises. When we trust and follow God, we realize (or understand better) that He is who He says He is and that He's faithful to His word (v. 13). And, like David, we respond by praising Him and telling others about Him (vv. 10–12).

When we face worrisome times, God can help us not falter in our walk with Him, for He is trustworthy (Hebrews 10:23).

Karen Huang

When we trust and follow God, we realize He's faithful to His Word.

GOD'S RADIANT BEAUTY

Romans 1:18–25

For since the creation of the world God's invisible qualities—
his eternal power and divine nature—have been clearly seen,
being understood from what has been made. —Romans 1:20

Lord Howe Island is a small paradise of white sands and crystal waters off Australia's east coast. When I visited some years ago, I was struck by its beauty. Here, one could swim with turtles and with fish like the shimmering trevally, while moon wrasses drifted nearby, flashing their neon colors like a billboard. In its lagoon I found coral reefs full of bright orange clownfish and yellow-striped butterfly fish that rushed to kiss my hand. Overwhelmed by such splendor, I couldn't help but worship God.

The apostle Paul gives the reason for my response. Creation at its best reveals something of God's nature (Romans 1:20). The wonders of Lord Howe Island were giving me a glimpse of His power and beauty.

When the prophet Ezekiel encountered God, he was shown a radiant Being seated on a blue throne surrounded by glorious colors (Ezekiel 1:25–28). The apostle John saw something similar: God sparkling like precious stones, encircled by an emerald rainbow (Revelation 4:2–3). When God reveals himself, He is found to be not only good and powerful but beautiful too. Creation reflects this beauty the way a piece of art reflects its artist.

People often worship nature instead of God (Romans 1:25). What a tragedy! Instead, earth's crystal waters and shimmering creatures should point us to the One standing behind them, who is more powerful and beautiful than anything in this world.

Sheridan Voysey

When God reveals himself, He is found to be not only good and powerful but beautiful too. Creation reflects this beauty.

RISE AGAIN

Proverbs 24:15–18

Though the righteous fall seven times,
they rise again. —Proverbs 24:16

Olympic runner Ryan Hall is the US record-holder for the half marathon. He completed the event distance of 13.1 miles (21 kilometers) in a remarkable time of fifty-nine minutes and forty-three seconds, making him the first US athlete to run the race in under an hour. While Hall has celebrated record-setting victories, he has also known the disappointment of not being able to finish a race.

Having tasted both success and failure, Hall credits his faith in Jesus for sustaining him. One of his favorite Bible verses is an encouraging reminder from the book of Proverbs that "though the righteous fall seven times, they rise again" (24:16). This proverb reminds us that the righteous, those who trust in and have a right relationship with God, will still experience difficulties and hardships. However, as they continue to seek Him even in the midst of difficulty, God is faithful to give them the strength to rise again.

Have you recently experienced a devastating disappointment or failure and feel like you will never recover? Scripture encourages us not to rely on our strength but to continue to put our confidence in God and His promises. As we trust God, His Spirit gives us strength for every difficulty we encounter in this life, from seemingly mundane to significant struggles (2 Corinthians 12:9).

Lisa M. Samra

Scripture encourages us not to rely on our strength but to continue to put our confidence in God and His promises.

MERCY AND GRACE

2 Chronicles 34:1–8

[Josiah] began to seek the God of his father
David. —2 Chronicles 34:3

A stately sunflower stood on its own in the center of a lonely stretch of national highway, just a few feet from the fast lane. As I drove past, I wondered how it had grown there with no other sunflowers visible for miles. Only God could create a plant so hardy it could thrive so close to the roadway in the gray gravel lining the median. There it was, thriving, swaying gently in the breeze— cheerfully greeting travelers as they hurried by.

The Old Testament tells the story of a faithful king of Judah who also showed up unexpectedly. His father and grandfather had enthusiastically served other gods; but after Josiah had been in power for eight years, "while he was still young, he began to seek the God of his father David" (2 Chronicles 34:3). He sent workmen to "repair the temple of the LORD" (v. 8). As they did, they discovered the Book of the Law—the first five books of the Old Testament (v. 14). God then inspired Josiah to lead the entire nation of Judah to return to the faith of their ancestors, and they served the Lord "as long as [Josiah] lived" (v. 33).

Our God is the master of unanticipated mercies. He's able to cause great good to spring up unexpectedly out of the hard gravel of life's most unfavorable circumstances. Watch Him closely. He may do it again today. *James Banks*

Our God is the master of unanticipated mercies.

STEP-BY-STEP

1 Peter 4:7–11

How good and pleasant it is when God's people
live together in unity! —Psalm 133:1

A dozen teams, each including three people standing shoulder to shoulder, prepared for the four-legged race. Bound to the person in the middle by colorful rags at their ankles and knees, each trio locked their eyes on the finish line. When the whistle blew, the teams lunged forward. Most of them fell and struggled to regain their footing. A few groups chose to hop instead of walk. Some gave up. But one team delayed their start, confirmed their plan, and communicated as they moved forward. They stumbled along the way but pressed on and soon passed all the teams. Their willingness to cooperate, step-by-step, enabled them to cross the finish line together.

Living for God within the community of believers in Jesus often feels as frustrating as trying to move forward during a four-legged race. We often stumble when interacting with people who hold different opinions from us. Frequently, we push forward when others aren't with us on the same page.

Peter speaks of prayer, hospitality, and using our gifts to align ourselves in unity for life ahead. He urges believers in Jesus to "love each other deeply" (1 Peter 4:8), to be hospitable without complaining, and to "serve others, as faithful stewards of God's grace in its various forms" (v. 10). When we ask God to help us communicate and cooperate, we can lead the race in showing the world how to celebrate differences and live together in unity.   *Xochitl Dixon*

**Peter urges believers in Jesus to love, be
hospitable, and serve others.**

BREAK THE CYCLE

Philippians 4:1–7

I plead with Euodia and I plead with Syntyche to be
of the same mind in the Lord. —Philippians 4:2

I have no idea why Euodia and Syntyche were fussing at each other. Knowing human nature, I suppose it was something minor that had put them at odds. Whatever it was, their disagreement had apparently become a distraction to the whole church.

What we do know, however, is that unless the women were willing to break the cycle by apologizing and offering forgiveness, the feud would continue. It was already serious enough to have been called to Paul's attention.

We're not much different today. I once attended a church where feuding families sat on opposite sides of the sanctuary. They didn't speak to one another and avoided any kind of contact. The issue? They were split on the matter of whether to serve coffee in the foyer or in the church basement!

It's sad, but too many times, brothers and sisters in Christ have taken sides and waited months or even years for the other to make the first move—and neither has.

It's hard to take that first step. It takes humility and grace. But God, who gives us grace for all things, will enable us to make the first move toward reconciliation. Be the first to break the cycle!

David Egner

**God, who gives us grace for all things, will enable
us to make the first move toward reconciliation.**

ASTONISHED JOY!

Philippians 3:20–41

They will see his face. —Revelation 22:4

Do you sometimes wonder what heaven will be like? We all do, I suppose. I confess, however, that the nearer I come to the end of earth's journey the more often I indulge in "sanctified curiosity" about the home Jesus has promised to believers. What will be my reaction when I "cross the river" and enter glory?

British theologian Stephen Neill asked himself the same question. At first, he was inclined to think his emotion would be astonishment. But then he decided that his emotion, "to put it a little more precisely," would be "astonished joy."

Yes, astonished joy indeed! The apostle Paul called believers in Christ citizens of heaven, and wrote, "We eagerly await a Savior." He "will transform our lowly bodies so that they will be like his glorious body" (Philippians 3:20–21). Paul looked forward to a day when sin and pain and grief would be gone forever.

What a soul-thrilling vision that will be when we see our Lord! What indescribable ecstasy we will experience! Fully aware at last of the sheer marvel of redemptive grace that has brought us into the presence of unparalleled beauty, we will be filled with astonished joy!

Vernon Grounds

**What a soul-thrilling vision that will
be when we see our Lord!**

TASTE AND SAY!

Psalm 34:1–10

Taste and see that the LORD is good; blessed is the
one who takes refuge in him. —Psalm 34:8

Do you believe God is good, even when life isn't? Mary did, and
I gasped in amazement the day I heard her pastor share her
story at her funeral.

Mary had been a widow—very poor, and housebound because
of her ailments in old age. But like the psalmist, she had learned to
praise God amid her hardships. Over the years, she had come to
savor with deep gratitude every good thing He sent her way.

Her pastor had occasionally visited her at home. Because of her
crippling pain, it took her a long time to inch her way to the door
to let him in. So he would call her phone and tell her he was on his
way and what time he'd get there. Mary would then begin the slow,
arduous journey to the door, reaching it about the time he arrived.
Without fail, she would greet him with these triumphant words:
"God is good!"

Many believers who speak often about God's goodness are our
friends with the most trials. They focus on the Lord's mercy and
grace rather than on their troubles, and in so doing they taste His
goodness. Mary's example challenges us to not only "taste and see"
but also to taste and *say* that the Lord is good—even when life isn't.

Joanie Yoder

**Focus on the Lord's mercy and grace rather than on
troubles, and in so doing taste His goodness.**

WISE ADVICE

Proverbs 6:20–23

The way of fools seems right to them, but the
wise listen to advice. —Proverbs 12:15

When the roof of Notre-Dame Cathedral in Paris caught fire in April 2019, its ancient wood beams and lead sheeting created a furnace so hot it couldn't be contained. After the cathedral's spire dramatically fell, attention turned to its bell towers. If the giant steel bells' wooden frames also burned, their collapse would bring both towers down, leaving the cathedral in ruins.

Pulling his firefighters back for safety, General Jean-Claude Gallet, commander of the Paris fire department, pondered what to do next. A firefighter named Remi nervously approached. "Respectfully, General," he said, "I propose that we run hoses up the exterior of the towers." Given the building's fragility, the commander dismissed the idea, but Remi spoke on. Soon General Gallet faced a decision: follow the junior firefighter's advice or leave the cathedral to fall.

Scripture has much to say about taking advice. While this is sometimes in the context of youth respecting elders (Proverbs 6:20–23), most is not. Proverbs says, "the wise listen to advice" (12:15), wars are won with it (24:6), and only a fool fails to heed it (12:15). Wise people listen to good advice, whatever the age or rank of those giving it.

General Gallet listened to Remi. The burning bell frames were hosed down just in time, and the cathedral was saved. What problem do you need godly advice on today? Sometimes God guides the humble through a junior's lips.   *Sheridan Voysey*

**Wise people listen to good advice, whatever
the age or rank of those giving it.**

CORINE

1 Peter 4:7–11

Offer hospitality to one another without
grumbling. —1 Peter 4:9

A group of us were helping put together packets of material at an *Our Daily Bread* event in Orlando one winter when Corine greeted us. It was midmorning, and she was sure we must be hungry and thirsty. I told her we were "fine," and she replied, "I know you're fine, but you need something to eat." A few minutes later she came back with cold water and snacks.

Throughout the two days we were at this event, Corine came by regularly to check on us, bring us food or water, and take away our trash. On one occasion, I thanked her and said, "You have the gift of hospitality, don't you, Corine!" She looked down and replied, "I don't know. But you write the devotional articles, and I'll clean up. And God will be glorified."

Corine's desire is to bring God glory by helping people. She definitely has the gift of hospitality and practices it well. God has graced each of His children with skills and abilities so He can minister to others through us. You can find those gifts listed in Romans 12:4–13; 1 Corinthians 12:27–31; Ephesians 4:7–12; and 1 Peter 4:9–11.

The Lord has gifted us "that in all things God may be praised through Jesus Christ. To him be the glory and the power for ever and ever" (1 Peter 4:11).   *Anne Cetas*

**God has graced each of His children with skills and
abilities so He can minister to others through us.**

APPROACHING GOD

Isaiah 6:1–8

Holy, holy, holy is the LORD Almighty; the whole
earth is full of his glory. —Isaiah 6:3

It used to bother me that the closer I drew to God in my walk with Him, the more sinful I felt. Then a phenomenon I observed in my room enlightened me. A tiny gap in the curtain covering my window threw a ray of light into the room. As I looked, I saw particles of dirt drifting in the beam. Without the ray of light, the room seemed clean, but the light revealed the dirty particles.

What I observed shed light on my spiritual life. The closer I approach the Lord of light, the clearer I see myself. When the light of Christ shines in the darkness of our lives, it exposes our sin—not to discourage us, but to humble us to trust in Him. We can't depend on our own righteousness, since we are sinners and fall short of God's standards (Romans 3:23). When we are proud, the light reveals our heart and we cry as Isaiah did, "Woe to me! . . . For I am a man of unclean lips, . . . and my eyes have seen the King, the LORD Almighty" (Isaiah 6:5).

God is perfect in every way. Approaching Him calls for humility and childlike trust, not self-importance and pride. For it is by grace that He draws us to himself. It is good for us that we feel unworthy as we draw closer to God, for it humbles us to rely on Him alone.

Lawrence Darmani

**Approaching God calls for humility and childlike
trust, not self-importance and pride.**

AN ENCOUNTER WITH STONES

Isaiah 53:1–6

He was pierced for our transgressions, he was
crushed for our iniquities. —Isaiah 53:5

After centuries of war and destruction, the modern city of Jerusalem is literally built on its own rubble. During a family visit, we walked the Via Dolorosa (the Way of Sorrow), the route tradition says Jesus followed on His way to the cross. The day was hot, so we paused for a rest and descended to the cool basement of the Convent of the Sisters of Zion. There I was intrigued by the sight of ancient pavement stones unearthed during recent construction—stones etched with games played by Roman soldiers during their idle moments.

Those stones, even though they were likely from a period later than Jesus's time, caused me to ponder my spiritual life. Like a bored soldier passing time in idle moments, I had become complacent and uncaring toward God and others. I was deeply moved by remembering that near the place I was standing, the Lord was beaten, mocked, insulted, and abused as He took all my failure and rebellion on himself.

"He was pierced for our transgressions, he was crushed for our iniquities; the punishment that brought us peace was on him, and by his wounds we are healed" (Isaiah 53:5).

My encounter with the stones still speaks to me of Jesus's loving grace that is greater than all my sin.   *David McCasland*

Jesus's loving grace is greater than all my sin.

COMFORT ON DOORFRAMES

Deuteronomy 6:4–9

Write [these commandments] on the doorframes of
your houses and on your gates. —Deuteronomy 6:9

As I scanned my social media feed in the aftermath of a major
flood in southern Louisiana, I came across a friend's post. After
realizing her home would have to be gutted and rebuilt, my friend's
mom encouraged her to look for God even in the heart-wrenching
work of cleaning up. My friend later posted pictures of Bible verses
she uncovered on the exposed doorframes of the home, apparently
written at the time the home had been built. Reading the Scriptures
on the wooden planks gave her comfort.

The tradition of writing Bible verses on doorframes may stem
from God's command to Israel. God instructed the Israelites to post
His commands on doorframes as a way of remembering who He is.
By writing the commandments on their hearts (Deuteronomy 6:6),
teaching them to their children (v. 7), using symbols and other means
to recall what God commands (v. 8), and placing the words on doorframes and entry ways (v. 9), the Israelites created constant reminders
of God's words. They were encouraged never to forget what He said
or their covenant with Him.

Displaying God's words in our homes as well as planting their
meaning in our hearts can help us to build a foundation that relies
on His faithfulness as revealed in Scripture. And He can use those
words to bring us comfort, even in the midst of tragedy or heart-
wrenching loss.   *Katara Patton*

**Planting God's words and their meaning in our hearts can
help us build a foundation that relies on His faithfulness.**

SPIRITUAL CHECKUP

Colossians 3:1–14

Love the Lord your God with all your heart and
with all your soul and with all your mind and
with all your strength. —Mark 12:30

To detect health problems before they become serious, doctors recommend a routine physical exam. We can do the same for our spiritual health by asking a few questions rooted in the great commandment Jesus spelled out in Mark 12:30.

Do I love God with all my heart because He first loved me? Which is stronger, my desire for earthly gain or the treasures that are mine in Christ (Colossians 3:1)? He desires that His peace rule our hearts.

Do I love God with all my soul? Do I listen to God telling me who I am? Am I moving away from self-centered desires (v. 5)? Am I becoming more compassionate, kind, humble, gentle, and patient (v. 12)?

Do I love God with all my mind? Do I focus on my relationship with His Son, or do I let my mind wander wherever it wants to go (v. 2)? Do my thoughts lead to problems or solutions? To unity or division? Forgiveness or revenge (v. 13)?

Do I love God with all my strength? Am I willing to be seen as weak so God can show His strength on my behalf (v. 17)? Am I relying on His grace to be strong in His Spirit?

As we let "the message of Christ dwell among [us] richly . . . with all wisdom" (v. 16), He will equip us to build each other up as we become spiritually fit and useful to Him.   *Julie Ackerman Link*

**Do I focus on my relationship with God's Son, or do
I let my mind wander wherever it wants to go?**

IN ALL OUR DEALINGS

2 Corinthians 1:12–16

Our conscience testifies that we have conducted ourselves . . .
with integrity and godly sincerity. —2 Corinthians 1:12

In 1524, Martin Luther observed: "Among themselves the merchants have a common rule which is their chief maxim. . . . I care nothing about my neighbor; so long as I have my profit and satisfy my greed." More than two hundred years later, John Woolman, from Mount Holly, New Jersey, let his commitment to Jesus influence his tailor shop dealings. Out of support for the freeing of slaves, he refused to purchase any cotton or dye supplies from companies that used forced labor. With a clear conscience, he loved his neighbor and lived according to integrity and sincerity in all his dealings.

The apostle Paul strived to live out "integrity and godly sincerity" (2 Corinthians 1:12). When some people in Corinth tried to undermine his authority as an apostle for Jesus, he defended his conduct among them. He wrote that his words and actions could withstand the closest scrutiny (v. 13). He also showed that he was dependent on God's power and grace for effectiveness, not his own (v. 12). In short, Paul's faith in Christ permeated all his dealings.

As we live as ambassadors for Jesus, may we be careful to let the good news ring out in all our dealings—family, business, and more. When by God's power and grace we reveal His love to others, we honor Him and love our neighbors well.   *Marvin Williams*

**May we be careful to let the good news
ring out in all our dealings.**

AN UNDESERVED GIFT

1 Timothy 1:12–16

Here is a trustworthy saying that deserves full acceptance:
Christ Jesus came into the world to save sinners—
of whom I am the worst. —1 Timothy 1:15

When my friend gave me a gift recently, I was surprised. I didn't think I deserved such a nice present from her. She'd sent it after hearing about some work stress I was experiencing. Yet she was going through just as much stress, if not more, than I was, with an aging parent, challenging children, upheaval at work, and strain on her marriage. I couldn't believe she had thought of me before herself, and her simple gift brought me to tears.

In truth, we're all recipients of a gift we could never deserve. Paul put it this way: "Christ Jesus came into the world to save sinners—of whom I am the worst" (1 Timothy 1:15). The apostle had experienced a miraculous conversion from being a persecutor of Christians to becoming a faithful believer in Jesus. Although he "was once a blasphemer and a persecutor and a violent man, . . . the grace of our Lord was poured out on [him] abundantly" (vv. 13–14). He had a deep understanding of the free gift of grace and what it meant to be an undeserving recipient of that gift. As a result, Paul became a powerful instrument of God's love and told many people about what God had done for him.

It's only through God's grace that we receive love instead of condemnation and mercy instead of judgment. Today, let's celebrate the undeserved grace that God has given and be on the lookout for ways to demonstrate that grace to others.   *Karen Pimpo*

**It's only through God's grace that we receive love instead
of condemnation and mercy instead of judgment.**

FROM STRESS TO PEACE

Philippians 4:4–8

Do not be anxious about anything, but in every situation, by prayer and petition, with thanksgiving, present your requests to God. —Philippians 4:6

Moving from one house to another ranks as one of the biggest stressors in life. We moved to our current home after I'd lived in my previous one for nearly twenty years. I'd lived alone in that first home for eight years before I got married. Then my husband moved in, along with all his things. Later, we added a child, and that meant even more stuff.

Our moving day to the new house wasn't without incident. Five minutes before the movers arrived, I was still finishing up a book manuscript. And the new home had several sets of stairs, so it took double the time and twice as many movers as planned.

I was surprised that I wasn't feeling stressed out by the events of that day. Then it hit me: I'd spent many hours finishing writing a book—one chock-full of Scripture and biblical concepts. By God's grace, I'd been poring over the Bible, praying, and writing to meet my deadline. I believe the key to my calmness was my immersion in Scripture and in prayer.

Paul wrote, "Do not be anxious about anything, but in every situation, by prayer and petition, with thanksgiving, present your requests to God" (Philippians 4:6). When we pray—and "rejoice in" God (v. 4)—we refocus our mind from the problem to our Provider. We may be asking God to help us deal with a stressor, but we're also connecting with Him, which can provide a peace "which transcends all understanding" (v. 7). *Katara Patton*

When we pray, we refocus our mind from
the problem to our Provider.

ROADSIDE ASSISTANCE

Psalm 46

God is our refuge and strength, an ever-present help in trouble. —Psalm 46:1

A few years ago, an acquaintance of mine was hunting with friends near Balmoral, England, then the country estate of Queen Elizabeth II. As they walked through the woods, he twisted his ankle so badly that he couldn't go on. He told his friends to continue, and he would wait by the side of the road.

As he sat there, a car came down the road, slowed, and stopped. The woman driving rolled the window and asked if he was okay. He explained what happened and said he was waiting for his friends to return. She said, "Get in; I'll take you back to where you are staying." He limped to the car and opened the door—only to realize that it was Queen Elizabeth herself!

As shocking as receiving help from the queen of England may be, we have an offer of help that is even more astounding. The Creator-God of the universe descends into our world, sees our trouble, and offers to marshal His resources to help us. As the psalmist confidently affirms, "God is . . . an ever-present help in trouble" (Psalm 46:1). Our Savior helps by giving us grace to endure, His Word to sustain us, friends to encourage and pray for us, and the confidence that He will ultimately work it all together for our spiritual good.

Next time you feel stranded along life's road, look for your Helper.

Joe Stowell

Our Savior helps by giving us grace to endure.

THE SECRET

Philippians 4:10–19

I have learned the secret of being content in any
and every situation. —Philippians 4:12

Sometimes I suspect my cat Heathcliff suffers from a bad case of FOMO (fear of missing out). When I come home with groceries, Heathcliff rushes over to inspect the contents of the bags. When I'm chopping vegetables, he stands on his back paws peering at the produce and begging me to share. But when I actually give him whatever's caught his fancy, he quickly loses interest, walking away with an air of bored resentment.

But it would be hypocritical for me to be hard on my little buddy. In comical caricature, he reflects a bit of my own insatiable hunger for more, my assumption that "now" is never enough.

According to Paul, contentment isn't natural—it's learned (Philippians 4:11). On our own, we desperately pursue whatever we think will satisfy, moving on to the next thing the minute we realize it won't. Other times, our discontent takes the form of anxiously shielding ourselves from any and all suspected threats.

Ironically, sometimes it takes experiencing what we feared the most in order to stumble into real joy.

Having experienced much of the worst life has to offer, Paul could testify firsthand to "the secret" of true contentment (vv. 11–12)—the mysterious reality that as we lift up to God our longings for wholeness, we experience unexplainable peace (vv. 6–7), carried ever deeper into the depths of Christ's power, beauty, and grace.

Monica La Rose

**Sometimes it takes experiencing what we feared
the most in order to stumble into real joy.**

RECONCILING RELATIONSHIPS

Ephesians 4:22–32

Be kind and compassionate to one another, forgiving each
other, just as in Christ God forgave you. —Ephesians 4:32

My sister and I clashed frequently when we were younger, but
one time especially stands out in my memory. After a bout of
yelling back and forth where we'd both said hurtful things, she said
something that in the moment seemed unforgivable. Witnessing the
animosity growing between us, my grandmother reminded us of our
responsibility to love each other: "God gave you one sister in life.
You've got to show each other a little grace," she said. When we asked
God to fill us with love and understanding, He helped us acknowledge how we'd hurt each other and to forgive one another.

It can be so easy to hold on to bitterness and anger, but God
desires for us to experience the peace that can only come when we
ask Him to help us release feelings of resentment (Ephesians 4:31).
Instead of harboring these feelings, we can look to Christ's example
of forgiveness, which comes from a place of love and grace. Then
we can strive to be "kind and compassionate" and to "[forgive] each
other, just as in Christ God forgave [us]" (v. 32).

When we find it challenging to forgive, let's consider the grace
He extends to us each day. No matter how many times we fall short,
His compassion never fails (Lamentations 3:22). God can help us
remove bitterness from our hearts, so we're free to remain hopeful
and receptive to His love.   *Kimya Loder*

**When we find it challenging to forgive, may we
consider the grace that God extends to us each day.**

RHYTHMS OF GRACE

Matthew 11:25–30

Take my yoke upon you and learn from me, for
I am gentle and humble in heart, and you will
find rest for your souls. —Matthew 11:29

A friend and his wife, now in their early nineties and married for sixty-six years, wrote their family history for their children, grandchildren, and generations to come. The final chapter, "A Letter from Mom and Dad," contains important life lessons they've learned. One of those lessons caused me to pause and take inventory of my own life: "If you find that Christianity exhausts you, draining you of your energy, then you are practicing religion rather than enjoying a relationship with Jesus Christ. Your walk with the Lord will not make you weary; it will invigorate you, restore your strength, and energize your life" (See Matthew 11:28–29).

Eugene Peterson's paraphrase of Jesus's invitation in this passage begins, "Are you tired? Worn out? Burned out on religion? . . . Walk with me and work with me. . . . Learn the unforced rhythms of grace" (MSG).

When I think serving God is all up to me, I've begun working *for* Him instead of walking *with* Him. My spirit becomes dry and brittle. People are annoyances, not fellow humans created in God's image. Nothing seems right.

When I sense that I'm practicing religion instead of enjoying a relationship with Jesus, it's time to lay the burden down and walk with Him in His "unforced rhythms of grace."   *David McCasland*

**If I'm not walking with Christ, my
spirit becomes dry and brittle.**

THANKS FOR FLEAS

1 Thessalonians 5:12–18

Give thanks in all circumstances. —1 Thessalonians 5:18

Corrie ten Boom was an inspiration and challenge to thousands of people after World War II. Hearts were stirred and lives changed as she told with moving simplicity about God's sufficiency to meet her needs, even as a prisoner in a Nazi concentration camp.

The camp was filthy and there were fleas everywhere. Corrie's sister Betsie, who was imprisoned with her, insisted that 1 Thessalonians 5:18 was God's will for them: "In everything give thanks" (NKJV). But giving thanks in a flea-infested place seemed unrealistic to Corrie—until she realized why the guards didn't come into their barracks to make them stop praying and singing hymns. They wanted to avoid the fleas! So the prisoners were free to worship and study the Bible. The fleas, yes, even the fleas, were agents of grace and something to be thankful for.

What are some of the "fleas" in our lives? They aren't the big difficulties, but the petty annoyances. They are the little trials from which we can't escape. Is it possible that they are among the ways the Lord teaches us spiritual lessons and helps us to increase our endurance?

When we are tempted to grumble, let's remember the fleas and give thanks. *Vernon Grounds*

Little trials become one way the Lord teaches us spiritual lessons.

LET US PRAISE!

Psalm 67

May the nations be glad and sing for joy. —Psalm 67:4

When the alarm on Shelley's phone goes off every afternoon at 3:16, she takes a praise break. She thanks God and acknowledges His goodness. Although she communicates with God throughout the day, Shelley loves to take this break because it helps her celebrate her intimate relationship with Him.

Inspired by her joyful devotion, I decided to set a specific time each day to thank Christ for His sacrifice on the cross and to pray for those who have yet to be saved. I wonder what it would be like if all believers in Jesus stopped to praise Him in their own way and pray for others every day.

The image of a beautiful wave of worship rolling to the ends of the earth resounds in the words of Psalm 67. The psalmist pleads for God's grace, proclaiming his desire to make His name great in all the nations (vv. 1–2). He sings, "May the peoples praise you, God; may all the peoples praise you" (v. 3). He celebrates His sovereign rule and faithful guidance (v. 4). As a living testimony of God's great love and abundant blessings, the psalmist leads God's people into jubilant praise (vv. 5–6).

God's continued faithfulness toward His beloved children inspires us to acknowledge Him. As we do, others can join us in trusting Him, revering Him, following Him, and acclaiming Him as Lord.

Xochitl Dixon

God's faithfulness toward His beloved children inspires us to acknowledge Him.

THE LAW IN THE HEART

Romans 2:12–16

They show that the requirements of the law are
written on their hearts. —Romans 2:15

Marilyn Laszlo (1933–2021) dedicated her life to giving the Sepik Iwam people of New Guinea the Bible in their own language. As she worked on the translation, she came to the word for "sin." When Marilyn asked the people what they thought sin was, they told her, "It's when you lie." "It's when you steal." "It's when you kill." "It's when you take another man's wife."

Marilyn was astounded. They were giving her God's standards as spelled out in the Ten Commandments. "God's law is written on the heart of man," she later commented, underscoring the truth found in Romans 2:14–15.

What a remarkable verification of biblical truth! Our faith is strengthened by accounts like this. But there's something else. If each person on earth is aware of sin (which is true even though some deny it), we need to make sure everyone hears the remedy. Jesus paid the penalty for sin and offers all sinners a life free from bondage.

God put His law in our heart, but we can never live up to its requirements (Romans 3:23; James 2:10; 1 John 1:8). The law shows us how enslaved we are by sin, but God's grace to us through Christ brings liberty. If we have experienced this forgiveness and freedom, it's up to us to share the good news with others.   *Dave Branon*

We need to make sure everyone hears the remedy for sin.

SONGS OF GRACE

SEPTEMBER

"Come, Thou Fount of Every Blessing"

Robert Robinson and John Wyeth

Come, Thou Fount of every blessing,
tune my heart to sing Thy grace.

From Hoodlum to Hymn Writer

A wise and respected high school government teacher once pleaded with his fellow teachers not to judge teenagers too harshly but instead trust that God will reach them and use them even though they are troublesome at school.

Robert Robinson, an eighteenth-century troublesome teenager, was just the kind of guy this wise educator was talking about.

Young Robert was too much for his mother to handle. In 1743, when Robert was only eight years old, his father died. And then his

Sources: C. Michael Hawn, "History of Hymns: 'Come, Thou Fount of Every Blessing,'" Discipleship Ministries of The United Methodist Church, June 2013, http://tinyurl.com/mpsazr9a; "Hymn History: Come Thou Fount," *Enjoying the Journey*, February 2, 2022, http://tinyurl.com/4ca66zyw; Jerry Rushford. "Hymns of the Season: Come, Thou Fount of Every Blessing," *Pepperdine Library News*, May 14, 2020, http://tinyurl.com/mr2vphbs; all accessed November 6, 2023.

maternal grandfather abandoned his family, leaving Robert and his mother without needed resources. Robert was not an easy child to raise, and by the time he was fourteen, his mom had seen enough. She sent him off to London, about a hundred miles from their home in Swaffham, to be apprenticed to become a barber.

When Robert was seventeen, he and a group of friends, known for their rebellious ways, decided to attend a tent meeting where the renowned preacher George Whitfield was scheduled to deliver a sermon. The boys' plan was to heckle Rev. Whitfield—to "laugh at the poor, deluded Methodist," as one of them put it.

But Whitfield's words made an unexpected impression on Robert—especially when he hammered home the prospect of sinners facing "the wrath of God."

Robinson brooded over Whitfield's message for a while, later saying, "I could think of little else." When he finally felt the conviction of the Holy Spirit and trusted Jesus as Savior at age twenty, he said he "found full and free forgiveness through the precious blood of Jesus Christ."

He immediately embarked on a quest to learn God's Word and to be able to preach it.

Three years later, Robinson wrote the song "Come, Thou Fount of Every Blessing" as he was preparing a message for Pentecost Sunday. The tune that is used today was added by John Wyeth, an American printer.

Although Robinson became a successful pastor for many years, he was troubled by times of despair. One often-told story is that during one of those times, when he was riding in a stagecoach, a woman passenger began singing, "Come, Thou Fount of Every Blessing." Not knowing who he was, she told him how much the song meant to her and asked him what he thought of it. He replied that he was the unhappy man who wrote the hymn, and he wished he could enjoy again the feelings it expressed.

It is reported that she said, "Sir, the 'streams of mercy' are still flowing."

Indeed, Robinson found his way back into fellowship with the Lord after his times of discouragement. When he died at the age of fifty-five, he was again a dedicated pastor who preached the truths of God's Word.

Come, Thou Fount of Every Blessing

Come, Thou Fount of every blessing,
Tune my heart to sing Thy grace;
Streams of mercy, never ceasing,
Call for songs of loudest praise.
Teach me some melodious sonnet
Sung by flaming tongues above;
Praise the mount—I'm fixed upon it—
Mount of Thy redeeming love.

O to grace how great a debtor
Daily I'm constrained to be!
Let Thy goodness like a fetter
Bind my wandering heart to Thee:
Prone to wander—Lord, I feel it—
Prone to leave the God I love;
Here's my heart—O take and seal it,
Seal it for Thy courts above.

IN HIS PRESENCE

1 Corinthians 15:50–58

Death has been swallowed up in victory. —1 Corinthians 15:54

As the congregation around me sang the final verse of "Amazing Grace," I couldn't sing. I found myself instead wiping tears from my eyes as I stared at John Newton's words, "When we've been there ten thousand years, . . . we've no less days to sing God's praise than when we'd first begun."

At that moment, I wasn't interested in ten thousand years in heaven. All I could think of was that my seventeen-year-old daughter was already there. Melissa, who just a few months earlier had been looking forward to her senior year of high school, was in heaven. She was already experiencing an eternity that we can only talk and sing about.

When Melissa died in a car accident in the spring of that year, heaven took on new meaning for our family. Because our bright, beautiful teen had trusted Jesus Christ as her Savior, we knew she was there. As Paul said, "Death has been swallowed up in victory" (1 Corinthians 15:54). To us, heaven became even more real. We knew that as we talked with God, we were talking to Someone who had our Melissa in His presence.

The reality of heaven is one of the Bible's most glorious truths. It's a real place where our loved ones live in the presence of our great God, forever serving Him and singing His praises—all because of His amazing grace!

Dave Branon

The reality of heaven is one of the Bible's most glorious truths.

A SMALL FIRE

James 3:3–12

The tongue is a small part of the body, but it
makes great boasts. Consider what a great forest
is set on fire by a small spark. —James 3:5

It was a Sunday night in September and most people were sleeping when a small fire broke out in Thomas Farriner's bakery on Pudding Lane. Soon the flames spread from house to house, and London was engulfed in the Great Fire of 1666. Over 70,000 people were left homeless by the blaze that leveled four-fifths of the city. So much destruction from such a small fire!

The Bible warns us of another small but destructive fire. James was concerned about lives and relationships, not buildings, when he wrote, "The tongue is a small part of the body, but it makes great boasts. Consider what a great forest is set on fire by a small spark" (James 3:5).

But our words can also be *constructive*. Proverbs 16:24 reminds us, "Gracious words are a honeycomb, sweet to the soul and healing to the bones." The apostle Paul says, "Let your conversation be always full of grace, seasoned with salt, so that you may know how to answer everyone" (Colossians 4:6). As salt flavors our food, grace flavors our words for building up others.

Through the help of the Holy Spirit, our words can encourage people who are hurting, who want to grow in their faith, or who need to come to the Savior. Our words can put out fires instead of starting them.   *Bill Crowder*

**As salt flavors our food, grace flavors our
words for building up others.**

A FUTURE WITH FORGIVENESS

Romans 12:9–21

Do not be overcome by evil, but overcome
evil with good. —Romans 12:21

In 1994, when South Africa made the transition from government by apartheid (imposed racial segregation) to a democracy, it faced the difficult question of how to address the crimes committed under apartheid. The country's leaders couldn't ignore the past, but merely imposing harsh punishments on the guilty risked deepening the country's wounds. As Desmond Tutu, the first black Anglican Archbishop of South Africa, explained in his book *No Future Without Forgiveness*, "We could very well have had justice, retributive justice, and had a South Africa lying in ashes."

Through establishing the Truth and Reconciliation Committee, the new democracy chose the difficult path of pursuing truth, justice, and mercy. Those guilty of crimes were offered a path to restoration—if they were willing to confess their crimes and seek to make restitution. Only by courageously facing the truth could the country begin to find healing.

In a way, South Africa's dilemma mirrors the struggle we all face. We're called to pursue both justice and mercy (Micah 6:8), but mercy is often misunderstood to be a lack of accountability, while pursuing justice can become distorted into pursuing revenge.

Our only path forward is a love that will not only "hate what is evil" (Romans 12:9) but also long for the transformation and good of our "neighbor" (13:10). Through the power of Christ's Spirit, we can learn what it means to have a future of overcoming evil with good (12:21). *Monica La Rose*

Our only path forward is love that hates evil
and longs for the good of our neighbor.

LOVE IS WORTH THE RISK

John 21:15–19

If you love me, keep my commands. —John 14:15

After a friend ended our decade-long friendship without explanation, I began slipping back into my old habit of keeping people at arm's length. While processing my grief, I pulled a tattered copy of *The Four Loves* by C. S. Lewis from my shelf. Lewis makes a powerful observation about love requiring vulnerability. He states there's "no safe investment" when a person risks loving. He suggests that loving "anything [will lead to] your heart being wrung and possibly broken." Reading those words changed how I read the account of the third time Jesus appeared to His disciples after His resurrection (John 21:1–14), after Peter had betrayed Him not once but three times (18:15–27).

Jesus said, "Simon son of John, do you love me more than these?" (21:15).

After experiencing the sting of betrayal and rejection, Jesus spoke to Peter with courage, not fear; strength, not weakness; selflessness, not desperation. He displayed mercy, not wrath, by confirming His willingness to love.

Scripture reveals that "Peter was hurt because Jesus asked him the third time, 'Do you love me?'" (v. 17). But when Jesus asked Peter to prove his love by loving others (vv. 15–17) and following Him (v. 19), He invited all His disciples to risk loving unconditionally. Each of us will have to answer when Jesus asks, "Do you love me?" Our answer will impact how we love others.   *Xochitl Dixon*

**Jesus displayed mercy not wrath by
confirming His willingness to love.**

GRADED WITH GRACE

Romans 5:6–15

While we were still sinners, Christ died for us. —Romans 5:8

My son's blue eyes sparkled with excitement as he showed me a paper he had brought home from school. It was a math test, marked with a red star and a grade of 100 percent. As we looked at the exam, he said he had three questions left to answer when the teacher said time was up. Puzzled, I asked how he could have received a perfect score. He replied, "My teacher gave me grace. She let me finish the test although I had run out of time."

As my son and I discussed the meaning of grace, I pointed out that God has given us more than we deserve through Christ. We deserve death because of our sin (Romans 3:23). Yet, "while we were still sinners, Christ died for us" (5:8). We were unworthy, yet Jesus—sinless and holy—gave up His life through death on the cross so we could escape the penalty for our sin and one day live forever in heaven.

Eternal life is a gift from God. It's not something we earn by working for it. We are saved by God's grace, through faith in Christ (Ephesians 2:8–9).

Jennifer Benson Schuldt

God has given us more than we deserve through Christ.

JUST DO WHAT'S RIGHT

Philippians 2:12–18

That you may become blameless and pure,
"children of God without fault in a warped and
crooked generation." —Philippians 2:15

On a trip out of the country, I happened to meet an attorney who was from my hometown in New Jersey. We were surprised at how much we had in common. In the course of the conversation, he asked, "Did you say your name was Stillwell?" I said, "No, it's Stowell." He then mentioned that he had a client named Stillwell. "Is it Art Stillwell?" I asked, and, to my surprise, he said yes. Art Stillwell attended my church and was an influential businessman in the community.

The attorney admitted that he had no client quite like Art. He explained that most of his clients want him to do whatever it takes to get them out of their problems, but Art was different. Whenever he asked Art what to do in any given situation, Art always replied, "Just do what's right!" Obviously, it had made an impression on the attorney.

Yielding to Christ in all of our desires and decisions regardless of the outcome is what sets us apart in a world full of people consumed by their own interests. When we live blameless lives "without fault"—courageously reflecting the integrity, love, and grace of Jesus—we clearly "shine as lights in the world" (Philippians 2:15 NKJV).

So if you want to light up your world in a compelling way, just do what's right!   *Joe Stowell*

Yielding to Christ in all of our desires and decisions regardless of the outcome is what sets us apart.

ACTS OF GRATITUDE

Micah 6:1–8

And what does the LORD require of you? To act justly and to love mercy and to walk humbly with your God. —Micah 6:8

Few people knew me better as a boy than Francis Allen, the pastor who led me to Jesus Christ. A fire-and-brimstone preacher in the pulpit, he was a near-perfect example of the gentleness of God's love outside of it.

Early on, Francis recognized a tendency in me to try to "buy" approval by working harder than expected and doing more than people asked. "These are good traits to give as gifts to others," he would tell me, "but you should never use them to buy acceptance and love from people—or from God."

To help me understand this, he told me to read Jesus's promise in Matthew 11:30 that His "yoke is easy"—a statement that sometimes seems too simple to be true. Then, pointing to Micah 6:6–8, he said: "Now read this and ask yourself if there are any gifts you can give God that He doesn't already have." The answer, of course, is no.

Next, he went on to explain that God cannot be bought—the gift of grace is free. Since this is true, what should be our response? "To act justly and to love mercy and to walk humbly with your God" (v. 8). I learned that these were acts of gratitude—not of purchase.

Micah 6 is a helpful reminder that grace is free and that faithful living is our grateful response. *Randy Kilgore*

God cannot be bought—the gift of grace is free.

THE MIRACLE OF SALVATION

John 11:38–44

Did I not tell you that if you believe, you will
see the glory of God? —John 11:40

Blogger Kevin Lynn's life seemed to be falling apart. In a recent
article he recounted, "I actually put a gun to my head. . . . It
took for God to supernaturally step into my room and my life. And
at that moment, I really found what I know is God now." God intervened and prevented Lynn from taking his life. He filled him with
conviction and gave him an overwhelming reminder of His loving
presence. Instead of hiding this powerful encounter, Lynn shared his
experience with the world, creating a YouTube ministry where he
shares his own transformation story as well as the stories of others.

When Jesus's follower and friend Lazarus died, many assumed Jesus
was too late to help (John 11:32). Lazarus had been in his tomb for
four days before Christ arrived, but Jesus turned this moment of anguish into a miracle when He raised Lazarus from the dead (v. 38).
"Did I not tell you that if you believe, you will see the glory of God?"
(v. 40).

Just as Jesus raised Lazarus from death to life, He offers us new
life through Him. By sacrificing His life on the cross, Christ paid the
penalty for our sins and offers us forgiveness when we accept His gift
of grace. We're freed from the bondage of our sins, renewed by His
everlasting love, and given the opportunity to change the course of
our lives. *Kimya Loder*

**By sacrificing His life on the cross, Christ paid the
penalty for our sins and offers us forgiveness.**

MERCY FOR YOU AND ME

Psalm 103:8–12

He will not always accuse, nor will he harbor
his anger forever. —Psalm 103:9

One of the consequences of the COVID-19 pandemic was the docking of cruise ships and the quarantining of passengers. *The Wall Street Journal* featured an article that included interviews with some of the tourists. Commenting about how being quarantined provided more opportunities for conversations, one passenger joked how his spouse—who possessed an excellent memory—was able to bring up every transgression he ever had, and he sensed she wasn't done yet!

Accounts like this might make us smile, remind us of our humanness, and serve to caution us if we're prone to hold too tightly to the things we should release. Yet what helps us to be kindly disposed to those who hurt us? Glimpses of our great God, as He is portrayed in passages such as Psalm 103:8–12.

The Message's rendering of verses 8–10 is noteworthy: "God is sheer mercy and grace; not easily angered, he's rich in love. He doesn't endlessly nag and scold, nor hold grudges forever. He doesn't treat us as our sins deserve, nor pay us back in full for our wrongs." Asking for God's help as we prayerfully read Scripture can cause us to have second thoughts about ill-conceived payback or plans to punish. And it can prompt prayers for ourselves and for those we may be tempted to harm by withholding grace, mercy, and forgiveness.   *Arthur Jackson*

**Asking for God's help as we prayerfully read Scripture can
cause us to have second thoughts about ill-conceived ideas.**

"SLACKERS, GET MOVING!"

Ephesians 1:1–14

God created mankind in his own image. —Genesis 1:27

A drill sergeant barked out an order to a bunch of recruits: "All you slackers, get moving!" All but one obeyed. Angered by his seeming defiance, the sergeant marched up to him and growled, "Well?" The young recruit replied, "There certainly were a lot of them, Sir!"

It would be great if more of us as Christians felt that good about ourselves. It's not wrong to affirm our worth. The Bible does. We have been created to reflect the moral and personal nature of God (Genesis 1:26). Sin has marred that image, but because of love, God sent His Son to die for our sins. By trusting Jesus as our Savior, we are "accepted," just as the Father accepts Him (Ephesians 1:6).

We may feel unworthy of such love and grace, but we can still have a healthy sense of self-worth, belonging, and confidence. Because Christ has removed the guilt of our sin by paying its penalty on the cross, we know we are fully accepted by Him (vv. 7–14).

Feelings of self-condemnation may still come over us, but we must affirm our worth in Christ. When an inner voice keeps shouting, "You're a slacker!" silence it by saying to yourself, "God made me. Christ saved me. And that makes me a person of great worth!"

Dennis DeHaan

We must affirm our worth in Christ.

TOUGH TREES

Romans 5:1–5

Suffering produces perseverance; perseverance,
character; and character, hope. —Romans 5:3–4

Bristlecone pines are the world's oldest living trees. Several are estimated to be 3,000 to 4,000 years old. In 1957, scientist Edmund Schulman found one he named "Methuselah." This ancient, gnarled pine is nearly 5,000 years old! It was an old tree when the Egyptians were building the pyramids.

Bristlecones grow atop the mountains of the western United States at elevations of 10,000 to 11,000 feet. They've been able to survive some of the harshest living conditions on earth: arctic temperatures, fierce winds, thin air, and little rainfall.

Their brutal environment is one of the reasons they've survived for millennia. Hardship has produced extraordinary strength and staying power.

Paul taught that "suffering produces . . . character" (Romans 5:3–4). Adversity is part of the process God uses to produce good results in our lives. Trouble, if it turns us to the Lord, could be the best thing for us. It leaves us wholly dependent on Him.

So, we should pray not just for relief from our affliction but also for the grace to turn it into greater openness to God and His will for us. Then we can be strong in calamity and at peace in the place where God has planted us.   *David Roper*

**Adversity is part of the process God uses to
produce good results in our lives.**

NEW LIFE ON DEATH ROW

John 19:16–18

Jesus answered him, "Truly I tell you, today you
will be with me in paradise." —Luke 23:43

We see two opposite responses to Jesus from the two thieves
who were crucified next to Him: One blasphemed; the other
believed (Luke 23:39–42). We rejoice over the conversion of the
one as we read Christ's words to him: "Today you will be with me
in paradise" (v. 43). Now, as then, Jesus saves those who truly repent—even at "the eleventh hour."

One such person was Lester Ezzell, who was on death row in
Florida. When his former Sunday school teacher Curtis Oakes traveled 750 miles to visit him in prison, Lester said, "You don't give up,
do you?" Though Lester still wouldn't listen to the gospel, Curtis
gave him a New Testament and urged him to read it.

Later, Lester wrote several letters to Curtis. The first one brought
news of his conversion. His final letter in early 1957 read: "By the
time you receive this, my life will have been taken. I will have paid
for the wrong I have done. But I want you to know this—with that
little Testament, and by the grace of God, I have led forty-seven
people to the saving knowledge of Jesus Christ. Thank you for not
giving up on me."

When we witness to others about Jesus Christ, some may not
repent until late in life. So let's never give up on anyone.

Joanie Yoder

Let's never give up on anyone.

WHAT'S BENEATH?

Matthew 15:7–20

Out of the heart come evil thoughts. . . . These are
what defile a person. —Matthew 15:19–20

*A*s long as you keep your mouth closed, I told myself, *you won't
be doing anything wrong.* I'd been outwardly holding back my
anger toward a colleague after misinterpreting things she had said.
Since we had to see each other every day, I decided to limit communication to only what was necessary (and retaliate with my silent
treatment). How could a quiet demeanor be wrong?

Jesus, however, said that sin begins in the heart (Matthew
15:18–20). My silence may have fooled people into thinking all was
well, but it wasn't fooling God. He knew I was hiding a heart filled
with anger. I was like the Pharisees, who "honor [Jesus] with their
lips, but their hearts [were] far from [Him]" (v. 8). Even though
my outward appearance didn't show my true feelings, the bitterness
was festering inside me. The joy and closeness I'd always felt with
my heavenly Father were gone. Nurturing and hiding sin does that.

By God's grace, I told my colleague how I was feeling and apologized. She graciously forgave me and, eventually, we became good
friends. "Out of the heart come evil thoughts" (v. 19), Jesus said.
The state of our heart matters because evil residing there can overflow into our lives. Both our actions and our heart matter.

Karen Huang

Jesus says that the state of our heart matters.

KNOWN FOR COMPASSION

Acts 11:19–26

He was a good man, full of the Holy Spirit and faith, and a great number of people were brought to the Lord. —Acts 11:24

During Major General Mark Graham's two years as commander of Fort Carson, Colorado, he became known and loved for the way he treated others. One US Army colleague said: "I have never come across another general officer who was so compassionate and so concerned about the well-being of soldiers and their families." After losing one son to suicide and another who was killed in action, Mark and his wife, Carol, dedicated themselves to helping soldiers and their families cope with service-related stress, depression, and loss.

In the book of Acts, a follower of Christ was well-known for his care and concern toward others. His name was Joseph, but in the early church, the apostles called him Barnabas, "son of encouragement." It was Barnabas who vouched for the newly converted Saul when others doubted the sincerity of his faith (Acts 9:26–27). Later, Barnabas brought Saul from Tarsus to teach the believers in Antioch (11:25–26). And it was Barnabas who wanted to give John Mark a second chance after his failure on a previous missionary journey (15:36–38).

Compassion is an inner feeling resulting in outward action. It should be our daily uniform of service (Colossians 3:12). By God's grace, let's make sure we are known for our compassion.

David McCasland

Compassion is an inner feeling resulting in outward action.

TWO RULES TO LIVE BY

Matthew 22:34–40

All the Law and the Prophets hang on these
two commandments. —Matthew 22:40

Have you ever felt overwhelmed by rules and expectations? Think of how the Jewish people must have felt as they tried to keep up with more than six hundred rules from the Old Testament and many more that had been imposed on them by the religious leaders of their day. And imagine their surprise when Jesus simplified the pursuit of righteousness by narrowing the list down to only two— "love the Lord your God" (Matthew 22:37) and "love your neighbor as yourself" (v. 39).

In essence, Jesus is telling us that the way God knows we love Him is by how we treat people. All of them. Let's face it—loving our neighbor can be a challenge. But when we do it to express our love to God, we unleash a powerful motivation that helps us love, whether the person deserves it or not. And as we love God and our neighbor, everything else falls into place. If I love my neighbor, I won't bear false witness against him, covet his wealth or his wife, or steal from him. Loving others for God's sake even provides the grace and strength to forgive those who have treated us unjustly.

Who needs to see God's love today through you? The more unlovable the person, the greater the statement about how much you love God!

Joe Stowell

**Loving others for God's sake provides the grace and
strength to forgive those who treated us unjustly.**

USEFUL TEMPTATION

James 1:2–5, 12–21

Humbly accept the word planted in you,
which can save you. —James 1:21

Fifteenth-century monk Thomas à Kempis, in the beloved classic *The Imitation of Christ*, offers a perspective on temptation that might surprise you. Instead of focusing on the pain and difficulties temptation can lead to, he writes, "[temptations] are useful because they can make us humble, they can cleanse us, and they can teach us." Kempis explains, "The key to victory is true humility and patience; in them we overcome the enemy."

Humility and patience. How different my walk with Christ would be if this were how I naturally responded to temptation! More often, I react with shame, frustration, and impatient attempts to get rid of the struggle.

But as we learn from James 1, the temptations and trials we face don't have to be without purpose or merely a threat we endure. Although giving in to temptation can bring heartbreak and devastation (vv. 13–15), when we turn to God with humble hearts seeking His wisdom and grace, we find He "gives generously to all without finding fault" (v. 5). Through His power in us, our trials and struggles to resist sin build perseverance, "so that [we] may be mature and complete, not lacking anything" (v. 4).

As we trust in Jesus, we have no reason to live in fear. As God's dearly loved children, we can find peace as we rest in His loving arms—even as we face temptation.   *Monica La Rose*

When we turn to God with humble hearts seeking His wisdom and grace, we find He gives generously.

THE TELLING ROOM

1 Samuel 18:1–4

Jonathan made a covenant with David because
he loved him as himself. —1 Samuel 18:3

Some residents of northern Spain produced a beautiful way of expressing communion and friendship. With the countryside full of handmade caves, after each harvest some farmers would sit in a room built above a cave and inventory their various foods. As time passed, the room became known as the "telling room"—a place of communion where friends and families would gather to share their stories, secrets, and dreams. If you needed the intimate company of safe friends, you would head for the telling room.

Had Jonathan and David lived in northern Spain, the deep friendship they shared might have led them to create a telling room. When King Saul became so jealous that he wanted to kill David, Jonathan, Saul's oldest son, protected and befriended him. The two became "one in spirit" (1 Samuel 18:1). And Jonathan "loved him as himself" (vv. 1, 3) and—though Saul's son was heir apparent to the throne—he recognized David's divine selection to be king. He gave David his robe, sword, bow, and belt (v. 4). Later, David declared that Jonathan's deep love for him as a friend was wonderful (2 Samuel 1:26).

As believers in Jesus, let's ask Him to help us build our own relational "telling rooms"—friendships that reflect Christlike love and care. Then we can take the time to linger with friends, open our hearts, and live in true communion with one another in Him.

Marvin Williams

**As believers in Jesus, let's seek friendships
that reflect Christlike love and care.**

JUST AS I AM

Matthew 10:1, 5–10, 16–20

Jesus called his twelve disciples to him and
gave them authority. —Matthew 10:1

The young woman couldn't sleep. A church bazaar was being held the next day to raise funds for educating daughters of clergymen. Having suffered a physical disability for many years, she alone of all her family members was unable to help. *I'm useless*, she thought. As Charlotte Elliott tossed and turned, she gave in to her distress and was soon questioning every aspect of her spiritual life.

Still restless the next day, Charlotte determined to focus instead on what she knew to be true of God. She moved to a desk and picked up paper and pen to write down the words of the now classic hymn, "Just as I Am."

"Just as I am, without one plea, But that Thy blood was shed for me, And that Thou bidst me come to Thee, O Lamb of God, I come, I come."

Her words, written in 1835, express the right attitude to have as we contemplate service for our Savior. We don't have to be ready— we have to be willing. Think about the team Jesus sent out to serve Him. It was a ragtag group, including a tax collector, a zealot, two overly ambitious brothers (see Mark 10:35–37), and Judas Iscariot "who betrayed him" (Matthew 10:4). But they were willing to go, just as they were. And Jesus gave them authority to "heal the sick, raise the dead, cleanse those who have leprosy, drive out demons" (v. 8)—all without taking any money, luggage, extra shirt or sandals, or even a walking stick with them (vv. 9–10).

"I am sending you," He said (v. 16), and He was enough. For each of us who say yes to Jesus, He still is.   *Patricia Raybon*

Jesus is still enough.

DAILY DEPENDENCE

Matthew 6:6–13

Give us today our daily bread. —Matthew 6:11

One morning our younger kids decided to get up early and fix breakfast for themselves. Tired from a grueling week, my wife and I were trying to sleep until at least 7:00 a.m. on that Saturday morning. Suddenly, I heard a loud crash! I jumped out of bed and raced downstairs to find a shattered bowl, oatmeal all over the floor, and Jonas—our five-year-old—desperately trying to sweep (more like smear) the gooey mess off the floor. My children were hungry, but they chose not to ask for help. Instead of reaching out in dependence, they chose independence, and the result was definitely not a culinary delight.

In human terms, children are meant to grow from dependence to independence. But in our relationship with God, maturity means moving from independence to dependence on Him. Prayer is where we practice such dependent ways. When Jesus taught His disciples—and all of us who have come to believe in Him—to pray, "Give us today our daily bread" (Matthew 6:11), He was teaching a prayer of dependence. Bread is a metaphor for sustenance, deliverance, and guidance (vv. 10, 13). We're dependent on God for all of this and more.

There are no self-made believers in Jesus, and we'll never graduate from His grace. Throughout our lives, let's always begin our day by taking the posture of dependence as we pray to "our Father in heaven" (v. 9).   *Glenn Packiam*

**There are no self-made believers in Jesus, and
we'll never graduate from His grace.**

A GIFT OF GRACE

2 Corinthians 8:7–15

You know the grace of our Lord Jesus Christ, that though he
was rich, yet for your sake he became poor. —2 Corinthians 8:9

In high schools in the United States, being elected homecoming
queen is a great honor for any young woman. But when a high
school near Houston, Texas, crowned Shannon Jones, it was a special
moment for her and for everyone in the community. Nineteen-year-
old Shannon, who is an award-winning athlete and an active member of her church youth group, has Down syndrome.

Shannon knew this once-in-a-lifetime experience was a gift from
her younger sister Lindsey, who was the catalyst to elect her. Their
dad said, "I'm so proud of Lindsey. Probably somewhere in the back
of her mind, this is something she'd like to do." But she made it
happen for Shannon.

The most inspiring acts of human love are only a shadow of the
immeasurable gift our Savior has given us. Paul wrote, "You know
the grace of our Lord Jesus Christ, that though he was rich, yet for
your sake he became poor, so that you through his poverty might
become rich" (2 Corinthians 8:9).

Christ left His glory in heaven and died on the cross for our sin
so we could be forgiven through faith in Him. His sacrifice was
based on His love, not on our merit. All we are and all we have are
the Savior's loving gifts of grace to us.   *David McCasland*

**The most inspiring acts of human love are only a shadow
of the immeasurable gift our Savior has given us.**

BETTER TOGETHER

Acts 2:42–47

All the believers were together and had
everything in common. —Acts 2:44

Marie, a single working mom, rarely missed church or Bible study. Each week, she rode the bus to and from church with her five children and helped with setup and cleanup.

One Sunday, the pastor told Marie that some church members had donated gifts for the family. One couple provided the family a house with reduced rent. Another couple offered her a job with benefits at their coffee shop. A young man gave her an old car he'd rebuilt, and he promised to serve as her personal mechanic. Marie thanked God for the joy of living in a community devoted to serving God and each other.

Although we may not all be able to give as generously as Marie's church family, God's people are designed to help each other. The gospel writer Luke described believers in Jesus as "devoted" to the "apostles' teaching and to fellowship" (Acts 2:42). When we combine our resources, we can work together to help those in need like the first believers in Jesus did (vv. 44–45). As we grow closer to God and each other, we can care for one another. Witnessing God's love demonstrated through His people's actions can lead others to a saving relationship with Jesus (vv. 46–47).

We can serve others with a smile or a kind deed. We can offer a financial gift or a prayer. As God works in and through us, we're simply better together. *Xochitl Dixon*

**As we grow closer to God and each other,
we can care for one another.**

LEAVE THE LIGHT ON

Matthew 5:13–16

You are the light of the world. A town built on
a hill cannot be hidden. —Matthew 5:14

A hotel chain's commercial featured one little building standing amidst a dark night. Nothing else was around. The only light in the scene came from a small lamp near the door on the porch of the building. The bulb cast enough illumination for a visitor to walk up the steps and enter the building. The commercial ended with the phrase, "We'll leave the light on for you."

A porch light is akin to a welcome sign, reminding weary travelers that there's a comfortable place still open where they can stop and rest. The light invites those passing by to come on in and escape from their dark, weary journey.

Jesus says the lives of those who believe in Him should resemble a welcoming light. He told His followers, "You are the light of the world. A town built on a hill cannot be hidden" (Matthew 5:14). As believers, we're to illuminate a dark world.

As He directs and empowers us, "[others] may see [our] good deeds and glorify [our] Father in heaven" (v. 16). And as we leave our lights on, they will feel welcomed to come to us to learn more about the one true Light of the World—Jesus (John 8:12). In a weary and dark world, His light always remains on.

Have you left your light on? As Jesus shines through you today, others may see and begin radiating His light too.   *Katara Patton*

In a weary and dark world, Jesus's light always remains on.

NO LOSS

Matthew 13:44–46

The kingdom of heaven is like treasure. —Matthew 13:44

My friend Ruel attended a high school reunion held in a former classmate's home. The waterfront mansion near Manila Bay could accommodate two hundred attendees, and it made Ruel feel small.

"I've had many happy years of pastoring remote rural churches," Ruel told me, "and even though I know I shouldn't, I couldn't help but feel envious of my classmate's material wealth. My thoughts strayed to how different life might be if I'd used my degree to become a businessman instead."

"But I later reminded myself there's nothing to feel envious about," Ruel continued with a smile. "I invested my life in serving God, and the results will last for eternity." I'll always remember the peaceful look on his face as he said those words.

Ruel drew peace from Jesus's parables in Matthew 13:44–46. He knew that God's kingdom is the ultimate treasure. Seeking and living for His kingdom might take various forms. For some, it might mean full-time ministry, while for others, it may be living out the gospel in a secular workplace. Regardless of how God chooses to use us, we can continue to trust and obey His leading, knowing, like the men in Jesus's parables, the value of the imperishable treasure we've been given. Everything in this world has infinitely less worth than all we gain by following God (1 Peter 1:4–5).

Our life, when placed in His hands, can bear eternal fruit.

Karen Huang

**Everything in this world has infinitely less
worth than all we gain by following God.**

SIGN LANGUAGE

John 1:14–18

May the Lord make your love increase and overflow in love
for each other and for everyone else. —1 Thessalonians 3:12

A friend of mine pastors a church in a small mountain community not far from Boise, Idaho. The community is nestled in a wooded valley through which a pleasant little stream meanders. Behind the church and alongside the stream is a grove of willows, a length of grass, and a sandy beach. It's an idyllic spot that has long been a place where members of the community gather to picnic.

One day, a man in the congregation expressed concern over the legal implications of "outsiders" using the property. "If someone is injured," he said, "the church might be sued." Although the elders were reluctant to take any action, the man convinced them that they should post a sign on the site informing visitors that this was private property. So the pastor posted a sign. It read: "Warning! Anyone using this beach may, at any moment, be surrounded by people who love you." I read his sign the week after he put it up and was charmed. "Exactly," I thought. "Once again grace has triumphed over law!"

This love for one's neighbor springs from God's kindness, forbearance, and patience with us. It's not the law, but the goodness of God that draws men and women to repentance (Romans 2:4) and to saving faith in His Son Jesus Christ.   *David Roper*

**Love for one's neighbor springs from God's
kindness, forbearance, and patience with us.**

SERVING WITHOUT DISTRACTION

Luke 10:38–42

Martha was distracted by all the preparations
that had to be made. —Luke 10:40

While Martha served Jesus unsparingly, her sister Mary sat at His feet, listening and learning. Renowned British preacher Charles Spurgeon believed that Martha's mistake wasn't her serving but rather that she allowed it to distract her attention from Jesus. Spurgeon believed we should be both Martha and Mary! He wrote, "We should do much service and have much communion at the same time. For this we need great grace. It is easier to serve than to commune."

I once met a young mother who found the grace to do both. She hungered after God and His Word but was unavoidably immersed in family life each day. Then an idea came to her. In each room she placed paper and a pencil on a high surface, away from tiny hands. As she served the Lord in household responsibilities, she also kept herself open to God. Whenever a Scripture came to mind, or something to confess, to correct, or to pray about, she jotted it on the nearest pad of paper. In the evening after the children were asleep, she gathered her pieces of paper and pondered them prayerfully over her open Bible.

This woman found a way to be Martha and Mary at the same time. We too can discover ways to both serve God and commune with Him.

Joanie Yoder

"We should do much service and have much communion at the same time." —Charles Spurgeon

GIVING OUR BEST

Malachi 1:8–14

He will purify . . . and refine them like gold and
silver. Then the LORD will have men who will bring
offerings in righteousness. —Malachi 3:3

We stared at the piles of donated shoes as we entered a local
homeless shelter. The director had invited our youth group
to help sort through the heaps of used footwear. We spent the morning searching for matches and lining them up in rows across the concrete floor. At the end of the day, we threw away more than half of the shoes because they were too damaged for others to use. Although the shelter couldn't stop people from giving poor quality items, they refused to distribute shoes that were in bad condition.

The Israelites struggled with giving God their damaged goods too. When the Lord spoke through the prophet Malachi, He rebuked the Israelites for sacrificing blind, lame, or diseased animals when they had strong animals to offer (Malachi 1:6–8). He announced His displeasure (v. 10), affirmed His worthiness, and reprimanded the Israelites for keeping the best for themselves (v. 14). But God also promised to send the Messiah, whose love and grace would transform people's hearts and ignite their desire to bring offerings that would be pleasing to Him (3:1–4).

At times, it can be tempting to give God our leftovers. We praise Him and expect Him to give us His all, yet we offer Him our crumbs. When we consider all God has done, we can rejoice in celebrating His worthiness and giving Him our very best.

Xochitl Dixon

**God promised to send the Messiah, whose love
and grace would transform people's hearts.**

UNIMAGINABLE PROMISES

2 Peter 1:2–8

He has given us his very great and
precious promises. —2 Peter 1:4

In our moments of greatest failure, we can easily believe it's too late
for us, that we've lost our chance at a life of purpose and worth.
That's how Elias, a former inmate at a maximum-security prison in
New York, described feeling as a prisoner. "I had broken . . . promises, the promise of my own future, the promise of what I could be."

It was Bard College's "Prison Initiative" college degree program
that began to transform Elias's life. While in the program, he partic-
ipated on a debate team, which debated a team from Harvard—and
won. For Elias, being "part of the team . . . [was] a way of proving
that these promises weren't completely lost."

A similar transformation happens in our hearts when we begin
to understand that the good news of God's love in Jesus is good
news for us too. It's not too late, we begin to realize with wonder.
God still has a future for me.

It's a future we can neither earn nor forfeit, dependent only on
God's extravagant grace and power (2 Peter 1:2–3). A future where
we're set free from the despair in the world and in our hearts into
one filled with His "glory and goodness" (v. 3). A future secure in
Christ's unimaginable promises (v. 4). It's a future transformed into
the "freedom and glory of the children of God" (Romans 8:21).

Monica La Rose

**A transformation happens in our hearts when
we understand that the good news of God's
love in Jesus is good news for us too.**

GOD HEALS OUR BROKENNESS

Ephesians 2:1–10

It is by grace you have been saved. —Ephesians 2:5

Collin and his wife, Jordan, wandered through the craft store, looking for a picture to hang in their home. Collin thought he'd found just the right piece and called Jordan over to see it. On the right side of the ceramic artwork was the word "grace." But the left side held two long cracks. "Well, it's broken!" Jordan said as she started looking for an unbroken one on the shelf. But then Collin said, "No. That's the point. We're broken and then grace comes in—period." They decided to purchase the one with the cracks. When they got to the checkout, the clerk exclaimed, "Oh, no, it's broken!" "Yes, so are we," Jordan whispered.

What does it mean to be a "broken" person? Someone defined it this way: "A growing awareness that no matter how hard we try, our ability to make life work gets worse instead of better." It's a recognition of our need for God and His intervention in our lives.

The apostle Paul talked about our brokenness in terms of being "dead in [our] transgressions and sins" (Ephesians 2:1). The answer to our need to be forgiven and changed comes in verses 4 and 5: "Because of his great love for us, God, who is rich in mercy, made us alive . . . it is by grace [we] have been saved."

God is willing to heal our brokenness with His grace when we admit, "I'm broken." *Anne Cetas*

**To be broken is a recognition of our need for
God and His intervention in our lives.**

SEPTEMBER 29

SET APART

Romans 1:1–6

Paul [was] . . . set apart for the gospel of God. —Romans 1:1

The three-wheeled taxis of Sri Lanka, known as "tuk tuks," are a convenient and delightful mode of transport for many. Lorraine, a resident of the capital of Colombo, also realized that they're a mission field. Hopping onto a tuk tuk one day, she found the friendly driver more than happy to engage in conversation about religion. The next time, she told herself, she would talk to the driver about the good news.

The book of Romans starts with Paul declaring himself as "set apart for the gospel of God" (Romans 1:1). The Greek word for *gospel* is *evangelion*, which means "good news." Paul was essentially saying that his main purpose was to tell God's good news.

What is this good news? Romans 1:3 says that the gospel of God is "regarding his Son." The good news is Jesus! It's God who wants to tell the world that Jesus came to save us from sin and death, and He's chosen us to be His mode of communication. What a humbling fact!

Sharing the good news is a privilege all believers in Jesus have been given. We've "received grace" to call others to this faith (vv. 5–6). God has set us apart to carry the exciting news of the gospel to those around us, whether on tuk tuks or wherever we are. Like Lorraine, let's look for opportunities in our daily life to tell others the good news that is Jesus.   *Asiri Fernando*

**Sharing the good news is a privilege all
believers in Jesus have been given.**

MERCY THROUGH PIZZA

Jude 1:17–23

Be merciful to those who doubt. —Jude 1:22

The invitation for dinner from my church leader Harold and his wife, Pam, warmed my heart but also made me nervous. I had joined a college Bible study group that taught ideas that contradicted some of the teachings in the Bible. Would they lecture me about that?

Over pizza, Harold and Pam shared about their family and asked about mine. They listened as I talked about homework, my dog Buchi, and the guy I had a crush on. Only later did they gently caution me about the group I had been attending and explain what was wrong with its teachings.

Their warning took me away from the lies presented in the Bible study and close to the truths of Scripture. In his letter, Jude uses strong language about false teachers, urging believers to "contend for the faith" (Jude 1:3). He reminded them that "in the last times there will be scoffers . . . who divide you . . . and do not have the Spirit" (vv. 18–19). However, Jude also calls on believers to "be merciful to those who doubt" (v. 22) by coming alongside them, showing compassion without compromising the truth.

Harold and Pam knew I wasn't firmly grounded in my faith, but instead of judging me, they first offered their friendship and then their wisdom. We can ask the Lord to give us this same love and patience, using wisdom and compassion as we interact with those who have doubts.

Karen Huang

Jude calls on believers to "be merciful to those who doubt" by coming alongside them. —Jude 1:22

OCTOBER

"How Firm a Foundation"

Author Unknown

When thru fiery trials thy pathway shall lie,
my grace, all-sufficient, shall be thy supply.

A Song for the People

December 24, 1898. Christmas Eve in Havana, Cuba.

The Spanish-American War ended when the Treaty of Paris was signed on December 10, but American troops stayed behind in Cuba for four more years to protect US interests. Spain had relinquished its sovereignty over Cuba, and Cuba would become independent in 1902.

Surely, the American troops stationed on the island ninety miles from Florida wished to be home with their families for the holiday. At midnight, a sentinel standing guard over the camp of the

Sources: "How Firm a Foundation: A Hymn of Sure Promises," *Hymns for Worship*, http://tinyurl.com/ym3ftbjr; "Letter from Theodore Roosevelt to Thomas E. Stewart," *Digital Library, Theodore Roosevelt Center*, http://tinyurl.com/3e4n4u2j; "President Andrew Jackson—7th President of the USA," *Discover Ulster-Scots*, http://tinyurl.com/4d33et2t; Louis F. Benson, *Studies of Familiar Hymns* (Philadelphia: Westminster Press, 1903), 37–50, http://tinyurl.com/59nudhvz; all accessed November 6, 2023.

Forty-ninth Regiment from Iowa, which had arrived in Cuba just three days earlier, belted out, "Twelve o'clock, and all's well!"

Now it was Christmas.

Suddenly, there was a commotion in the tent of the bandsmen of the Forty-ninth, followed by music. The first strains of a famous old hymn broke across the encampment, and a rich baritone voice belted out these words, "How firm a foundation, ye saints of the Lord." Soldiers from the Iowa regiment joined in, as did military men from the newly arriving Sixth Missouri Infantry and Fourth Virginia Infantry.

Soon the song rang out across the encampment of American soldiers as men who had volunteered for service to their country joined to praise God, the One who promises to "strengthen thee, and cause thee to stand, upheld by my righteous, omnipotent hand."

Everyone from soldiers to politicians have depended on this classic hymn, written in 1787 by an unknown writer, to provide hope and confidence through God's power and promises.

Numerous people of note have told stories of their connection to the song.

The Rev. James Gallagher visited America's seventh president, Andrew Jackson, in the waning years of his life. Later, Gallagher revealed that Jackson, in speaking of his personal faith, quoted the first stanza of "How Firm a Foundation" as a tribute to his departed wife Rachel, who claimed the song as her favorite.

In 1903, Thomas E. Stewart, a former congressman, asked Theodore Roosevelt which of the great hymns was his favorite. Roosevelt replied, "I like 'How Firm a Foundation' as much as any other." Reportedly, this hymn was sung at Roosevelt's funeral after the twenty-sixth president died in 1919.

The song has also been sung at Washington's National Cathedral on America's National Day of Prayer.

While we don't know for sure who wrote this song, it has certainly become a vital encouragement to Christians both famous and ordinary as it reminds us that God will uphold us with His "righteous, omnipotent hand."

How Firm a Foundation

How firm a foundation, ye saints of the Lord,
Is laid for your faith in His excellent Word!
What more can He say than to you He hath said—
To you, who for refuge to Jesus have fled?

"Fear not, I am with thee, O be not dismayed,
For I am thy God, and will still give thee aid;
I'll strengthen thee, help thee, and cause thee
        to stand,
Upheld by My righteous, omnipotent hand."

CONFRONTED BY THE CROSS

Luke 23:33–43

When they came to the place called the Skull,
they crucified [Jesus]. —Luke 23:33

World-famous Russian author Aleksandr Solzhenitsyn was sent to a Siberian prison because he criticized communism. Languishing there under intolerable conditions year after year, he decided to end his life. But suicide, he firmly believed, would be against God's will. He thought it would be better for a guard to shoot him.

So at a public assembly of the prisoners, he sat in a front row, planning to get up and walk toward an exit, compelling a guard to kill him. But to his surprise, another prisoner sat down, blocking his exit. That unknown man leaned over and, to Solzhenitsyn's astonishment, drew a cross on the dirt floor.

The cross! Wondering if that fellow prisoner might be a messenger from God, Solzhenitsyn resolved to endure his imprisonment. There in prison he became a Christian and was eventually set free to bear witness to the world.

Are you in the grip of difficult circumstances? Have you wondered if life is worth living? Focus your heart on the cross—it is the message of God's love, forgiveness, and saving grace for you. Invite the Christ of Calvary with His transforming power into your life. Discover for yourself that the Christ of the cross can change you.

Vernon Grounds

**Focus your heart on the cross—it is the message of
God's love, forgiveness, and saving grace for you.**

GOD KNOWS YOU

Psalm 139:1–12

You have searched me, LORD, and you
know me. —Psalm 139:1

It seems my mother can sense trouble from a mile away. Once, after a rough day at school, I tried to mask my frustration, hoping that no one would notice. "What's the matter?" she asked. Then she added, "Before you tell me it's nothing, remember I'm your mother. I gave birth to you, and I know you better than you know yourself." My mom has consistently reminded me that her deep awareness of who I am helps her be there for me in the moments I need her most.

As believers in Jesus, we're cared for by a God who knows us intimately. The psalmist David praised Him for His attentiveness to the lives of His children saying, "You have searched me, LORD, and you know me. You know when I sit and when I rise; you perceive my thoughts from afar" (Psalm 139:1–2). Because God knows who we are—our every thought, desire, and action—there's nowhere we can go where we're outside the bounds of His abundant love and care (vv. 7–12). David wrote, "If I settle on the far side of the sea, even there your hand will guide me" (vv. 9–10). We can find comfort knowing that no matter where we are in life, when we call out to God in prayer, He'll offer us the love, wisdom, and guidance we need.

Kimya Loder

**God knows who we are—our every thought,
desire, and action. There's nowhere we can go
where we're outside of His love and care.**

IGNORING GRACE

Matthew 7:13–23

Small is the gate and narrow the road that leads to
life, and only a few find it. —Matthew 7:14

In the hectic downtown of one of Asia's great cities, I marveled at the busy sidewalks filled with people. There seemed to be no room to move in the crush of humanity, yet it also seemed that everyone was moving at top speed.

My attention was drawn to the soft, almost mournful sound of a single trumpeter playing "Amazing Grace." The crowds appeared oblivious to both the musician and the music. Still, he played—sending a musical message of the love of God out to whoever knew the song and would think about the words as he played.

I thought of this experience as a parable. The music seemed to be an invitation to the masses to follow Christ. As with the gospel message, some believe in God's amazing grace and choose the narrow way. Others ignore His grace, which is the broad way that leads to everlasting destruction. Jesus said, "Enter through the narrow gate. For wide is the gate and broad is the road that leads to destruction, and many enter through it. But small is the gate and narrow the road that leads to life, and only a few find it" (Matthew 7:13–14).

Jesus died so that "everyone who calls" on His name (Romans 10:13) can find forgiveness in His grace.   *Bill Crowder*

**Some believe in God's amazing grace
and choose the narrow way.**

SWEET PRAISE

Colossians 3:12–17

Let the message of Christ dwell among you richly as you
teach and admonish one another with all wisdom through
psalms, hymns, and songs from the Spirit, singing to
God with gratitude in your hearts. —Colossians 3:16

Several years ago, my husband helped lead a work crew of high
school students on a short-term mission trip to a Christian
school in an urban community. Unfortunately, Tom had broken
his foot shortly before the trip and was supervising the work from
a wheelchair. He was discouraged because he couldn't get around
as he had hoped.

While he worked on the ground floor, a few of the girls were
painting on the third floor. He could hear them singing praise cho-
ruses in harmony as their voices echoed down the wide-open stair-
cases. Song after song ministered to him. "It was the most beautiful
sound I'd ever heard," he told me later. "And it lifted my spirits."

Colossians 3 reminds us, "Let the message of Christ dwell among
you richly as you teach and admonish one another with all wisdom
through psalms, hymns, and songs from the Spirit, singing to God
with gratitude in your hearts" (v. 16). Not only were those teenage
girls giving sweet praise to God, but they were also ministering to
one of their leaders.

Whatever you're doing today, cultivate an attitude of praise.
Whether it is through song or conversation, let your joy in the Lord
reverberate to others. You never know who you might encourage.

Cindy Hess Kasper

Cultivate an attitude of praise.

PRAYING AND ASKING

2 Chronicles 6:12–21

The heavens, even the highest heavens, cannot contain you.
How much less this temple I have built! —2 Chronicles 6:18

Teen Challenge, a ministry to at-risk youth that started in New York City, was born from an unusual commitment to prayer. Its founder, David Wilkerson, sold his television set and spent his TV-watching time (two hours each night) praying. In the months that followed, he not only gained clarity about his new endeavor but also learned about the balance between praising God and asking Him for help.

King Solomon's temple dedication prayer shows this balance. Solomon began by highlighting God's holiness and faithfulness. Then he gave God credit for the success of the project and emphasized God's greatness, declaring, "The heavens, even the highest heavens, cannot contain you. How much less this temple I have built!" (2 Chronicles 6:18).

After exalting God, Solomon asked Him to pay special attention to everything that happened inside the temple. He asked God to show mercy to the Israelites and provide for them when they confessed their sin. Immediately after Solomon's prayer, "fire came down from heaven and consumed the burnt offering and the sacrifices, and the glory of the LORD filled the temple" (7:1). This incredible response reminds us that the mighty One we praise and speak to when we pray is the same One who listens to and cares about our requests.

Jennifer Benson Schuldt

The One we praise and speak to when we pray is the same God who listens to and cares about our requests.

DEALING WITH DISAGREEMENT

Colossians 3:12–14

Bear with each other and forgive one another if any of you
has a grievance against someone. —Colossians 3:13

The social media powerhouse X created a platform where people all over the world express opinions in short sound bites. In recent years, however, this formula has become more complex as individuals have begun to leverage X as a tool to reprimand others for attitudes and lifestyles they disagree with. Log on to the platform on any given day, and you'll find the name of at least one person "trending." Click on that name, and you'll find millions of people expressing opinions about whatever controversy has emerged.

We've learned to publicly criticize everything from the beliefs people hold to the clothes they wear. The reality, however, is that a critical and unloving attitude doesn't align with who God has called us to be as believers in Jesus. While there will be times when we must deal with disagreement, the Bible reminds us that as believers, we're always to conduct ourselves with "compassion, kindness, humility, gentleness and patience" (Colossians 3:12). Instead of being harshly critical, even of our enemies, God urges us to "bear with each other and forgive one another if [we have] a grievance" (v. 13).

This treatment isn't limited to the people whose lifestyles and beliefs we agree with. Even when it's difficult, let's extend grace and love to everyone we encounter as Christ guides us, recognizing that we've been redeemed by His love.   *Kimya Loder*

**As believers, we're to always conduct ourselves
with "compassion, kindness, humility, gentleness
and patience." —Colossians 3:12**

CHANGING YOUR WORLD

1 Corinthians 13:1–7

I have been crucified with Christ and I no longer
live, but Christ lives in me. —Galatians 2:20

A young woman lived in a home where she was very unhappy. She often complained to her friends and told them how difficult it was for her to stay there. She blamed her parents and other family members for her discontent and threatened to move out as soon as she could afford to live on her own.

One day, though, her face was graced with a happy smile. Gone was her usual glum expression. Her eyes were sparkling. There was a spring in her step.

When a friend noticed the difference, she exclaimed, "Things must have improved at home. I'm so glad!" "No," the young woman responded, "I'm the one who's different!"

That young woman's outlook was brighter and her relationships with others were transformed. It wasn't because her circumstances had improved, but because she had experienced a change in her heart.

When we are confronted with irritating situations and we begin to feel sorry for ourselves, we should ask these questions: Is the trouble really with others? Or could it be me? As we ask the Lord to fill us with His perfect love, it's amazing how life begins to look better. Letting God change us is the best way to change our world.

Richard DeHaan

**As we ask the Lord to fill us with His perfect love,
it's amazing how life begins to look better.**

LOVING LIKE JESUS

1 John 3:11–18

Dear children, let us not love with words or speech
but with actions and in truth. —1 John 3:18

While waiting for a train at a station in Atlanta, Georgia, a young man wearing dress pants and a button-down shirt sat on a bench. As he struggled with his tie, an older woman encouraged her husband to help. When the elderly man hunched over and began teaching the young man how to knot the tie, a stranger took a photo of the trio. When this photo went viral online, many viewers left comments about the power of random acts of kindness.

For believers in Jesus, kindness to others reflects the self-sacrificing care He showed for people like us. It's an expression of God's love, and it's how He desired His disciples to live out "love one another" (1 John 3:11). John equates hating a brother or sister to murder (v. 15). Then he turns to Christ as an example of love in action (v. 16).

Selfless love doesn't have to be an extravagant display of sacrifice. Selfless love simply requires us to acknowledge the value of all God's image-bearers by placing their needs above our own . . . every day. Those seemingly ordinary moments when we care enough to notice the needs of others and do what we can to help are selfless, when we're motivated by love. When we see beyond our personal space, step out of our comfort zones to serve others and give, especially when we aren't required to give, we're loving like Jesus loves.

Xochitl Dixon

**Selfless love simply requires us to acknowledge the value of all
God's image-bearers by placing their needs above our own.**

SWEETER THAN HONEY

Psalm 119:97–105

How sweet are your words to my taste, sweeter
than honey to my mouth! —Psalm 119:103

On Chicago Day in October 1893, the city's theaters shut down because the owners figured everyone would be attending the city's World's Fair. Over seven hundred thousand people went, but Dwight L. Moody wanted to fill a music hall at the other end of Chicago with preaching and teaching. His friend R. A. Torrey was skeptical that Moody could draw a crowd on the same day as the fair. But by God's grace, he did. As Torrey later concluded, the crowds came because Moody knew "the one Book that this old world most longs to know—the Bible." Torrey longed for others to love the Bible as Moody did, reading it regularly with dedication and passion.

God through His Spirit brought people back to himself at the end of the nineteenth century in Chicago, and He continues to speak today. We can echo the psalmist's love for God and His Scriptures as he exclaims, "How sweet are your words to my taste, sweeter than honey to my mouth!" (119:103). For the psalmist, God's messages of grace and truth acted as a light for his path, a lamp for his feet (v. 105).

How can we grow more in love with the Savior and His message? As we immerse ourselves in Scripture, God will increase our devotion to Him and guide us, shining His light along the paths we walk.

Amy Boucher Pye

**For the psalmist, God's messages of grace
and truth acted as a light for his path.**

PLAYING IN CONCERT

Romans 12:3–8

In Christ we, though many, form one body, and each member
belongs to all the others. We have different gifts, according
to the grace given to each of us. —Romans 12:5–6

During our granddaughter's school band concert, I was impressed
by how well this group of eleven- and twelve-year-olds played
together. If each of them had wanted to be a solo performer, they
could not have achieved individually what the band did collectively.
The woodwinds, brass, and percussion sections all played their parts,
and the result was beautiful music!

To the followers of Jesus in Rome, Paul wrote, "In Christ we,
though many, form one body, and each member belongs to all
the others. We have different gifts, according to the grace given
to each of us" (Romans 12:5–6). Among the gifts Paul mentioned
are service, teaching, encouragement, giving, leadership, and mercy
(vv. 7–8). Each gift is to be exercised freely for the good of all (1 Corinthians 12:7).

One definition of *in concert* is "agreement in design or plan; com-
bined action; harmony or accord." That's the Lord's plan for us as His
children through faith in Jesus Christ. "Be devoted to one another in
love. Honor one another above yourselves" (Romans 12:10). The goal
is cooperation, not competition.

In a sense, we are "on stage" before a watching and listening world
every day. There are no soloists in God's concert band, but every instrument is essential. The music is best when we each play our part in
unity with others.   *David McCasland*

There are no soloists in God's concert band.

HAPPILY EVER AFTER

1 Peter 3:1–12

Your beauty should not come from outward adornment, . . .
Rather, it should be that of your inner self. —1 Peter 3:3–4

Despite what we've heard in countless fairy tales, there's no guarantee that people who get married will live happily ever after. Things go wrong—sometimes terribly wrong. Even with the best of intentions, we may find ourselves in a house full of resentment, hostility, unrest, and misery. There is no heartache quite like the heartache of an unhappy marriage.

Yet, a difficult marriage can be the setting in which God can deal with "the hidden person of the heart" (1 Peter 3:4 NKJV). Instead of focusing only on what's wrong with our spouse, we need to ask the Lord to confront the wrong in us. He will begin to do so—gently, gradually, graciously. We will begin to see ourselves as we are—and not as the thoughtful, patient, polite, gracious, giving, and self-controlled person we had imagined ourselves to be. We will come to see how much we ourselves need the Savior's forgiveness and the Spirit's help to do what is right and loving (vv. 1–12), even when we have been wronged.

Our growth in grace may change our spouse, or it may not. There are no guarantees in life except God's love. But with His help, *we* can change. Although all our marriage ills may not be cured, God's grace can make *us* well.   *David Roper*

Instead of focusing only on what's wrong with our spouse,
we need to ask the Lord to confront the wrong in us.

THE WORD

John 1:1–14

In the beginning was the Word, and the Word was
with God, and the Word was God. —John 1:1

Michellan faced challenges while growing up in the Philippines,
but she always loved words and found comfort in them. Then
one day while attending university, she read the first chapter in the
gospel of John, and her "stone heart stirred." She felt like someone
was saying, "Yes, you love words, and guess what? There is an Eternal Word, one who . . . can cut through the darkness, now and always. A Word who took on flesh. A Word who can love you back."

She was reading the gospel that begins with words that would
have reminded John's readers of the opening of Genesis: "In the
beginning . . ." (Genesis 1:1). John sought to show that Jesus was
not only *with* God at the beginning of time but also *was* (and is)
God (John 1:1). And this living Word became a man "and made his
dwelling among us" (v. 14). Further, those who receive Him, believing in His name, become His children (v. 12).

Michellan embraced God's love that day and was "born of God"
(v. 13). She credits God for saving her from her family's pattern of
addiction, and now she writes about the good news of Jesus—de-
lighting in sharing her words about the Living Word.

If we're believers in Christ, we too can share God's message and
His love. What grace-filled words can we speak to our friends, relatives, and coworkers?   *Amy Boucher Pye*

We can share God's message and His love.

TURNING PAIN INTO PRAISE

2 Corinthians 1:7–11

Our hope for you is firm, because we know that
just as you share in our sufferings, so also you
share in our comfort. —2 Corinthians 1:7

After years of a remarkable and fruitful ministry in India, Amy Carmichael (1867–1951) became a bedridden sufferer. As the courageous founder and dynamic heart of the Dohnavur Fellowship, she had been instrumental in rescuing hundreds of girls and boys from a terrible life of sexual servitude.

While she carried on her rescue operation of bringing young people into spiritual freedom through faith in Jesus Christ, she wrote books and poems that are still blessing readers around the world.

Then arthritis made Amy a pain-wracked sufferer. Did she bemoan her affliction or question God? No. Amy was still the guiding inspiration of Dohnavur, and she kept on writing. Her meditations, letters, and poems are filled with praise to God and encouragement to her fellow pilgrims.

When affliction strikes us, how do we react? Are we embittered, or do we trustfully appropriate God's sustaining grace (2 Corinthians 12:9)? And do we prayerfully encourage those around us by our Spirit-enabled cheerfulness, our courage, and our confidence in God?

When we rely on the Lord, He will help us turn pain into praise.

Vernon Grounds

**When we rely on the Lord, He will
help us turn pain into praise.**

ENGRAVED GRIEF

Job 19:19–27

Oh, that my words were recorded, that they were
written on a scroll, . . . inscribed with an iron tool on
lead, or engraved in rock forever! —Job 19:23–24

After receiving the devastating diagnosis of a rare and incurable brain cancer, Caroline found renewed hope and purpose through providing a unique service: volunteering photography services for critically ill children and their families. Through this service, families could capture the precious moments shared with their children, both in grief and in "the moments of grace and beauty we assume don't exist in those desperate places." She observed that "in the hardest moments imaginable, those families . . . choose to love, despite and because of it all."

There's something unspeakably powerful about capturing the truth of grief—both the devastating reality of it and the ways in which we experience beauty and hope in the midst of it.

Much of the book of Job is like a photograph of grief—honestly capturing Job's journey through devastating loss (1:18–19). After sitting with Job for several days, his friends wearied of his grief, resorting to minimizing it or explaining it away as God's judgment. But Job would have none of it, insisting that what he was going through mattered, and wishing that the testimony of his experience would be "engraved in rock forever!" (19:24).

Through the book of Job, it was "engraved"—in a way that points us in our grief to the living God (vv. 26–27), who meets us in our pain, carrying us through death into resurrection life.

Monica La Rose

The living God meets us in our pain.

FOOD THAT SAYS I LOVE YOU

Luke 22:14–20

He took bread, gave thanks and broke it,
and gave it to them. —Luke 22:19

I attended a family birthday gathering where the hostess wove the theme of "favorite things" into the decor, the gifts, and—best of all—the food. Because the birthday girl loved steak and salad—and white chocolate raspberry Bundt cake—the hostess grilled steak, spun spinach, and ordered that favorite cake. Favorite foods say, "I love you."

The Bible contains many references to banquets, feasts, and festivals, pairing the physical act of eating with celebrations of God's faithfulness. Feasting was a part of the sacrificial system of worship practiced by the Israelites (see Numbers 28:11–31), with Passover, the festival of weeks, and new moon feasts held every month. And in Psalm 23:5, God prepares a table with an abundant meal and cups overflowing with mercy and love. Perhaps the most lavish pairing of food and wine ever expressed was when Jesus broke a piece of bread and took a cup of wine, illustrating the gift of His death on a cross for our salvation. He then challenged us to "do this in remembrance of me" (Luke 22:19).

As you partake of food today, take a moment to consider our God, who made both mouth and stomach and offers food to you as a language of His love in celebration of His faithfulness. He feasts with the faithful, pairing His perfect provision with our great need, saying, "I love you."   *Elisa Morgan*

**God prepares a table with an abundant meal
and cups overflow with mercy and love.**

CLINGING TO WHAT'S GOOD

Romans 12:9–13

Love must be sincere. Hate what is evil; cling
to what is good. —Romans 12:9

When we park our car near an open field and walk across it to get to our house, we almost always get some sticky cockleburs on our clothes—especially in the fall. These tiny "hitchhikers" attach to clothing, shoes, or whatever is passing by and ride to their next destination. It's nature's way of spreading cocklebur seeds in my local field and around the world.

As I have tried to carefully remove clinging cockleburs, I've often thought about the message that admonishes believers in Jesus to "cling to what is good" (Romans 12:9). When we're trying to love others, it can be challenging. However, as the Holy Spirit helps us hold on to what's good with all we have, we can repel evil and be "sincere" in our love as He guides us (v. 9).

Cocklebur seeds don't fall off with a mere brush of the hand; they hang on to you. And when we focus on what's good, keeping our mind on God's mercy, compassion, and commands, we too—in His strength—can hang on tightly to those we love. He helps us stay "devoted to one another in love," remembering to place others' needs before our own (v. 10). *Katara Patton*

**As the Holy Spirit helps us hold on to what's good,
we can repel evil and be sincere in our love.**

LIBERATED BY JESUS

Mark 5:1–20

The man went away and began to tell . . . how
much Jesus had done for him. —Mark 5:20

"I lived with my mother so long that she moved out!" These were the words of KC, whose life before sobriety and surrender to Jesus was not pretty. He candidly admits supporting his drug habit by stealing—even from loved ones. That life is behind him now, and he rehearses this by noting the years, months, and days he's been clean. When KC and I regularly sit down to study God's Word together, I'm looking at a changed man.

Mark 5:15 speaks of a former demon-possessed individual called Legion, who had also been changed. Prior to his healing, *helpless, hopeless, homeless*, and *desperate* were words that fit the man (vv. 3–5). But all of that changed after Jesus liberated him (v. 13). But, as with KC, his life before Jesus was far from normal. His internal turmoil that he expressed externally is not unlike what people experience today. Some hurting people dwell in abandoned buildings, vehicles, or other places; some live in their own homes but are emotionally alone. Invisible chains shackle hearts and minds to the point that they distance themselves from others.

In Jesus, we have the One who can be trusted with our pain and the shame of the past and present. And as He did with Legion and KC, Jesus waits with open arms of mercy for all who run to Him today (v. 19).   *Arthur Jackson*

**In Jesus, we have the One who can be trusted with
our pain and the shame of the past and present.**

GOD'S GIFT OF GRACE

Ephesians 4:4–8

To each one of us grace has been given as
Christ apportioned it. —Ephesians 4:7

As I was grading another stack of papers for a college writing class I was teaching, I was impressed with one particular paper. It was so well written! Soon, though, I realized it was *too* well written. Sure enough, a little research revealed that the paper had been plagiarized from an online source.

I sent the student an email to let her know that her ruse had been discovered. She was getting a zero on this paper, but she could write a new paper for partial credit. Her response: "I am humiliated and very sorry. I appreciate the grace you are showing me. I don't deserve it." I responded by telling her that we all receive Jesus's grace every day, so how could I deny showing her grace?

There are many ways God's grace enhances our lives and redeems us from our errors. Peter says it gives salvation: "We believe it is through the grace of our Lord Jesus that we are saved" (Acts 15:11). Paul says it helps us not to be overtaken by sin: "Sin shall no longer be your master, because you are not under the law, but under grace" (Romans 6:14). Elsewhere, Peter says grace allows us to serve: "Use whatever gift you have received . . . as faithful stewards of God's grace" (1 Peter 4:10).

Grace. So freely given by God (Ephesians 4:7). It's a gift we can use to love and encourage others. *Dave Branon*

Grace allows us to serve others.

LEAP OF FAITH

Proverbs 3:5–8

In all your ways submit to him, and he will
make your paths straight. —Proverbs 3:6

As I prepared to ride a zip line from the highest point of a rain-forest on the Caribbean Island of St. Lucia, fear welled up inside me. Seconds before I jumped from the platform, thoughts of everything that could go wrong filled my mind. But with all the courage I could muster (and few options for turning back), I released. Dropping from the pinnacle of the forest, I whizzed through the lush green trees, wind flowing through my hair and my worries slowly fading. As I moved through the air allowing gravity to carry me, my view of the next platform became clearer and, with a gentle stop, I knew I'd arrived safely.

My time on the zip line pictured for me the times God has us undertake new, challenging endeavors. Scripture teaches us to put our trust in God and "lean not on [our] own understanding" (Proverbs 3:5) when we feel doubt and uncertainty. When our minds are filled with fear and doubt, our paths can be unclear and distorted. But once we've made the decision to step out in faith by submitting our way to God, "He will make [our] paths straight" (v. 6). We become more confident taking leaps of faith by learning who God is through spending time in prayer and the Scriptures.

We can find freedom and tranquility even in life's challenges as we hang on to God and allow Him to guide us through the changes in our lives. *Kimya Loder*

**Once we've made the decision to step out in
faith by submitting our way to God, "He will
make [our] paths straight." —Proverbs 3:6**

BLESSED ROUTINE

Ecclesiastes 2:17–26

Without [God], who can eat or find
enjoyment? —Ecclesiastes 2:25

Watching the morning crowd pour onto the train, I felt the Monday blues kick in. From the sleepy, grumpy faces of those in the jam-packed cabin, I could tell no one looked forward to going to work. Frowns broke out as some jostled for space and more tried to squeeze in. Here we go again, another mundane day at the office.

Then it struck me that just a year before, the trains would have been empty because COVID-19 lockdowns had thrown our daily routines into disarray. We couldn't even go out for a meal, and some actually missed going to the office. But now we were almost back to normal, and many were going back to work—as usual. "Routine," I realized, was good news, and "boring" was a blessing!

King Solomon came to a similar conclusion after reflecting on the seeming pointlessness of daily toil (Ecclesiastes 2:17–23). At times, it appeared endless, "meaningless," and unrewarding (v. 21). But then he realized that simply being able to eat, drink, and work each day was a blessing from God (v. 24).

When we're deprived of routine, we can see that these simple actions are a luxury. Let's thank God that we can eat and drink and find satisfaction in all our toil, for this is His gift (3:13).   *Leslie Koh*

**Simply being able to eat, drink, and work
each day is a blessing from God.**

TIME FOR A CHANGE

2 Corinthians 5:11–21

If anyone is in Christ, he is a new creation.
—2 Corinthians 5:17 NKJV

Even after my ministry to drug-addicted people ended, I continued to discover that God is in the rehabilitation business—bringing about personal change. Christian rehabilitation is unique, for it relies on Christ's power to change people from the inside out.

Drug addicts aren't the only people who need to be changed. All of us, without exception, have fallen short of God's standards. We may not be slaves to alcohol or drugs, but we are addicted to sin and self. Every person needs to be rescued from sin's grip and become a new creature in Christ (2 Corinthians 5:17).

We enter the Lord's unique life-changing program the day we put our faith in Jesus, and this program continues for life—not just for a few months. The apostle Paul put it this way: "He who began a good work in you will carry it on to completion until the day of Christ Jesus" (Philippians 1:6).

Whatever our sin-habits are, we all need the same Savior. And everyone who comes to Him echoes the same testimony: "Amazing grace, how sweet the sound, that saved a wretch like me."

Are you letting Jesus Christ change you from the inside out?

Joanie Yoder

We all need the same Savior.

LIKE A HYPOCRITE

Ephesians 2:1–10

Because of his great love for us, God, who is rich
in mercy, made us alive with Christ even when we
were dead in transgressions. —Ephesians 2:4–5

Pastor and author Ray Stedman (1917–1992) told about a young man who had stopped attending the church Ray was pastoring. The young man said that when he was at work, he would sometimes lose his temper and treat coworkers poorly. Then, when Sunday rolled around, he didn't want to go to church because he felt like a hypocrite.

Stedman told his young friend, "A hypocrite is someone who acts like something he isn't. When you come to church, you are acting like a Christian. You are not a hypocrite at church." Suddenly, the young man realized where he was being a hypocrite. He recognized that the answer was not in avoiding church but in changing the way he was at work.

The term *hypocrite* is from a Greek word that means "play-actor." It means we pretend to be something we aren't. Sometimes we forget our true identity as believers in Jesus. We forget that we are accountable to God. When we do that, we live the way we "used to live" (Ephesians 2:2) and thus are hypocrites.

Let's not let our old ways make us act like someone we're not. Instead, through God's grace, let's live in a way that shows we are "alive with Christ" (v. 5). That's a sure cure for hypocrisy. *Dave Branon*

Sometimes we forget our true identity as believers in Jesus.

ALL WE NEED TO KNOW

Romans 7:18–25

For I have the desire to do what is good, but
I cannot carry it out. —Romans 7:18

In a Fernando Ortega rendition of "Just as I Am," Billy Graham's voice can be heard faintly in the background. Dr. Graham is reminiscing about an illness during which he believed he was dying. As he mused on his past, he realized what a great sinner he was and how much he continued to need God's daily forgiveness.

Billy Graham was putting an end to the notion that apart from God we're okay. We can feel good about ourselves, but that confidence must come from the knowledge that we're greatly loved children of God (John 3:16), not that we're very good children (Romans 7:18).

The first step in becoming a truly "good" person as a follower of Christ is to stop pretending we're good on our own and to ask God to make us as good as we can be. We will fail many times, but He will keep growing us and changing us. God is faithful and—in His time and in His way—He'll do it.

In his final years, the writer of "Amazing Grace," John Newton, suffered from dementia and lamented the loss of his memory. Yet he confided, "I remember two things very clearly: I am a great sinner, and Christ is a great Savior." When it comes to faith, these are the only things anyone needs to know. *David Roper*

**"I am a great sinner, and Christ is a
great Savior." —John Newton**

THROWING STONES

John 8:1–11

"Neither do I condemn you," Jesus declared. "Go now and leave your life of sin." —John 8:11

Lisa felt no sympathy for people who cheated on their spouse . . . until she found herself deeply unsatisfied with her marriage and struggling to resist a dangerous attraction. That painful experience helped her gain a new compassion for others and greater understanding of Christ's words: "Let any one of you who is without sin be the first to throw a stone" (John 8:7).

Jesus was teaching in an area just outside the temple in Jerusalem when He made that statement. A group of teachers of the law and Pharisees had just dragged a woman caught in adultery before Him and challenged, "In the Law Moses commanded us to stone such women. Now what do you say?" (v. 5). Because they considered Jesus a threat to their authority, the question was "a trap, in order to have a basis for accusing him" (v. 6) . . . and getting rid of Him.

Yet when Jesus replied, "Let any one of you who is without sin . . ." (v. 7), not one of the woman's accusers could bring themselves to pick up a stone. One by one, they walked away.

Before we critically judge another's behavior while looking lightly at our own sin, let's remember that all of us "fall short of the glory of God" (Romans 3:23). Instead of condemnation, our Savior showed this woman—and you and me—grace and hope (John 3:16; 8:10–11). How can we not do the same for others?

Alyson Kieda

Let's remember that we all "fall short of the glory of God." —Romans 3:23

DYING GRACE

Psalm 23:1–4

Though I walk through the darkest valley, I will fear
no evil, for you are with me. —Psalm 23:4

Several years ago, I read a pamphlet that quoted the dying words of various people who did not profess faith in Jesus Christ. The English atheist Thomas Hobbes said, "I am taking a great leap in the dark!" Renowned atheist Sir Francis Newport wailed in anguish, "Oh, eternity, eternity forever and forever! Oh, the unsufferable pangs of hell!"

What a sobering contrast to the last words of people who knew and loved Christ as their Lord and Savior. Evangelist Dwight L. Moody said, "I see earth receding; heaven is opening; God is calling me!" Scottish physicist Sir David Brewster declared, "I will see Jesus—see Him as He is. I have had the light for many years. Oh, how bright it is! I feel so safe, so satisfied!" And these words from a man being burned at the stake: "Blessed be the time that ever I was born for this day. We shall not lose our lives in this fire," he said to his fellow martyrs, "but only change them for something better."

Even if physical pain and heartache are a part of our closing days, the heavenly Father will give us dying grace. When we pass through that dark valley, we need not fear. The Great Shepherd will be with us.

Richard DeHaan

The heavenly Father will give us dying grace.

TEARS OF PRAISE

Psalm 30

Sing the praises of the LORD, you his faithful
people; praise his holy name. —Psalm 30:4

Years ago, I cared for my mom as she was in hospice. I thanked
God for the four months He allowed me to serve as her care-
giver, and I asked Him to help me through the grieving process. I
often struggled to praise God as I wrestled with my mixed emotions. But as my mom breathed her last breath and I wept uncon-
trollably, I whispered, "Hallelujah." I felt guilty for praising God in
that devastating moment until, years later, I took a closer look at
Psalm 30.

In David's song "For the dedication of the temple" (as the title
for Psalm 30 explains), he worshiped God for His faithfulness and
mercy (vv. 1–3). He encouraged others to "praise his holy name"
(v. 4). Then David explored how intimately God entwines hardship
and hope (v. 5). Next, he acknowledged times of grief and rejoicing, times of feeling secure and being dismayed (vv. 6–7). His cries
for help remained laced with confidence in God (vv. 7–10). The
echo of his praise wove through David's moments of wailing and
dancing, grief and joy (v. 11). As if acknowledging the mystery and
complexity of enduring affliction and anticipating God's faithfulness, David proclaimed his endless devotion to God (v. 12).

Like David, we can sing, "LORD my God, I will praise you forever"
(v. 12). Whether we're happy or hurting, God can help us declare our
trust in Him and lead us to worship Him with joyful shouts and tears
of praise.   *Xochitl Dixon*

**God can help us declare our trust in Him
and lead us to worship Him.**

FROM RAGS TO RICHES

Ephesians 3:8–21

This grace was given me: to preach to the Gentiles
the boundless riches of Christ. —Ephesians 3:8

During the Great Depression, a man named Mr. Yates owned a huge piece of land in Texas where he raised sheep. Financial problems had brought him to the brink of bankruptcy. Then an oil company, believing there might be oil on his land, asked for permission to drill.

With nothing to lose, Mr. Yates agreed. Soon, at a shallow depth, the workmen struck the largest oil deposit found at that time on the North American continent. Overnight, Mr. Yates became a billionaire. The amazing thing, though, is that the untapped riches were there all along. He just didn't know it!

Are you a spiritual "Mr. Yates" who is unaware of the riches you already own in Christ? When Paul wrote his letter to the Ephesians, he revealed hidden treasure by preaching "the boundless riches of Christ" (3:8). His goal was to make sure all Christians could see how wealthy they actually are (v. 9).

Paul not only preached but he also prayed that believers might recognize and use their spiritual wealth, and that they would be strengthened within, established in love, powerful in prayer, and filled with God himself.

Read Ephesians 3:14–21 again, and claim your unlimited spiritual resources today. *Joanie Yoder*

Claim your unlimited spiritual resources today.

GRACE FOR ONE DAY AT A TIME

2 Corinthians 12:7–10

My grace is sufficient for you, for my power is made
perfect in weakness. —2 Corinthians 12:9

The important word in 2 Corinthians 12:9 is the little verb "is."
It's in the present tense. If God's grace is sufficient now, it will
be sufficient tomorrow—for tomorrow will be the "present," and
today will be in the past. We do not need tomorrow's grace until
tomorrow.

A man can no more take in a supply of grace for the future than
he can eat enough food today to last him for the rest of the week.
God's grace is supplied moment by moment as we need it. Yes, the
Lord's "grace *is* sufficient for you" and me (v. 9).

Paul suffered from what he described as "a thorn in my flesh"
(v. 7), and he prayed three times that it might be removed. The
Lord did not take away Paul's affliction, but He said, "My grace is
sufficient for you, for my power is made perfect in weakness" (v. 9).

If you are passing through deep waters and God has not seen fit
to relieve your trouble, then remember this: There is grace available
to you so that by faith you can receive an even greater blessing. If
you had known beforehand the trial of today, you would have de-
spaired and felt you could never bear it; but today His grace is there.
You didn't need grace for this trial until the trial came.

We must draw upon God's grace as we need it, and then we find
out that His grace *is* sufficient.   *M. R. DeHaan*

You don't need grace for the next trial until the trial comes.

ANYWHERE WITH JESUS

Exodus 33:12–17

Do not be afraid; do not be discouraged; . . . the
LORD will be with you. —2 Chronicles 20:17

When our son Brian was small, I took him with me to pick up our babysitter. As I approached the house, I noticed that her dog, usually penned in the backyard, was lying on the front porch. At first glance, the dog looked benign. But to my alarm he sprang to his feet and attacked Brian, who leaped for my leg, shinnied up to my waist, and somehow ended up wrapped around my neck and shoulders.

I, on the other hand, was left to fend off the dog. We danced for a while—the dog trying to get in a bite and I a kick—until, to my relief, the owner came around the house and called off the beast. All of us—dog, boy, and I—escaped unscathed.

Later, as we were walking to the car, Brian looked up to me and said, "Dad, I'll go anywhere with you." His confidence was misplaced; I can fail him. But I often think of his words when I grapple with fear.

As Moses faced uncertain circumstances, he implored God, "Teach me your ways so I may know you and continue to find favor with you" (Exodus 33:13). The Lord replied, "My Presence will go with you" (v. 14).

Whenever we enter frightening circumstances or face furious assaults, we can say with confidence, "Lord, I'll go anywhere with you."

David Roper

"My Presence will go with you." —Our Lord (Exodus 33:14)

ARENA OF VICTORY

Acts 4:1–13

When they saw the courage of Peter and John and realized that they were unschooled, ordinary men, they were astonished and they took note that these men had been with Jesus. —Acts 4:13

I suffered one of my most humiliating defeats as a Christian in the break room of a factory. Some of the people I worked with were foul-mouthed, angry, and godless. They needed the Lord. Yet, when I had a wonderful opportunity to tell them about Christ, I sat in silence and fear.

I'm not alone. Peter did a similar thing in the temple courtyard. Three times he denied the Lord, but then he wept bitterly (Luke 22:54–62).

After the resurrection, the Lord Jesus confronted Peter and lovingly restored him (John 21:15–19). A few days later, Peter stood in that same temple courtyard where he had previously denied the Lord, and this time he proclaimed Christ. When he and John were brought before the high priest, Peter spoke with courage and boldness (Acts 4:1–13).

For Peter, the place of defeat had become an arena of victory. It did for me too. Later, in that same break room where I had been silent, God gave me the grace to speak out for Christ.

Do you have a place of defeat? A break room? Cafeteria? Office? Talk to the Lord about it. Admit your fears and trust Him to provide the courage to witness for Him. Jesus can turn your place of defeat into an arena of victory!   *David Egner*

**Admit your fears and trust Him to
provide the courage to witness.**

HOW TO BE UNPOPULAR

Jeremiah 23:16–23

Woe to the shepherds who are destroying and scattering
the sheep of my pasture! —Jeremiah 23:1

In 1517, Martin Luther nailed his Ninety-Five Theses to the door of the castle church in Wittenberg, Germany. Luther became known as a reformer, and we remember his bold stand as a turning point in church history.

The fiery priest demonstrated great courage in expressing outrage at the church's practice of selling forgiveness through indulgences, which allowed the people to sin intentionally in exchange for money.

Luther's passion to stop these practices did not make him popular with the religious authorities of his day. In fact, his efforts resulted in a series of attempts to silence him.

Long before Luther, the prophet Jeremiah felt the power of God's Word in his heart like "a fire shut up in my bones. I am weary of holding it in; indeed, I cannot" (Jeremiah 20:9). Jeremiah and Luther refused to allow God's truth to be compromised.

Living for God is not only about grace and forgiveness. It's also about boldly standing for the truth. Having God's Word in our heart doesn't always result in warm, pleasant feelings. Sometimes His truth becomes a blazing fire that causes us to challenge corruption—even though we may be attacked for it.   *Julie Ackerman Link*

**Living for God is not only about grace and forgiveness.
It's also about boldly standing for the truth.**

NOVEMBER

"When We All Get to Heaven"

Eliza Hewitt and Emily D. Wilson

Sing the wondrous love of Jesus, Sing His mercy and His grace.

Camp Meetings and Heaven

One of the most interesting worship phenomena of the nineteenth century was the camp meeting. These outdoor evangelistic events brought hundreds and sometimes thousands of people together to sing Christian songs and listen to circuit-riding evangelists and local preachers. The camp meetings placed great emphasis on spiritual revival, morality, and heaven.

One famous camp meeting site was Ocean Grove, New Jersey. Both Eliza Hewitt and Emily Wilson attended the Ocean Grove revivals. Hewitt was a schoolteacher from Philadelphia who was

Sources: "Camp Meeting," Wikipedia, http://tinyurl.com/38vydwn5; C. Michael Hawn, "History of Hymns: 'When We All Get to Heaven,'" April 2019, Discipleship Ministries of United Methodist Church, http://tinyurl.com/4k6ssehu; "When We All Get to Heaven," Hymnary.org, http://tinyurl.com/9945w75v; "When We All Get to Heaven," *Hymnology Archive*, http://tinyurl.com/2tahetcm; "When We All Get to Heaven," *Hymn Studies* (blog), September 21, 2011, http://tinyurl.com/4wytx46t; "When We All Get to Heaven," *OChristian.com*, http://tinyurl.com/276uth5z; all accessed November 6, 2023.

heavily involved in her church's Sunday schools. She'd overcome an injury that had left her partially incapacitated, and she dedicated herself to teaching children the basic truths of the faith.

Wilson, whose husband was a Methodist leader in the Philadelphia area, was a noted singer and musician.

It is speculated that Hewitt and Wilson were introduced to each other at an Ocean Grove camp meeting by John Sweney, himself a songwriter and composer.

One recurring theme of camp meetings was the return of Jesus. It's been suggested that Paul's words to the church at Thessalonica in 1 Thessalonians 4:17 about being "caught up in the clouds together . . . to meet the Lord in the air" may have been part of the impetus for Hewitt to pen the song "When We All Get to Heaven." Others suggest the spirit of unity as hundreds of believers gathered to worship helped Hewitt anticipate what it would be like when we all gather in heaven.

Whatever sparked Hewitt to pen this song, it's clear that the camp meetings had an inspirational effect. And, of course, they were vital in bringing songwriter (Miss Hewitt) and musician (Mrs. Wilson) together. The song was written in 1898 and has appeared in most Christian hymnals ever since.

The first line of the chorus, "When we *all* get to heaven," has sparked some controversy. Some have said the wording is too inclusive. A few songbook editors have changed Hewitt's words to "When the saved get to heaven." Since it's presumably only believers in Jesus who are singing these songs as affirmations of their faith, it seems reasonable to understand this as "all" who trust in Jesus.

Hewitt wrote other songs that have been sung by congregations through the years, including "More about Jesus" and "Sunshine in My Soul."

When We All Get to Heaven

Sing the wondrous love of Jesus,
Sing His mercy and His grace;
In the mansions bright and blessed
He'll prepare for us a place.

Chorus:
When we all get to heaven,
What a day of rejoicing that will be!
When we all see Jesus,
We'll sing and shout the victory.

Onward to the prize before us!
Soon His beauty we'll behold;
Soon the pearly gates will open—
We shall tread the streets of gold.

LET THE WHOLE WORLD HEAR!

Acts 1:1–8

Go into all the world and preach the gospel
to all creation. —Mark 16:15

Fritz Kreisler (1875–1962), a world-famous violinist, earned a fortune with his concerts and compositions, but he generously gave most of it away. So, when he discovered an exquisite violin on one of his trips, he wasn't able to buy it.

Later, having raised enough money to meet the asking price, he returned to the seller, hoping to purchase the beautiful instrument. But to his great dismay, it had been sold to a collector. Kreisler made his way to the new owner's home and offered to buy the violin. The collector said it had become his prized possession, and he would not sell it. Keenly disappointed, Kreisler was about to leave when he had an idea. "Could I play the instrument once more before it is consigned to silence?" he asked. The owner agreed, and the great virtuoso filled the room with heart-moving music that deeply stirred the collector's emotions. "I have no right to keep that to myself," he exclaimed. "It's yours, Mr. Kreisler. Take it into the world, and let people hear it."

To sinners saved by grace, the gospel is like the rapturous harmonies of heaven. We have no right to keep it to ourselves. Jesus tells us to take it out into the world and let it be heard. *Vernon Grounds*

The gospel is like the rapturous harmonies of heaven.

LAUGHING OUT LOUD

Genesis 21:1–7

God has brought me laughter, and everyone who hears
about this will laugh with me. —Genesis 21:6

Comedian John Branyan said, "We didn't think up laughter; that wasn't our idea. That was given to us by [God who] knew we were going to need it to get through life. [Because] He knew we were going to have hardship, He knew we were going to have struggles, He knew . . . stuff was going to happen. . . . Laughter is a gift."

A quick look at the creatures God made can bring laughter, whether because of their oddities (such as duck-billed platypuses) or antics (such as playful otters). God made mammals that live in the ocean and long-legged birds that can't fly. God clearly has a sense of humor, and because we're created in His image, we too have the joy of laughter.

We first see the word *laughter* in the Bible in the story of Abraham and Sarah. God promised this elderly couple a child: "A son who is your own flesh and blood will be your heir" (Genesis 15:4). And God had said, "Look up at the sky and count the stars. . . . So shall your offspring be" (v. 5). When Sarah finally gave birth at ninety, Abraham named their son Isaac, which means "laughter." As Sarah exclaimed, "God has brought me laughter, and everyone who hears about this will laugh with me" (21:6). It amazed her that she could nurse a child at her age! God transformed her skeptical laughter when she'd heard she'd give birth (18:12) into laughter of sheer joy.

Thank God for the gift of laughter! *Alyson Kieda*

A quick look at the creatures God made can bring laughter.

EVERYBODY WORSHIPS

Acts 17:24–32

People of Athens! I see that in every way
you are very religious. —Acts 17:22

I recently visited Athens, Greece. Walking around its ancient Agora—the marketplace where philosophers taught and Athenians worshiped—I found altars to Apollo and Zeus, all in the shadow of the Acropolis, where a statue of the goddess Athena once stood.

We may not bow to Apollo or Zeus today, but society is no less religious. "Everybody worships," novelist David Foster Wallace said, adding this warning: "If you worship money and things . . . then you will never have enough. . . . Worship your body and beauty. . . and you will always feel ugly. . . . Worship your intellect . . . [and] you will end up feeling stupid." Our secular age has its own gods, and they're not benign.

"People of Athens!" Paul said while visiting the Agora, "I see that in every way you are very religious" (Acts 17:22). The apostle then described the one true God as the Creator of all (vv. 24–26) who wants to be known (v. 27) and who has revealed himself through the resurrection of Jesus (v. 31). Unlike Apollo and Zeus, this God isn't made by human hands. Unlike money, looks, or intelligence, worshiping Him won't ruin us.

Our "god" is whatever we rely on to give us purpose and security. Thankfully, when every earthly god fails us, the one true God is ready to be found (v. 27).   *Sheridan Voysey*

**Unlike money, looks, or intelligence, worshiping
the one true God won't ruin us.**

THE GOD WHO RESTORES

Ezekiel 37:1–14

I will make breath enter you, and you
will come to life. —Ezekiel 37:5

On November 4, 1966, a disastrous flood swept through Florence, Italy, submerging Giorgio Vasari's renowned work of art *The Last Supper* under a pool of mud, water, and heating oil for more than twelve hours. With its paint softened and its wooden frame significantly damaged, many believed the piece was beyond repair. However, after a tedious fifty-year conservation effort, experts and volunteers were able to overcome monumental obstacles and restore the valuable painting.

When the Babylonians conquered Israel, the people felt hopeless—surrounded by death and destruction and in need of restoration (Lamentations 1). During this period of turmoil, God took the prophet Ezekiel to a valley and gave him a vision where he was surrounded by dry bones. "Can these bones live?" He asked. Ezekiel responded, "Lord, you alone know" (Ezekiel 37:3). God then told him to prophesy over the bones so they might live again. "As I was prophesying," Ezekiel recounted, "there was a noise, a rattling sound, and the bones came together" (v. 7). Through this vision, God revealed to Ezekiel that Israel's restoration could only come through Him.

When we feel as if things in life have been broken and are beyond repair, God assures us He can rebuild our shattered pieces. He'll give us new breath and new life.   *Kimya Loder*

God can rebuild our shattered pieces.

A FULL SURRENDER

Romans 11:13–12:2

I urge you, brothers and sisters, in view of God's mercy, to
offer your bodies as a living sacrifice, holy and pleasing to
God—this is your true and proper worship. —Romans 12:1

When someone asked William Booth (1829–1912), founder
of the Salvation Army, the secret of his success, Booth remained silent for several moments. Finally, with tear-filled eyes, he
said, "There have been men with greater brains or opportunities
than I, but I made up my mind that God would have all of William
Booth there was."

Several years later when General Booth's daughter heard about
her father's comment regarding his full surrender to God, she said,
"That wasn't really his secret—his secret was that he never took that
comment back."

We may never be a William Booth, but all of us can, in response
to God's grace and mercy in saving us, give Him our all—and never
take it back.

In Romans 11 and 12, the apostle Paul made an appeal based
on what he had discussed earlier in his letter. In consideration of
all that the Lord in His mercy has done for us, we are to give our
bodies as living sacrifices to God.

Elisha A. Hoffman, the hymn writer, asks: "Is your all on the altar
of sacrifice laid? Your heart, does the Spirit control?" Those are penetrating questions. How would you answer them?   *Richard DeHaan*

**All of us can, in response to God's grace and
mercy in saving us, give Him our all.**

WE ARE STRANGERS

Leviticus 19:32–37

The foreigner residing among you must be treated
as your native-born. —Leviticus 19:34

Everything felt drastically different in their new country—new language, schools, customs, traffic, and weather. They wondered how they would ever adjust. People from a nearby church gathered around them to help them in their new life in a new land. Patti took the couple shopping at a local food market to show them what's available and how to purchase items. As they wandered around the market, their eyes widened, and they smiled broadly when they saw their favorite fruit from their homeland—pomegranates. They bought one for each of their children and even placed one in Patti's hands in gratefulness. The small fruit and new friends brought big comfort in their strange, new land.

God, through Moses, gave a list of laws for His people, which included a command to treat foreigners among them "as your native-born" (Leviticus 19:34). "Love them as yourself," God further commanded. Jesus called this the second greatest commandment after loving God (Matthew 22:39). For even God "watches over the foreigner" (Psalm 146:9).

Besides obeying God as we help new friends adapt to life in our country, we may be reminded that we too in a real sense are "strangers on earth" (Hebrews 11:13). And we'll grow in our anticipation of the new heavenly land to come.   *Anne Cetas*

**God gave a list of laws for His people, which
included a command to treat foreigners
among them "as your native-born."**

WHERE SINNERS GO

Romans 5:6–15

God demonstrates his own love for us in this: While we
were still sinners, Christ died for us. —Romans 5:8

My friend was having a conversation with a man who didn't
have much good to say about the Christian faith. My friend
knew that if he were to sound too "religious," he would jeopardize
any chance to witness. So, in the middle of their discussion, he said,
"Hey, Bob, do you know where sinners go?"

"That's easy," he replied. "You're going to tell me they go to hell."

"No," my friend responded. "They go to church."

Bob was speechless. That wasn't what he expected. He wasn't
ready to hear from a Christian who realized he wasn't perfect. My
friend had a chance to share that Christians understand their sinfulness and their need for continual spiritual restoration. He was able
to explain grace—the unmerited favor we have with God despite
our sinfulness (Romans 5:8–9; Ephesians 2:8–9).

Perhaps we don't give those outside the church a clear picture of
what's happening inside. They may not understand that we're there
to praise our Savior for providing "redemption, the forgiveness of
sins" (Colossians 1:14).

Yes, sinners go to church. And sinners—forgiven ones—go to
heaven because of God's grace.   *Dave Branon*

**Grace is the unmerited favor we have
with God despite our sinfulness.**

IN THE GARDEN

Matthew 26:36–42

My father, . . . may your will be done. —Matthew 26:42

My forefathers were pioneers in Michigan. They cleared the land, planted crops, and cultivated gardens to raise food for their families. This agrarian bent has been passed down through the generations. My dad grew up on a Michigan farm and loved gardening, which may explain why I love gardening and the smell of fertile soil. Cultivating plants that bear beautiful flowers and tending roses that fragrantly grace our yard with beauty are enjoyable pastimes for me. If it weren't for the weeds, it would be wonderful!

When I have to wrestle with the weeds, I am reminded of the garden of Eden. It was a perfect garden until Adam and Eve disobeyed God, and thorns and thistles became a reality for them and every gardener since then (Genesis 3:17–18).

The Bible also mentions another garden—the garden of Gethsemane where Christ, in deep distress, pleaded with His Father to find another way to reverse sin's consequences that were born in Eden. In Gethsemane, Jesus surrendered to His Father by uttering words of full obedience in the face of great pain: "Your will be done" (Matthew 26:42).

Because Jesus surrendered in that garden, we now harvest the benefits of His amazing grace. May this lead us to surrender to His weeding of sin from our lives. *Joe Stowell*

**Jesus surrendered to His Father by uttering
words of full obedience in the face of great pain:
"Your will be done." —Matthew 26:42**

GREAT THINGS!

Psalm 126

What, then, shall we say in response to these things? If
God is for us, who can be against us? —Romans 8:31

On November 9, 1989, the world was astonished by the news
that the Berlin Wall had fallen. The wall that had divided Berlin, Germany, was coming down, and the city that had been split
in two for twenty-eight years would be united again. Although the
epicenter of joy was Germany, an onlooking world shared in the
excitement. Something great had taken place!

When Israel returned to her homeland in 538 BC after being exiled
for almost seventy years, it was also momentous. Psalm 126 begins
with an over-the-shoulder look at that joy-filled time in the history of
Israel. The experience was marked by laughter, joyful singing, and international recognition that God had done great things for His people
(v. 2). And what was the response of the recipients of His rescuing
mercy? Great things from God prompted great gladness (v. 3). Furthermore, His works in the past became the basis for fresh prayers for
the present and bright hope for the future (vv. 4–6).

You and I need not look far in our own experiences for examples
of great things from God, especially if we believe in God through
His Son, Jesus. Nineteenth-century hymn writer Fanny Crosby captured this sentiment when she wrote, "Great things He hath taught
us, great things He hath done, and great our rejoicing through Jesus
the Son." Yes, to God be the glory, great things He has done!

Arthur Jackson

**God's works in the past became the basis for fresh
prayers for the present and bright hope for the future.**

BETTER WITH GOD

Daniel 1:11–16; 2:19–20

Wisdom and power are his. —Daniel 2:20

On her college volleyball team, my granddaughter learned a winning principle. When the ball came her way, no matter what, she could "better the ball." She could make a play that left her teammates in a better situation—without throwing tantrums, blaming, or making excuses. Always make the situation better.

That was Daniel's response when he and three Hebrew friends were taken into captivity by Babylon's king Nebuchadnezzar. Although they were given pagan names and ordered to take three years of "training" in the enemy's palace, Daniel didn't rage. Instead, he asked permission not to defile himself in God's sight by eating or drinking the king's rich food and wine. As this intriguing Bible story shows, after consuming nothing but vegetables and water for ten days (Daniel 1:12), Daniel and his friends "looked healthier and better nourished than any of the young men who ate the royal food" (v. 15).

Another time, Nebuchadnezzar threatened to kill Daniel and all palace wise men if they couldn't repeat the king's disturbing dream and interpret it. Again, Daniel didn't panic, but sought mercy "from the God of heaven" (2:18), and the mystery was revealed to him in a vision (v. 19). Then Daniel declared of God that "wisdom and power are his" (v. 20). Throughout his captivity, Daniel sought God's best despite the conflicts he faced. In our own troubles, let's strive to follow his example, making the situation better by taking it to God.

Patricia Raybon

Daniel sought God's best despite the conflicts he faced. What a great example!

ALWAYS PRAY AND DON'T GIVE UP

Luke 18:1–8

Jesus told his disciples a parable to show them that they
should always pray and not give up. —Luke 18:1

A re you going through one of those times when it seems every
attempt to resolve a problem is met with a new difficulty? You
thank the Lord at night that it's taken care of but awake to find that
something else has gone wrong and the problem remains.

During an experience like that, I was reading the gospel of Luke
and was astounded by the opening words of chapter 18: "Then Jesus
told his disciples a parable to show them that they should always
pray and not give up" (v. 1). I had read the story of the persistent
widow many times but never grasped why Jesus told it (vv. 2–8).
Now I connected those opening words with the story. The lesson to
His followers was very clear: "Always pray and never give up."

Prayer is not a means of coercing God to do what we want. It is
a process of recognizing His power and plan for our lives. In prayer
we yield our lives and circumstances to the Lord and trust Him to
act in His time and in His way.

As we rely on God's grace, not only for the outcome of our requests but for the process as well, we know we can keep coming to
the Lord in prayer over and over, trusting His wisdom and care for us.

David McCasland

**Prayer is a process of recognizing God's
power and plan for our lives.**

BUCKLING UP

Hebrews 4:11–16

This High Priest of ours understands our weaknesses, for he faced all of the same testings we do, yet he did not sin. —Hebrews 4:15 NLT

"The captain has turned on the fasten seat belt sign. We are experiencing some turbulence. Please remain in your seats with your seat belts securely fastened." Flight attendants give this warning when necessary because in rough air, unbuckled passengers can be injured. Secured in their seats, they can safely ride out the turbulence.

Most of the time, life doesn't warn us of the unsettling experiences coming our way. But our loving Father knows and cares about our struggles, and He invites us to bring our cares, hurts, and fears to Him. The Scriptures tell us, "This High Priest of ours understands our weaknesses, for he faced all of the same testings we do, yet he did not sin. So let us come boldly to the throne of our gracious God. There we will receive his mercy, and we will find grace to help us when we need it most" (Hebrews 4:15–16 NLT).

In seasons of turbulence, going to our Father in prayer is the best thing we can do. The phrase "grace to help us when we need it"—means that in His presence we can be "buckled" in peace during threatening times, since we bring our concerns to the One who is greater than all! When life feels overwhelming, we can pray. He can help us through the turbulence. *Bill Crowder*

Our loving Father knows and cares about our struggles, and He invites us to bring our cares, hurts, and fears to Him.

FOLLOWED BY GOD'S GOODNESS

Psalm 23:5–6

Surely your goodness and love will follow me
all the days of my life. —Psalm 23:6

At my first job during my high school years, I worked at a women's clothing store where a female security guard dressed as a shopper followed women she thought might steal the merchandise. Certain people fit profiles of those the store owners thought were suspicious. Others not considered a threat were left alone. I've been profiled in stores myself and followed—an interesting experience since I still recognize the tactic.

In sharp contrast, David declared he was followed by a divine blessing—God's goodness and mercy. These two gifts always stay close, following him not with suspicion but with real love. The "twin guardian angels," as evangelist Charles Spurgeon described the pair, follow believers closely during both bleak days and bright. "The dreary days of winter as well as the bright days of summer. Goodness supplies our needs, and mercy blots out our sins," Spurgeon wrote in his book *The Treasury of David*.

As a onetime shepherd, David understood this intentional pairing of goodness and mercy as it's provided by God. Other things could follow believers—fear, worry, temptation, doubts. But "surely," David declares with undoubting certainty, God's kind goodness and loving mercy follow us always.

David rejoiced, "Surely your goodness and love will follow me all the days of my life, and I will dwell in the house of the LORD forever" (Psalm 23:6). What an amazing gift to follow us home!

Patricia Raybon

God's kind goodness and loving mercy follow us always.

BETTER THAN EVER

Psalm 51:9–13

Restore to me the joy of your salvation and grant me
a willing spirit, to sustain me. —Psalm 51:12

The story is told of a group of salmon fishermen who gathered in a Scottish inn after a long day of fishing. As one was describing a catch to his friends, his arm swept across the table and knocked a glass against the wall, shattering it and leaving a stain on the white plaster surface. The man apologized to the innkeeper and offered to pay for the damage, but there was nothing he could do; the wall was ruined. A man seated nearby said, "Don't worry." Rising, he took a painting implement from his pocket and began to sketch around the ugly stain. Slowly there emerged the head of a magnificent deer with majestic antlers. The man was Sir E. H. Landseer, Scotland's foremost animal artist.

David, Israel's illustrious king who penned Psalm 51, brought shame on himself and his nation by his sins. He "slept with" the wife of one of his friends (2 Samuel 11:4) and engineered the death of that friend—both deeds worthy of death. It would seem his life was ruined. But he pled with God: "Restore to me the joy of your salvation and grant me a willing spirit, to sustain me" (v. 12).

Like David, we have shameful acts in our past and the memories that accompany them—recollections that taunt us in the middle of the night. There's so much we wish we could undo or redo.

But remember this: There is a grace that not only forgives sin but also uses it to make us better than before. God wastes nothing.

David Roper

There is a grace that forgives sin and makes us better.

THE ADVANTAGE OF WEAKNESS

2 Corinthians 12:1–10

For Christ's sake, I delight in weaknesses, in insults, in
hardships, in persecutions, in difficulties. For when I
am weak, then I am strong. —2 Corinthians 12:10

It is always a joy to talk with my old college friend Tom and get
caught up on what the Lord has been teaching us since we last met.

One time Tom began with a sheepish grin, "You know, I can't
believe how many years it's taken me to learn my latest lesson—and
I'm a Bible teacher!" He went on to list some of the trials and testings he and his family had been facing and how unworthy he felt
teaching an adult Sunday school class. "Week after week I felt I was
a total failure," he confided, "and I kept wondering if this might be
my last Sunday before announcing my resignation."

Then one Sunday Tom noticed a young woman who stayed behind to speak to him. She was a friend of his family, so she knew
what they had been going through. "Tom," she said, "I hope you
won't take this the wrong way, but you're a much better teacher
when you're going through tough times!"

Another sheepish grin crept across Tom's face as he told me, "Only
then did I feel I grasped the Lord's response to Paul's thorn in the
flesh: 'My grace is sufficient for you, for my power is made perfect in
weakness.'"

Weakness helps us relate to others and lets God's power work in
our lives. This may be our greatest asset. *Joanie Yoder*

**Weakness helps us relate to others and lets
God's power work in our lives.**

NEVER TOO FAR

Luke 22:31–34, 54–62

When you have turned back, strengthen
your brothers. —Luke 22:32

Raj had trusted Jesus as Savior in his youth, but soon afterward, he drifted from the faith and led a life apart from God. Then one day he made the decision to renew his relationship with Jesus and go back to church—only to be scolded by a woman who berated him for being absent for all these years. The scolding added to Raj's sense of shame and guilt for his years of drifting. *Am I beyond hope?* he wondered. Then he recalled how Christ had restored Simon Peter (John 21:15–17) even though Peter had denied Jesus (Luke 22:34, 60–61).

Whatever scolding Peter might have expected, all he received was forgiveness and restoration. Jesus didn't even mention Peter's denial but instead gave him a chance to reaffirm his love for Christ and take care of His followers (John 21:15–17). Jesus's words before Peter disowned Him were being fulfilled: "When you have turned back, strengthen your brothers" (Luke 22:32).

Raj asked God for that same forgiveness and restoration, and today he's not only walking closely with Jesus but also serving in a church and supporting other believers. No matter how far we've strayed from God, He's always ready to forgive us, welcome us back, and restore us so we can love, serve, and glorify Him. We're never too far from God: His loving arms are always wide open.

Leslie Koh

**No matter how far we've strayed from God, He's
always ready to forgive us and welcome us back.**

READY TO GO

Ephesians 4:1–16

I urge you to live a life worthy of the calling
you have received. —Ephesians 4:1

The book *Hidden Figures* recounts preparations for John Glenn's flight into space. Computers were new-fangled inventions in 1962, subject to glitches. Glenn didn't trust them and worried about calculations for the launch. He knew one brainy woman in the back room who could run the numbers. He trusted her. "If she says the numbers are good," Glenn said, "I'm ready to go."

Katherine Johnson was a teacher and mother of three. She loved Jesus and served in her church. God had blessed Katherine with a remarkable mind. NASA tapped her in the late 1950s to help with the space program. She was Glenn's "brainy woman," one of the "human computers" they hired at the time.

We may not be called to be brilliant mathematicians, but God calls us to other things: "To each one of us grace has been given as Christ apportioned it" (Ephesians 4:7). We're to "live a life worthy of the calling" we've received (v. 1). We're part of one body, in which "each part does its work" (v. 16).

Katherine Johnson's calculations confirmed the course trajectory. Glenn's launch into orbit was like "hitting a bull's-eye." But this was just one of Katherine's callings. Remember, she was also called to be a mother, teacher, and church worker. We might ask ourselves what God has called us to, whether big or small. Are we "ready to go," exercising the grace-gifts He's bestowed, living "a life worthy of [our] calling" (v. 1)?

Kenneth Petersen

**We should ask ourselves: What has God
called us to do? Are we ready to go?**

TACKLING INDECISION

Proverbs 3:5–8

Trust in the LORD with all your heart and lean not
on your own understanding. —Proverbs 3:5

We live in a world that offers a wide range of choices—from paper towels to life insurance. In 2004, psychologist Barry Schwartz wrote a book titled *The Paradox of Choice* in which he argued that while freedom of choice is important to our well-being, too many choices can lead to overload and indecision. While the stakes are certainly lower when deciding which paper towel to buy, indecision can become debilitating when making major decisions that impact the course of our lives. So how can we overcome indecision and move forward confidently in living for Jesus?

As believers in Christ, seeking God's wisdom helps us as we face difficult decisions. When we're deciding on anything in life, large or small, the Scriptures instruct us to "trust in the LORD with all [our] heart and lean not on [our] own understanding" (Proverbs 3:5). When we rely on our own judgment, we can become confused and worry about missing an important detail or making the wrong choice. When we look to God for the answers, however, He'll "make [our] paths straight" (v. 6). He'll give us clarity and peace as we make decisions in our day-to-day lives.

God doesn't want us to be paralyzed or overwhelmed by the weight of our decisions. We can find peace in the wisdom and direction He provides when we bring our concerns to Him in prayer.

Kimya Loder

**As believers in Christ, seeking God's wisdom
helps us as we face difficult decisions.**

TELL THE STORY

Psalm 78:1–8

Tell the next generation the praiseworthy deeds of the LORD,
his power, and the wonders he has done. —Psalm 78:4

In an interview with *Wired* magazine, filmmaker George Lucas was asked how he wanted to be remembered. He replied: "I'll be remembered as a filmmaker. . . . Hopefully some of the stories I told will still be relevant. . . . If you've raised children, you know you have to explain things to them, and if you don't, they end up learning the hard way. . . . So the old stories have to be reiterated again in a form that's acceptable to each new generation. I don't think I'm ever going to go much beyond the old stories, because I think they still need to be told."

In Psalm 78, the psalmist was aware of the possibility of God's mighty works being forgotten and a generation being lost, so he called on God's people to never tire of telling the old story of His redemptive acts to future generations (v. 4). The goal of this perpetual rehearsing of their history wasn't just for memorizing historical data; it was to inspire faith, obedience, and hope in the Lord (v. 7) and to keep future generations from groping in the darkness of unbelief and rebellion like the generations before them (v. 8).

Because of God's mighty power and grace in our lives, we desire to be faithful to tell His stories, which can inspire faith and obedience in future generations. *Marvin Williams*

The psalmist called God's people to never tire of telling the old story of His redemptive acts to future generations.

A HEART FOR SERVICE

2 Corinthians 9:12–13

Because of the service by which you have proved yourselves,
others will praise God. —2 Corinthians 9:13

A ministry in Carlsbad, New Mexico, supports that community by offering more than 24,000 pounds of free food each month to residents. The leader of the ministry said, "People can come here, and we will accept them and meet them right where they are. Our goal is . . . to meet their practical needs to get to their spiritual needs." As believers in Christ, God desires for us, as believers in Christ, to use what we've been given to bless others, drawing our communities closer to Him. How can we develop this in our lives—having a heart for service that brings glory to God?

We develop a heart for service by asking God to show us how to use the gifts He's given us to benefit others (1 Peter 4:10). In this way, we offer "many expressions of thanks to God" for the abundance He's blessed us with (2 Corinthians 9:12).

Serving others was an important part of Jesus's ministry. When He healed the sick and fed the hungry, many were introduced to God's goodness and love. By caring for our communities, we're following His model of discipleship. God's wisdom reminds us that when we demonstrate God's love through our actions, "others will praise God" (v. 13). Service isn't about self-gratification. It's about showing others the extent of God's love plus the miraculous ways He works through those who are called by His name. *Kimya Loder*

**We develop a heart for service by asking God to show us
how to use the gifts He's given us to benefit others.**

FIRST THINGS FIRST

1 Chronicles 28:5–10

Acknowledge the God of your father, and serve
him with wholehearted devotion and with a
willing mind. —1 Chronicles 28:9

When our granddaughter Sarah was very young, she told us she wanted to be a basketball coach like her daddy when she grew up. But she couldn't be one yet, she said, because first she had to be a player, and a player had to be able to tie her shoelaces, and she couldn't tie hers yet!

First things first, we say. And the first thing in all of life is to know God and enjoy Him.

Acknowledging and knowing God helps us become what we were meant to be. Here is King David's counsel to his son Solomon: "Know the God of your father, and serve Him with a loyal heart and with a willing mind" (1 Chronicles 28:9 NKJV).

Remember, God can be known. He is a Person, not a logical or theological concept. He thinks, wills, enjoys, feels, loves, and desires as any person does.

A. W. Tozer writes, "He is a person and can be known in increasing degrees of intimacy as we prepare our hearts for the wonder of it." Ah, there's the rub: We must "prepare our hearts."

The Lord is not playing hard to know; those who want to know Him can. He will not foist His love on us, but He does wait patiently, for He wants to be known by you. Knowing Him is the first thing in life.   *David Roper*

"[God] is a person and can be known in increasing
degrees of intimacy." —A. W. Tozer

SHINING STARS

Philippians 2:12–16

You will shine among them like stars in the sky as you
hold firmly to the word of life. —Philippians 2:15–16

The first thing I noticed about the city was its gambling outlets. Next, its cannabis shops, "adult" stores, and giant billboards for opportunistic lawyers making money off others' mishaps. While I had visited many shady cities before, this one seemed to reach a new low.

My mood brightened, however, when I spoke to a taxi driver the next morning. "I ask God every day to send me the people He wants me to help," he said. "Gambling addicts, prostitutes, people from broken homes tell me their problems in tears. I stop the car. I listen. I pray for them. This is my ministry."

After describing Jesus's descent into our fallen world (Philippians 2:5–8), the apostle Paul gives believers in Christ a calling. As we pursue God's will (v. 13) and hold to the "word of life"—the gospel (v. 16)—we'll be "children of God without fault in a warped and crooked generation" who "shine . . . like stars in the sky" (v. 15). Like that taxi driver, we're to bring Jesus's light into the darkness.

A believer in Christ has only to live faithfully in order to change the world, historian Christopher Dawson said, because in that very act of living "there is contained all the mystery of divine life." Let's ask God's Spirit to empower us to live faithfully as Jesus's people, shining His light in the world's darkest places.   *Sheridan Voysey*

**A believer in Christ has only to live faithfully
in order to change the world.**

WHO DESERVES THE PRAISE?

Hebrews 3:1–6

Every house is built by someone, but God is the
builder of everything. —Hebrews 3:4

From the spiral staircase to the expansive bedroom, from the hardwood floors to the plush carpeting, from the huge laundry room to the well-organized office, the realtor showed a potential home to the young couple. At every corner they turned, they raved about its beauty: "You've picked the best place for us. This house is amazing!" Then the realtor responded with something they thought a bit unusual yet true: "I'll pass along your compliment to the builder. The one who built the house deserves the praise, not the house itself or the one who shows it off."

The realtor's words echo the writer of Hebrews: "The builder of a house has greater honor than the house itself" (3:3). The writer was comparing the faithfulness of Jesus, the Son of God, with the prophet Moses (vv. 1–6). Although Moses was privileged to speak to God face-to-face and to see His form (Numbers 12:8), he was still only "a servant" in the house of God (Hebrews 3:5). Christ, as Creator (1:2, 10), deserves honor as divine "builder of everything" and as Son "over God's house" (3:6). God's house is His people.

When we serve God faithfully, it's Jesus the divine builder who deserves the honor. Any praise we, God's house, receive ultimately belongs to Him.

Anne Cetas

**When we serve God faithfully, it's Jesus the
divine builder who deserves the honor.**

GIVE THANKS TO GOD

Luke 24:28–35

When he was at the table with them, he took bread, gave
thanks, broke it and began to give it to them. —Luke 24:30

My friend hurried from her stressful job at the hospital, wondering what she would prepare for dinner before her husband
returned from his equally demanding job. She had made chicken
on Sunday and served leftovers on Monday. Then, they had yet another round of chicken—this time baked—on Tuesday. She found
two pieces of fish in the freezer, but she knew the fillets weren't her
husband's favorite. Not finding anything else she could prepare in
just a few minutes, she decided the fish would have to do.

As she placed the dish on the table, she said somewhat apologetically to her husband who had just arrived home: "I know this isn't
your favorite." Her husband looked up and said, "Honey, I'm just
happy we have food on the table."

His attitude reminds me of the importance of being grateful and
thankful for our daily provisions from God—whatever they are. Giving thanks for our daily bread, or meals, models Jesus's example. When
He ate with two disciples after His resurrection, Christ "took bread,
gave thanks, [and] broke it" (Luke 24:30). He thanked His Father as
He had earlier when He'd fed the five thousand with five "loaves and
two small fish" (John 6:9).

When we give thanks for our daily meals and for other provisions, our gratitude reflects Jesus's ways and honors our heavenly
Father. Let's give thanks to God today.   *Katara Patton*

**Giving thanks for our daily bread, or
meals, models Jesus's example.**

PEOPLE POWER

Ephesians 4:7–16

The whole body, joined and held together by every
supporting ligament, grows and builds itself up in
love, as each part does its work. —Ephesians 4:16

A man was boarding a train in Perth, Australia, when he slipped and his leg got caught in the gap between the train carriage and the station platform. Dozens of passengers quickly came to his rescue. They used their sheer might to tilt the train away from the platform, and the trapped man was freed! The train service's spokesman, David Hynes, said in an interview, "Everyone sort of pitched in. It was people power that saved someone from possibly a quite serious injury."

In Ephesians 4, we read that people power is God's plan for building up His family. He has given each of us a special gift of His grace (v. 7) for the specific purpose that "the whole body, joined and held together by every supporting ligament, grows and builds itself up in love, as each part does its work" (v. 16).

Every person has a job to do in God's family; there are no spectators. In God's family we weep and laugh together. We bear each other's burdens. We pray for and encourage one another. We challenge and help each other to turn from sin. *Show us, Father, our part in helping your family today.*   *Poh Fang Chia*

**Every person has a job to do in God's
family; there are no spectators.**

NOTHING BUT GRACE

Luke 17:6–10

We are unworthy servants; we have only
done our duty. —Luke 17:10

In 1914, before the use of insulin injections, Corrie ten Boom's Aunt Jans was diagnosed with diabetes. She knew she did not have long to live. Yet, within a few days after learning this, she went right back to working in God-honoring causes. Several months later, a blood test indicated that the end was near.

The family was gathered in Aunt Jans's room when Corrie's father gently broke the news to her. Then he added, "Jans, some must go to their Father empty-handed, but you will run to Him with hands full."

Jans's response touched them all. She said that her good deeds were as "little tricks and trinkets." Then she prayed, "Dear Jesus, I thank you that we must come with empty hands. I thank you that you have done all—all—on the cross, and that all we need in life or death is to be sure of this."

Jesus reminded us that even after we've served Him faithfully, we have merely done our duty (Luke 17:10). Yet, on another occasion He indicated that one day He would honor us for our faithfulness (12:37). How can this be? Because all that we have, even the ability to serve the Lord, comes to us as a gracious gift from Him.

Remember, from beginning to end, everything is of grace.

Herb Vander Lugt

**Everything we have, even the ability to serve the
Lord, comes to us as a gracious gift from Him.**

GOD'S GREAT LOVE

Lamentations 3:19–26

Because of the LORD's great love we are not consumed,
for his compassions never fail. —Lamentations 3:22

When a friend asked me to speak with teenage girls at a workshop promoting purity, I declined. As a teenage runaway myself, I struggled and had decades of scars caused by my immorality. After getting married and losing our first child to a miscarriage, I thought God was punishing me for my past sins.

When I finally surrendered my life to Christ at the age of thirty, I confessed my sins and repented . . . repeatedly. Still, guilt and shame consumed me. How could I share about God's grace when I couldn't even bring myself to fully receive the gift of His great love for me? Thankfully, over time, God has abolished the lies that chained me to who I was before I confessed my sins. By His grace, I've finally received the forgiveness God had been offering me all along.

God understands our laments over our afflictions and the consequences of our past sins. However, He empowers His people to overcome despair, turn from our sins, and arise with hope in His great "love," "compassions," and "faithfulness" (Lamentations 3:19–23). Scripture says God himself is our "portion"—our hope and salvation—and we can learn to trust His goodness (vv. 24–26).

Our compassionate Father helps us believe His promises. When we receive the fullness of His great love for us, we can spread the good news about His grace. *Xochitl Dixon*

Our compassionate Father helps us believe His promises.

RECKLESS DECISIONS

Numbers 20:1–12

Because you did not trust in me . . . , you will not bring
this community into the land. —Numbers 20:12

As a teen, I was driving way too fast trying to follow my friend to his home after high school basketball practice. It was raining hard, and I was having a hard time keeping up with his car. Suddenly, my wipers cleared the watery windshield only to reveal my friend's sedan stopped in front of me! I slammed on the brakes, slid off the street, and struck a large tree. My car was destroyed. Later, I awoke in the comatose ward of a local hospital. While by God's grace I survived and was even able to continue playing basketball, my reckless ways had proved to be very costly.

Moses made a reckless decision that cost him greatly. His poor choice, however, involved a lack of water—not too much of it (as in my case). The Israelites were without water in the Desert of Zin, and "the people gathered in opposition to Moses" (Numbers 20:2). God told the frazzled leader to speak to a rock and it would "pour out its water" (v. 8). Instead, he "struck the rock twice" (v. 11). God said, "Because you did not trust in me . . . , you will not [enter the promised land]" (v. 12).

When we make reckless decisions, we pay the consequences. "Desire without knowledge is not good—how much more will hasty feet miss the way!" (Proverbs 19:2). May we prayerfully, carefully seek God's wisdom and guidance in the choices and decisions we make today.   *Tom Felten*

When we make reckless decisions, we pay the consequences.

"HE FOUND ME"

Luke 19:1–10

The Son of Man came to seek and to
save the lost. —Luke 19:10

The movie *Amazing Grace* was set in the late 1700s. It tells the story of William Wilberforce, a British politician who was driven by his faith in Christ to commit his money and energy to abolishing the slave trade in England. In one scene, Wilberforce's butler finds him praying. The butler asks, "You found God, Sir?" Wilberforce responds, "I think He found me."

The Bible pictures humanity as wayward and wandering sheep. It says, "All we, like sheep, have gone astray, each of us has turned to our own way" (Isaiah 53:6). In fact, this wayward condition is so deeply rooted in us that the apostle Paul said: "There is no one righteous, not even one; there is no one who understands; there is no one who seeks God. All have turned away" (Romans 3:10–12). This is why Jesus left heaven and came to earth. We would never seek Him, so He came seeking us. Jesus declared His mission with the words, "For the Son of Man came to seek and to save the lost" (Luke 19:10).

Wilberforce was exactly right. Jesus came to find us, for we could never have found Him if left to ourselves. It is a clear expression of the Creator's love for His lost creation that He pursues us and desires to make us His own.   *Bill Crowder*

Jesus came to find us, for we could never have found Him.

CHATTY BUS

Colossians 4:2–6

Let your conversation be always full of grace. —Colossians 4:6

In 2019, the Oxford Bus Company launched the instantly popular "Chatty Bus," a bus with designated people on board willing to talk with interested passengers. The route was initiated in response to government research, which found that thirty percent of Britons go at least one day each week without a meaningful conversation.

Many of us have likely experienced the loneliness that comes from not having someone to talk to in a time of need. As I reflect on the value of important conversations in my life, I'm especially reminded of discussions that were full of grace. Those times brought me joy and encouragement, and they helped to cultivate deeper relationships.

At the end of his letter to the Colossian church, Paul encouraged believers in Jesus with principles of authentic living, including ways their conversations could exhibit love to everyone they encountered. The apostle wrote, "Let your conversation be always full of grace" (4:6), reminding his readers that it is not simply the presence of words but the quality of those words—"full of grace"—that would make them a true encouragement to others.

The next time you have the opportunity to connect deeply in conversation—with a friend, coworker, or even a stranger seated next to you on a bus or in a waiting room—look for ways to use your time together to bring blessing into both your lives.   *Lisa M. Samra*

**Words "full of grace" allow us to be a
true encouragement to others.**

SONGS OF GRACE

DECEMBER

"Silent Night"

Josef Mohr and Franz Gruber

Radiant beams from Thy holy face
with the dawn of redeeming grace.

A Broken Organ, a Guitar, and a Nighttime Walk

The circumstances surrounding the origin, the first presentation, and the worldwide dissemination of the song "Silent Night" might make us think it was heaven-sent.

Let's start with the broken organ at St. Nicholas Church in December 1816. Whether it was rust or mischievous mice that shut down the church's organ during the Christmas season, we'll never know. All we know is that organist Franz Gruber couldn't get it to work.

That was bad news indeed, because the church was scheduled to host a Christmas play. The actors who had come to Oberndorf, Austria, to present the play were forced to secure another location

---

Sources: Ryan Reeves, "The History Behind 'Silent Night,'" December 11, 2016, *The Gospel Coalition*, http://tinyurl.com/2p8jr59c; "The Story Behind the Christmas Carol 'Silent Night,'" *Southern Nazarene University*, http://tinyurl.com /578dfv5f; all accessed November 6, 2023.

for their performance. The church's assistant pastor, Josef Mohr, went to see the drama. On his walk home, he decided to take a different route. That path took him to a location that overlooked the Austrian village.

With the Christmas play still fresh in his mind, Mohr stood amazed at the quiet winter's night scene in front of him. His mind drifted to a poem he had penned about the angels in Bethlehem's fields proclaiming Jesus's birth. It occurred to him that those words would work as a carol that could be used the next night—at St. Nicholas Church's Christmas Eve service.

But Mohr had no music for his words. So he enlisted the church's organist, Franz Gruber, to compose a tune for the guitar. Gruber took up his instrument and composed the tune to one of the most iconic and beautiful Christmas songs ever.

On Christmas Eve at St. Nicholas Church, Eve Mohr, accompanied by Gruber with his guitar, performed "Silent Night," or *Stille Nacht* in German.

A few weeks later, a man came to the Oberndorf church to fix the organ. Once he had it working, he asked Gruber to test it. Franz took his seat and played the new Christmas song he and the pastor had written. The repairman loved *Stille Nacht* and asked for a copy of it, which he took back to his village. There, a well-known family of singers heard it and began singing it in the area and beyond. Eventually, they took it to the United States, where its popularity continued to skyrocket.

Today "Silent Night" is considered by many to be the best Christmas carol of all time. In fact, Bing Crosby's version of the song is said to be the third-best selling song ever released.

It's amazing how God can use a broken organ and a silent night in Austria to bless His people for more than two hundred years!

Silent Night

Silent night, holy night,
All is calm, all is bright.
Round yon virgin,
Mother and Child.
Holy Infant, so tender and mild—

Sleep in heavenly peace,
Sleep in heavenly peace.

Silent night, holy night!
Shepherds quake at the sight;
Glories stream from heaven afar,
Heavenly hosts sing alleluia—
Christ the Savior is born!
Christ the Savior is born!

Silent night, holy night!
Son of God, love's pure light
Radiant beams from Thy holy face
With the dawn of redeeming grace—
Jesus, Lord at Thy birth,
Jesus, Lord at Thy birth.

ILLUSTRATING SCRIPTURE

Psalm 78:1–8

We will tell the next generation the praiseworthy deeds of the LORD, his power, and the wonders he has done. —Psalm 78:4

Decorative blue and white ceramic tiles commonly found in Dutch households were originally made in the city of Delft. They often depict familiar scenes of the Netherlands: beautiful landscapes, ubiquitous windmills, and people working and playing.

In the nineteenth century, Charles Dickens wrote in his book *A Christmas Carol* how these tiles were used to illustrate the Scriptures. He described an old fireplace built by a Dutchman paved with these quaint Delft tiles: "There were Cains and Abels, Pharaohs' daughters, Queens of Sheba, . . . [and] Apostles putting off to sea." Many households used these tiles as a teaching tool as the family gathered around the warmth of a fire and shared the stories of the Bible. They learned about God's character—His justice, compassion, and mercy.

The truths of the Bible continue to be relevant today. Psalm 78 encourages us to teach the "hidden lessons from our past—stories we have heard and known, stories our ancestors handed down to us" (vv. 2–3 NLT). The psalm goes on to instruct us to "tell the next generation the praiseworthy deeds of the LORD, his power, and the wonders he has done" and "they in turn [can] tell their children" (vv. 4, 6).

With God's help, and with or without Delft tiles, we can find creative and effective ways to illustrate the truths of Scripture to each generation. It's a great way to give God the full honor and praise He deserves.   *Cindy Hess Kasper*

The truths of the Bible continue to be relevant today.

THE GLOVES

Matthew 20:29–34

Jesus had compassion on them and touched
their eyes. —Matthew 20:34

When she shuffled into the subway, I wanted to look away. She was old, and she had only ragged clothes to protect her from the bitter Chicago winter wind. She took the nearest seat, her shoulders hunched against the cold and her eyes down. Her white, cracked, bony hands clutched a worn shawl tightly around her. I watched with wonder and pity.

At the next stop, an energetic young man strode confidently onto the train, his cheeks red with health. His clothes were sharp, his hair immaculate, his step graceful. He too saw the woman's silent misery. Three stops later, as the train slowed, he glided by her to the other door and disappeared into the tunnel.

On her lap lay his brown leather gloves.

I don't know if he was a believer in Christ or not. But I do know this: He saw her need and responded with compassion—while I just sat there. It never occurred to me to give her my gloves. That young man showed compassion in a way I'll never forget. It reminded me of the kind of compassion that moved Jesus to heal two blind men near Jericho (Matthew 20:34), and ultimately, to give His own life on the cross.

Let's follow our Lord's example by reaching out and giving hope to people in need. *David Egner*

Reach out and give hope to people in need.

LESSON FROM A TOOTHACHE

Hebrews 12:3–11

Endure hardship as discipline; God is treating
you as his children. —Hebrews 12:7

"When I was a child I often had a toothache," wrote C. S. Lewis in his classic book *Mere Christianity*. He continued, "And I knew that if I went to my mother she would give me something that would deaden the pain for that night and let me get to sleep. But I did not go to my mother—at least not till the pain became very bad . . . because I knew she would take me to the dentist the next morning. . . . I wanted immediate relief from pain, but I could not get it without having my teeth set permanently right."

Similarly, we might not always want to go to God right away when we have a problem or are struggling in a certain area. We know that He could provide immediate relief from our pain but that He is more concerned with dealing with the root of the problem. We may be afraid He will reveal issues we are unprepared or unwilling to deal with.

In times like these, it is helpful to remind ourselves that the Lord "is treating you as his children" (Hebrews 12:7). His discipline, though perhaps painful, is wise, and His touch is loving. He loves us too much to let us remain as we are; He wants to conform us to the likeness of His Son, Jesus (Romans 8:29). God's purposes of love can be trusted more than any of our emotions of fear.   *Poh Fang Chia*

**The Lord's discipline, though perhaps painful,
is wise, and His touch is loving.**

GROW, BABY, GROW!

1 Peter 2:1–12

Like newborn babies, crave pure spiritual milk, so that by
it you may grow up in your salvation. —1 Peter 2:2

Whenever children visit relatives, they often hear this kind of greeting: "My, how you've grown!" This embarrasses the children, but inside they're glad they've outgrown babyhood. Not that babyhood is bad. How else can life begin? But it is sad when babies remain babies.

Sometimes mature Christians, eager to keep new converts from stagnating in their growth, make them feel guilty for being babies and rush them down the road to maturity before they are ready.

In 1 Peter 2, the apostle affirmed that spiritual babyhood is normal. Instead of forcing newborns to run before they can walk, he encouraged them to crave the wholesome milk of Christ's basic teaching. He knew that as they continued to take in milk, in time they would move on to solid food and maturity (Hebrews 5:14). What a joy to see that happen!

Several years ago, I received a phone call from a friend, a former drug addict and now a Christian. "Hi, Chris," I responded cheerily. "How are you doing?" A long, worrisome pause made me wonder, *Had he slipped back?* Then came words that uplifted my heart: "Growing, Joanie, growing!" That said it all.

I hope you can say the same. *Joanie Yoder*

Crave the wholesome milk of Christ's basic teaching.

THE LIFE THAT MATTERS

1 Peter 5:1–7

Remember your leaders, who spoke the word of
God to you. Consider the outcome of their way of
life and imitate their faith. —Hebrews 13:7

Isaac Hann was a little-known pastor who served a small church in
Loughwood, England, in the mid-eighteenth century. At the close
of his ministry, the membership of the church numbered twenty-six
women and seven men. And only four of the men attended with any
regularity.

In this age of mass media and megachurches, who would consider
Hann's work successful? Today, Isaac Hann would be considered one
of those pastors who never quite "made it." He certainly wouldn't have
been invited to speak at pastors' conferences, nor would he have written articles on church growth.

Yet, when he died at age eighty-eight, his parishioners placed a
plaque on the wall of their meetinghouse that remains to this day.
It reads in part:

Few ministers so humble were, yet few so much admired:
Ripened for heaven by grace divine, like autumn fruit he fell;
Reader think not to live so long, but seek to live as well.

First Peter 5:5–6 comes to mind: "'God opposes the proud but
shows favor to the humble.' Humble yourselves, therefore, under
God's mighty hand, that he may lift you up in due time." Rev. Isaac
Hann "made it big" in a way that matters—humility before God
and a reward in heaven. We can too. *David Roper*

**"Humble yourselves . . . under God's
mighty hand." —1 Peter 5:6**

WHEN SHARKS DON'T BITE

Proverbs 27:1–10

One who is full loathes honey from the comb. —Proverbs 27:7

My children were thrilled, but I felt uneasy. During a vacation, we visited an aquarium where people could pet small sharks kept in a special tank. When I asked the attendant if the creatures ever snapped at fingers, she explained that the sharks had recently been fed and then given extra food. They wouldn't bite, because they weren't hungry.

What I learned about shark petting makes sense according to a proverb: "One who is full loathes honey from the comb, but to the hungry even what is bitter tastes sweet" (Proverbs 27:7). Hunger—that sense of inner emptiness—can weaken our discernment as we make decisions. It convinces us that it's okay to settle for anything that fills us up, even if it causes us to take a bite out of someone.

God wants more for us than a life lived at the mercy of our appetites. He wants us to be filled with Christ's love so that everything we do flows from the peace and stability He provides. The constant awareness that we're unconditionally loved gives us confidence. It enables us to be selective as we consider the "sweet" things in life—achievements, possessions, and relationships.

Only a relationship with Jesus gives true satisfaction. May we grasp His incredible love for us so we can be "filled to the measure [with] all the fullness of God" (Ephesians 3:19) for our sake—and the sake of others.   *Jennifer Benson Schuldt*

God wants us to be filled with Christ's love so that everything we do flows from the peace and stability He provides.

MAKE PEACE

2 Corinthians 5:17–20

God . . . gave us the ministry of
reconciliation. —2 Corinthians 5:18

It was a dramatic story of forgiveness. In December of 2000, on the
Battleship Missouri Memorial in Hawaii, a dozen American sur-
vivors of the attack on Pearl Harbor embraced three of the Japanese
pilots who had flown attacking planes. The reconciliation ceremony
had been arranged by the American-Japan Friendship Committee.

That moving scene is only a dim reflection of what God's grace
does for us. Although we are sinful, we can be brought into a relationship with God through simple faith in Jesus. Because He died
on the cross in our place, God blots out the record of our sins and
makes us right with Him.

The Lord in His amazing love has not only forgiven us but has
given to us "the ministry of reconciliation" (2 Corinthians 5:18). We
have the honor of sharing the good news with others so they too can
be at peace with God. And when we're right with God, we're also
to do what we can to live at peace with everyone (Romans 12:18).

Have you accepted God's offer of forgiveness in Christ? Are you
telling others about His love? And are you an agent of God's grace
in your relationships? Start today—make peace.   *Vernon Grounds*

We have the honor of sharing the good news with others.

HOW A TREE GROWS

Philippians 1:1–7

Grow in the grace and knowledge of our Lord
and Savior Jesus Christ. —2 Peter 3:18

An impatient student at a Christian college went to a school official and asked if he could take an accelerated course that would allow him to graduate sooner. "Yes," the administrator replied, "but it depends on what you want to be. When God wants to make an oak, he takes a hundred years. But when He wants to make a squash, He takes six months."

Like that student did with his education, we sometimes get frustrated with the rate of our spiritual growth. We'd like to see ourselves a lot closer to maturity than we are. We're disappointed that we fall back into childish behavior we thought we had outgrown. We want "school" to be over.

But growth takes time, and it often comes in spurts. Trees grow rapidly during a four-to-six-week period in early summer, when woody fibers appear between the bark and the trunk. During the remainder of the year, these fibers solidify into the sturdy wood from which furniture is built, which will last several lifetimes.

Not growing as fast in your Christian life as you'd like to grow? Perhaps you're "solidifying." It's a vital part of the process that the One who began a good work in you will bring to completion (Philippians 1:6). Be patient. God isn't finished with you yet.

David Egner

Be patient; God's not done with you.

PUBLIC PRAISE

Psalm 96

Declare his glory among the nations, his marvelous
deeds among all peoples. —Psalm 96:3

I love the YouTube video of people in a food court of a mall, who
in the midst of their ordinary lives were suddenly interrupted by
someone who stood up and boldly began singing the "Hallelujah
Chorus."

To the surprise of everyone, another person got up and joined
the chorus, and then another, and another. Soon the food court was
resounding with the celebrative harmonies of Handel's masterpiece.
A local opera company had planted their singers in strategic places
so they could joyfully interject the glory of God into the everyday
lives of lunching shoppers.

Every time I watch that video, it moves me to tears. It reminds
me that bringing the glory of God into the ordinary situations of our
world through the beautiful harmonies of Christlikeness is exactly
what we are called to do. Think of intentionally interjecting God's
grace into a situation where some undeserving soul needs a second
chance; of sharing the love of Christ with someone who is needy; of
being the hands of Jesus that lift a weary friend; or of bringing peace
to a confusing and chaotic situation.

As the psalmist reminds us, we have the high and holy privilege of declaring "his glory among the nations, his marvelous deeds
among all peoples" (Psalm 96:3).   *Joe Stowell*

**Bringing the glory of God into the ordinary situations
of our world through the beautiful harmonies of
Christlikeness is exactly what we are called to do.**

GRACE AND GLORY

Psalm 84:5–12

The LORD will give grace and glory; no good thing will He withhold from those who walk uprightly. —Psalm 84:11 NKJV

There's a circular path in the park where I walk behind our home in Boise, Idaho. When I've walked three times around, I've gone one mile.

It's easy to lose count of the laps on my three-mile walk. So, each morning I pick up nine small stones and put them in my pocket, discarding one each time I finish a lap.

I always feel good when there's one stone left in my pocket. It puts spring in my step. I pick up the pace.

It occurs to me that my walk through life is a lot like these daily walks. I've completed fourscore and ten years and don't have far to go. This too puts spring in my step.

I'm in no hurry to leave this life, but my times are in God's hands. As my body is breaking down under the weight of the years, there is a grace within that sustains me. I go now "from strength to strength," and in good time I will appear "before God in Zion" (Psalm 84:7 NKJV). That will be glory for me.

Our Lord gives "grace and glory," the psalmist says—grace for our earthly walk and glory when we have finished it. "No good thing will He withhold from those who walk uprightly" (v. 11 NKJV).

Do you need grace today? God gives it with both hands. All you have to do is take it.   *David Roper*

**Our Lord gives grace for our earthly walk
and glory when we have finished it.**

SPIRITUAL RENEWAL

2 Corinthians 4:16–18

Though outwardly we are wasting away, yet inwardly we
are being renewed day by day. —2 Corinthians 4:16

Chinese medicine has practiced pearl powder exfoliation for thousands of years, using ground pearls to scrub away dead cells resting at the top of the skin. In Romania, rejuvenating therapeutic mud has become a widely sought-after exfoliant that's purported to make skin youthful and glowing. All over the world, people use body care practices they believe will renew even the dullest of skin.

The tools we've developed to maintain our physical bodies, however, can only bring us temporary satisfaction. What matters more is that we remain spiritually healthy and strong. As believers in Jesus, we're given the gift of spiritual renewal through Him. The apostle Paul wrote, "Though outwardly we are wasting away, yet inwardly we are being renewed day by day" (2 Corinthians 4:16).

The challenges we face daily can weigh us down when we hold on to things like fear, hurt, and anxiety. Spiritual renewal comes when we "fix our eyes not on what is seen, but on what is unseen" (v. 18). We do this by turning our daily worries over to God and praying for the fruit of the Holy Spirit—including love, joy, and peace—to emerge anew in our lives (Galatians 5:22–23). When we release our troubles to God and allow His Spirit to radiate through us each day, He restores our souls. *Kimya Loder*

**Spiritual renewal comes when we turn our daily worries
over to God and pray for the fruit of the Holy Spirit.**

SEPARATED—NOT ISOLATED

John 17:14–18

My prayer is not that you take them out of the world but
that you protect them from the evil one. —John 17:15

Having spent time on a deserted island, a marooned sailor was
overjoyed one day to see a ship drop anchor in the bay. A small
boat came ashore and an officer handed him a bunch of newspapers.
"The captain suggests," said the officer, "that you read what's going
on in the world, and then let us know if you want to be rescued!"

The Christian has no such choice. We have been placed by divine decree in the midst of this world of trouble, sin, and distress.
When God saved our souls by His grace, He could have transported
us immediately into heaven. At times we push the "panic button,"
as Elijah did, and cry, "I have had enough, LORD, . . . Take my life"
(1 Kings 19:4). However, it's God's purpose that we should remain
in the world—not to be partakers of its evil deeds or to compromise
with its iniquity, but to be examples of His grace. Having been redeemed, we are now left to serve Him.

We are to be a separated people, but not an isolated one. Jesus
prayed, "Protect them from the evil one," (John 17:15). The Christian is to "keep oneself from being polluted by the world" (James
1:27) and to be an example of holiness. Sanctified by His Word, we
are to be both "salt" and "light" here.

Isolation would mean losing any chance for sharing the gospel,
but separation from evil will result in a pure and powerful testimony.

Paul Van Gorder

We are to be a separated people, but not an isolated one.

WARTS AND ALL

Colossians 3:12–15

Forgive as the Lord forgave you. —Colossians 3:13

Oliver Cromwell, England's first Lord Protector, was also a military commander in the seventeenth century. It was common practice during those pre-photography days for people of importance to have their portraits painted. And it wasn't unusual for an artist to avoid depicting the less attractive aspects of a person's face. Cromwell, however, wanted nothing to do with a likeness that would flatter him. He cautioned the artist, "You must paint me just as I am—warts and all—or I won't pay you."

Apparently, the artist complied. The finished portrait of Cromwell displays a couple of prominent facial warts that today would surely be photoshopped out before being posted on social media.

The expression "warts and all" has come to mean that people should be accepted just as they are—with all their annoying faults, attitudes, and issues. In some cases, we feel this is too difficult a task. Yet, when we take a hard inward look, we might find some rather unattractive aspects of our own character.

We're grateful God forgives our "warts." And in Colossians 3, we're taught to extend grace to others. The apostle Paul encourages us to be more patient, kind, and compassionate—even to those who aren't easy to love. He urges us to have a forgiving spirit because of the way God forgives us (vv. 12–13). By His example, we're taught to love others the way God loves us—warts and all.

Cindy Hess Kasper

The apostle Paul encourages us to be more patient, kind, and compassionate—even to those who aren't easy to love.

GOD CLEANS THE STAINS

Isaiah 1:10–18

Though your sins are like scarlet, they shall be as
white as snow; though they are red as crimson,
they shall be like wool. —Isaiah 1:18

What if our clothes were more functional, having the ability to clean themselves after we dropped ketchup or mustard or spilled a drink on them? Well, according to the BBC, engineers in China have developed a special "coating which causes cotton to clean itself of stains and odors when exposed to ultraviolet lights." Can you imagine the implications of having self-cleaning clothes?

A self-cleaning coating might work for stained clothes, but only God can clean a stained soul. In ancient Judah, God was angry with His people because they had "turned their backs on" Him, given themselves to corruption and evil, and were worshiping false gods (Isaiah 1:2–4). To make matters worse, they tried to clean themselves by offering sacrifices, burning incense, saying many prayers, and gathering together in solemn assemblies. Yet their hypocritical and sinful hearts remained (vv. 12–13). The remedy was for them to come to their senses and with a repentant heart bring the stains on their souls to a holy and loving God. His grace would cleanse them and make them spiritually "white as snow" (v. 18).

When we sin, there's no self-cleaning solution. With a humble and repentant heart, we must acknowledge our sins and place them under the cleansing light of God's holiness. We must turn from them and return to Him. And He, the only One who cleans the stains of the soul, will offer us complete forgiveness and renewed fellowship.

Marvin Williams

**With a humble and repentant heart, we must
acknowledge our sins and place them under
the cleansing light of God's holiness.**

GOD-PAVED MEMORIES

Deuteronomy 4:3–10

Assemble the people before me to hear my words so that
they may learn to revere me. —Deuteronomy 4:10

When my grown son faced a difficult situation, I reminded him about God's constant care and provision during his dad's year of unemployment. I recounted the times God strengthened our family and gave us peace while my mom fought and lost her battle with leukemia. Highlighting the stories of God's faithfulness stitched into Scripture, I affirmed that He is good at keeping His word. I led my son down our family's God-paved memory lane, reminding him about the ways He remained reliable through our valley and mountaintop moments. Whether we were struggling or celebrating, God's presence, love, and grace proved sufficient.

Although I'd like to claim this faith-strengthening strategy as my own, God designed the habit of sharing stories to inspire the future generations' belief in Him. As the Israelites remembered everything they had seen God do in the past, He placed cobblestones of confidence down their divinely paved memory lanes.

The Israelites had witnessed God holding true to His promises as they followed Him (Deuteronomy 4:3–6). He'd always heard and answered their prayers (v. 7). Rejoicing and reminiscing with the younger generations (v. 9), the Israelites shared the holy words breathed and preserved by the one true God (v. 10).

As we tell of our great God's majesty, mercy, and intimate love, our convictions and the faith of others can be strengthened by the confirmation of His enduring trustworthiness.   *Xochitl Dixon*

**God designed the habit of sharing stories to
inspire the future generations' belief in Him.**

ALWAYS ACCEPTED

Luke 19:1–10

Today salvation has come to this house. —Luke 19:9

After a few years of struggling to keep up with her classmates, Angie was finally taken out of her elite elementary school and transferred to a "normal" one. In Singapore's intensely competitive education landscape, where being in a "good" school can improve one's future prospects, many would see this as a failure.

Angie's parents were disappointed, and Angie herself felt as if she had been demoted. But soon after joining her new school, the nine-year-old realized what it meant to be in a class of average students. "Mummy, I belong here," she said. "I'm finally accepted!"

This reminds me of how excited Zacchaeus must have felt when Jesus invited himself to the tax collector's home (Luke 19:5). Christ was interested in dining with those who knew they were flawed and didn't deserve God's grace (v. 10). Having found us—and loved us—as we were, Jesus gives us the promise of perfection through His death and resurrection. We are made perfect through His grace alone.

I've often found my spiritual journey to be one of constant struggle, knowing that my life falls far short of God's ideal. How comforting it is to know that we are always accepted, for the Holy Spirit is in the business of molding us to be like Jesus.   *Leslie Koh*

Christ was interested in dining with those who knew they were flawed and didn't deserve God's grace.

GOD'S ARMS ARE OPEN

1 John 1:5–10

If we confess our sins, he is faithful and just
and will forgive us. —1 John 1:9

I frowned at my cell phone and sighed. Worry wrinkled my brow. A friend and I had had a serious disagreement over an issue with our children, and I knew I needed to call her and apologize. I didn't want to do it, because our viewpoints were still in conflict. Yet I knew I hadn't been kind or humble the last time we discussed the matter.

Anticipating the phone call, I wondered, *What if she doesn't forgive me? What if she doesn't want to continue our friendship?* Just then, lyrics to a song came to mind and took me back to the moment when I confessed my sin in the situation to God. I felt relief because I knew God had forgiven me and released me from guilt.

We can't control how people will respond to us when we try to work out relational problems. As long as we own up to our part, humbly ask for forgiveness, and make any changes needed, we can let God handle the healing. Even if we have to endure the pain of unresolved "people problems," peace with God is always possible.

His arms are open, and He is waiting to show us the grace and mercy we need. "If we confess our sins, he is faithful and just and will forgive us our sins and purify us from all unrighteousness" (1 John 1:9).   *Jennifer Benson Schuldt*

God is waiting to show us the grace and mercy we need.

LIGHT UP THE WORLD!

1 John 2:7–11

I am the light of the world. Whoever follows me will never walk in darkness, but will have the light of life. —John 8:12

One dark and ominous night during World War II, a US aircraft carrier was plowing through heavy seas in the South Pacific. All lights were out because enemy submarines were nearby. One plane was missing. Somewhere in that pitch-black sky it was circling in a seemingly futile search for the carrier—its only landing place, its only hope of not being swallowed up by the giant ocean. The ship's captain, knowing the terrible risk involved, gave the order, "Light up the ship." Soon the plane zoomed onto the deck like a homing pigeon.

At Bethlehem, knowing the risk, God gave the command, "Light up the world." Then Jesus was born. A new and radiant light began to shine, pushing back the darkness of the world, of spiritual ignorance, and of sin and despair. Like a ship lit up in an otherwise darkened sea of sinful humanity, Christ came as "the light of the world" (John 8:12). John also wrote, "The darkness is passing and the true light is already shining" (1 John 2:8). When Jesus the Savior entered this world, it was like the sunrise breaking radiantly over the horizon of human history (Luke 1:78–79).

In fathomless grace, God allowed His Son to die on the cross to save us from eternal darkness. What a blessed message! The light has come!   *Vernon Grounds*

When Jesus the Savior entered this world, it was like the sunrise breaking radiantly over the horizon of human history.

GOD ALONE CAN SATISFY

Genesis 25:29–34

When Jacob was cooking some stew, Esau came in [and]
said to Jacob, . . . "I'm famished!" —Genesis 25:29–30

A thousand dollars of food—jumbo shrimp, shawarma, sal-
ads, and more—was delivered to a homeowner. But the man
wasn't having a party. In fact, he didn't order the smorgasbord; his
six-year-old son did.

How did this happen? The father let his son play with his phone
before bedtime, and the boy used it to purchase the expensive bounty
from a restaurant. "Why did you do this?" the father asked his son,
who was hiding under his comforter. The six-year-old replied, "I was
hungry." The boy's appetite and immaturity led to a costly outcome.

Esau's appetite cost him a lot more than a thousand dollars. The
story in Genesis 25 finds him exhausted and desperate for food.
He said to his brother, "Let me have some of that red stew! I'm
famished!" (v. 30). Jacob responded by asking for Esau's birthright
(v. 31). The birthright included Esau's special place as the firstborn
son, the blessing of God's promises, a double portion of the inheritance, and the privilege of being the spiritual leader of the family.
Giving in to his appetite, Esau "ate and drank" and "despised his
birthright" (v. 34).

When we're tempted and desiring something, instead of letting
our appetites lead us to costly mistakes and sin, let's reach out to
our heavenly Father—the One who alone satisfies the hungry soul
"with good things" (Psalm 107:9).   *Marvin Williams*

**When we're desiring something, instead of letting our
appetites lead us awry, let's reach out to our heavenly Father.**

NOT PERFECT

Romans 7:14–15

The evil I do not want to do—this I
keep on doing. —Romans 7:19

In his book *Jumping Through Fires*, David Nasser tells the story of
his spiritual journey. Before he began a relationship with Jesus,
he was befriended by a group of Christian teens. Although most of
the time his buddies were generous, winsome, and nonjudgmental,
David witnessed one of them lie to his girlfriend. Feeling convicted,
the young man later confessed and asked for her forgiveness. Reflecting on this, David said that the incident drew him closer to
his Christian friends. He realized they needed grace, just as he did.

We don't have to act like we're perfect with the people we know.
It's okay to be honest about our mistakes and struggles. The apostle
Paul openly referred to himself as the worst of all sinners (1 Timothy 1:15). He also described his wrestling match with sin in Romans 7, where he said, "I have the desire to do what is good, but
I cannot carry it out" (v. 18). Unfortunately, the opposite was also
true: "The evil I do not want to do—this I keep on doing" (v. 19).

Being open about our struggles puts us on the same level with
every other human alive—which is right where we belong! However, because of Jesus Christ, our sin will not follow us into eternity.
It's like the old saying goes, "Christians aren't perfect, just forgiven."

Jennifer Benson Schuldt

It's okay to be honest about our mistakes and struggles.

SEEING GOD IN FAMILIAR PLACES

Isaiah 6:1–6

The whole earth is full of [God's] glory. —Isaiah 6:3

Because of where I live, I'm treated to spectacular displays of the magnificent, creative glory of God. Recently, on a drive through the woods, I was struck with a breathtaking display of deep rich reds and a variety of yellows that decorated the trees of autumn—all artfully arranged against the backdrop of a brilliant blue sky.

And as soon as the temperatures plummet and winter blows in, I'm reminded that no two snowflakes are ever the same as they pile on top of one another to create a rolling landscape of pristine white drifts. After that comes the miracle of spring, when that which seemed hopelessly dead bursts into life with buds and blossoms that will grace the meadows with a multiplicity of colors.

Wherever we look in the world around us, we see evidence that "the whole earth is full of his glory" (Isaiah 6:3). What is amazing is that the creation that surrounds us is damaged by sin (see Romans 8:18–22), yet God has seen fit to grace our fallen landscape with these loving brushstrokes of His creative hand. It serves as a daily reminder that the beauty of His grace covers our sin and that His love for that which is fallen is always available to us.   *Joe Stowell*

**God has seen fit to grace our fallen landscape with
these loving brushstrokes of His creative hand.**

A MISSING SHEEP

Luke 15:1–10

We are [God's] people, the sheep of his pasture. —Psalm 100:3

Laura loaded a goat and a sheep that she had borrowed into a trailer to transport them to church for a rehearsal of a live nativity. The animals head-butted and chased each other for a bit and then settled down. Laura started for the church but first had to stop for gas.

While pumping the gas, she noticed the goat standing in the parking lot! And the sheep was gone! In the commotion of getting them settled, she had forgotten to lock one of the latches. Laura called the sheriff and some friends, who searched frantically along a stretch of businesses, cornfields, and woods during the last daylight hours. Many were praying that she would find the borrowed animal.

The next morning Laura and a friend went out to post "Lost Sheep" flyers at local businesses. Their first stop was the gas station. A customer overheard them asking the cashier about posting a flyer and said, "I think I know where your sheep is!" The sheep had wandered to his neighbor's farm, where he had put it in the barn for the night.

The Lord cares about lost sheep—including you and me. Jesus came from heaven to earth to show us His love and provide salvation (John 3:16). He goes to great lengths to seek and find us (Luke 19:10).

When the sheep was found, Laura nicknamed her Miracle. And God's salvation of us is a miracle of His grace.   *Anne Cetas*

The Lord cares about lost sheep—including you and me.

CHRISTMAS-CARD PERFECT

John 7:1–9

Even his own brothers did not believe in him. —John 7:5

The Barker family Christmas video was perfect. Three robe-clad shepherds (the family's young sons) huddled around a fire in a grassy field. Suddenly an angel descended from the hilltop—their big sister, looking resplendent, except for the pink high-top sneakers. As the soundtrack swelled, the shepherds stared skyward in amazement. A trek across a field led them to a real baby—their infant brother in a modern barn. Big sister now played the role of Mary.

Then came the "bonus features," when their dad let us peek behind the scenes. Whiny kids complained, "I'm cold." "I have to go to the bathroom right now!" "Can we go home?" "Guys, pay attention," said their mom more than once. Reality was far from Christmas-card perfect.

It's easy to view the original Christmas story through the lens of a well-edited final cut. But Jesus's life was anything but smooth. A jealous Herod tried to kill Him in infancy (Matthew 2:13). Mary and Joseph misunderstood Him (Luke 2:41–50). The world hated Him (John 7:7). For a time, "even his own brothers did not believe in him" (7:5). His mission led to a grisly death. But He did it all to honor His Father and rescue us.

The Barkers' video ended with these words of Jesus: "I am the way and the truth and the life. No one comes to the Father except through me" (John 14:6). That's a reality we can live with—forever.

Tim Gustafson

Jesus went through it all to honor His Father and rescue us.

THE POWER OF GOD'S WORD

Isaiah 55:6–13

[My word] will not return to me empty, but will
accomplish what I desire. —Isaiah 55:11

On Christmas Eve 1968, Apollo 8 astronauts Frank Borman, Jim
Lovell, and Bill Anders became the first humans to enter lunar
orbit. As they circled the moon ten times, they shared images of the
moon and the Earth. During a live broadcast, they took turns reading from Genesis 1.

At the fortieth anniversary celebration of the event, Borman said,
"We were told that on Christmas Eve we would have the largest audience that had ever listened to a human voice. And the only instruc-
tions that we got from NASA was to do something appropriate." The
Bible verses spoken by the Apollo 8 astronauts still plant seeds of truth
into the listening hearts of people who hear the historical recording.

Through the prophet Isaiah, God says, "Give ear and come to
me; listen, that you may live" (Isaiah 55:3). Revealing His free offer
of salvation, God invites us to turn from our sin and receive His
mercy and forgiveness (vv. 6–7). He declares the divine authority
of His thoughts and His actions, which are too vast for us to truly
understand (vv. 8–9). Still, God gives us opportunity to share His
life-transforming words of Scripture, which point to Jesus, and affirm that He is responsible for the spiritual growth of His people
(vv. 10–13).

The Holy Spirit helps us share the gospel as the Father fulfills all
His promises according to His perfect plan and pace. *Xochitl Dixon*

**God gives us opportunity to share His life-transforming
words of Scripture, which point to Jesus.**

ALL IS WELL

Psalm 46:1–3

I will never leave you nor forsake you. —Hebrews 13:5 NKJV

A few years ago, my husband and I were reacquainted with a young man we had known as a child many years earlier. We fondly reminisced about a Christmas program when Matthew had sung—in a perfect boy soprano—the song "All Is Well" by Wayne Kirkpatrick and Michael W. Smith. It was a wonderful memory of a song beautifully sung, telling us that all is well because our Savior has been born.

To hear the words of that song at Christmastime is comforting to many. But some people are unable to absorb the message because their lives are in turmoil. They've experienced the loss of a loved one, persistent unemployment, a serious illness, or depression that will not go away. Their hearts loudly cry out, "All is not well—not for me!"

For those of us who celebrate the birth of our Savior—despite the dark night of the soul we may experience—all is well because of Christ. We are not alone in our pain. God is beside us and promises never to leave (Hebrews 13:5). He promises that His grace will be sufficient (2 Corinthians 12:9). He promises to supply all our needs (Philippians 4:19). And He promises us the amazing gift of eternal life (John 10:27–28).

As we review God's promises, we can agree with the poet John Greenleaf Whittier, who wrote, "Before me, even as behind, God is, and all is well."

Cindy Hess Kasper

God is beside us and promises never to leave.

THE DAY AFTER CHRISTMAS

Luke 2:15–20

*Mary treasured up all these things and pondered
them in her heart. —Luke 2:19*

After all the joy of Christmas Day, the following day felt like a let-down. We'd stayed overnight with friends but hadn't slept well. Then our car broke down as we were driving home. Then it started to snow. We abandoned the car and taxied home in the snow and sleet feeling blah.

We're not the only ones who've felt low after Christmas Day. Whether it's from excessive eating, the way carols suddenly disappear from the radio, or the fact that the gifts we bought last week are now on sale half price, the magic of Christmas Day can quickly dissipate!

The Bible never tells us about the day after Jesus's birth. But we can imagine that after walking to Bethlehem, scrambling for accommodations, experiencing pain in childbirth, and having shepherds drop by unannounced (Luke 2:4–18), Mary and Joseph were exhausted. Yet as Mary cradled her newborn, I can imagine her reflecting on her angelic visitation (1:30–33), Elizabeth's blessing (vv. 42–45), and her own realization of her baby's destiny (vv. 46–55). Mary "pondered" such things in her heart (2:19), which must've lightened the tiredness and physical pain of that day.

We'll all have "blah" days, perhaps even the day after Christmas. Like Mary, let's face them by pondering the One who came into our world, forever brightening it with His presence.   *Sheridan Voysey*

**Let's ponder Jesus, the One who came into our
world, forever brightening it with His presence.**

PAIN'S PURPOSE

Hebrews 12:7–11

No discipline seems pleasant at the time, but
painful. Later on, however, it produces a harvest of
righteousness and peace. —Hebrews 12:11

Affliction, when we accept it with patience and humility, can
lead us to a deeper, fuller life. "Before I was afflicted I went
astray," David wrote, "but now I obey your word" (Psalm 119:67).
He goes on, saying, "It is good for me to be afflicted so that I might
learn your decrees" (v. 71).

Pain, far from being an obstacle to our spiritual growth, can actually be the pathway to it. If we allow pain to train us, it can lead
us closer to God and into His Word. It is often the means by which
our Father graciously shapes us to be like His Son, gradually giving
us the courage, compassion, contentment, and tranquility we long
and pray for. Without pain, God would not accomplish all that He
desires to do in and through us.

Is God instructing you through suffering and pain? By His grace,
you can endure His instruction patiently (2 Corinthians 12:9). He
can make the trial a blessing and use it to draw you into His heart
and into His Word. He can also teach you the lessons He intends for
you to learn and give you His peace in the midst of your difficulties.

The Bible tells us, "Consider it pure joy . . . whenever you face
trials of many kinds" (James 1:2). God is making more out of you
than you ever thought possible. *David Roper*

**If we allow pain to train us, it can lead us
closer to God and into His Word.**

OVERCOMING

Genesis 50:7–21

You intended to harm me, but God intended it
for good to accomplish what is now being done,
the saving of many lives. —Genesis 50:20

Anne grew up in poverty and pain. Two of her siblings died in infancy. At five, an eye disease left her partially blind and unable to read or write. When Anne was eight, her mother died from tuberculosis. Shortly after, her abusive father abandoned his three surviving children. The youngest was sent to live with relatives, but Anne and her brother, Jimmie, went to Tewksbury Almshouse, a dilapidated, overcrowded poorhouse. A few months later, Jimmie died.

At age fourteen, Anne's circumstances brightened. She was sent to a school for the blind, where she underwent surgery to improve her vision and learned to read and write. Though she struggled to fit in, she excelled academically and graduated valedictorian. Today we know her best as Anne Sullivan, Helen Keller's teacher and companion. Through effort, patience, and love, Anne taught blind and deaf Helen to speak, to read Braille, and to graduate from college.

Joseph too had to overcome extreme trials: at seventeen, he was sold into slavery by his jealous brothers and was later wrongly imprisoned (Genesis 37; 39–41). Yet God used him to save Egypt and his family from famine (50:20).

We all face trials and troubles. But just as God helped Anne and Joseph to overcome and to deeply impact the lives of others, He can help and use us. Seek Him for help and guidance. He sees and hears.   *Alyson Kieda*

**We all face trials and troubles. But just as God
helped Joseph, He can help and use us.**

WHERE TO LOOK

Romans 8:35–39

Let us run . . . , fixing our eyes on Jesus. —Hebrews 12:1–2

Let's see. What is the crisis of the day? It could be terrorism and its random threat. Or the economy and the fear that we'll run out of money before we run out of time. Maybe it's a personal crisis with no foreseeable solution—a tragedy or a failure too great to bear.

Before we fall under the weight of our accumulated fears, we would do well to look back to a twentieth-century woman who bore sadness, pain, and heartache with grace.

Corrie ten Boom lived through the hellish life of Nazi concentration camps—a place where hope was lost for most people. She survived to tell her story of unfaltering faith and tightfisted hope in God.

She saw the face of evil up close and personal. She saw some of the most inhumane acts man can do to man. And when she came out of it all, she said this: "If you look at the world, you'll be distressed. If you look within, you'll be depressed. But if you look at Christ, you'll be at rest."

Where are you looking? Are you focusing on the world and its dangers? Are you gazing at yourself, hoping to find your own answers? Or are you looking to Jesus, the author and finisher of your faith (Hebrews 12:1–2)? In an uncertain world, we must keep looking to Him. *Dave Branon*

"If you look at Christ, you'll be at rest." —Corrie ten Boom

GOD'S INEXHAUSTIBLE GRACE

1 Peter 5:6–11

And the God of all grace, . . . will himself
restore you. —1 Peter 5:10

In 1 Peter 5 our Father in heaven is referred to as "the God of all grace."

Let's see what this means: He provides *justifying grace* for the believer, *illuminating grace* for the seeker, *comforting grace* for the bereaved, *strengthening grace* for the weak, *sanctifying grace* for the unholy, *living grace* for the follower of Jesus, and *dying grace* for His world-weary sons and daughters as they come to the end of life's journey. His grace is sufficient for every need.

On the island of Trinidad is a crater called La Brea Pitch Lake, which contains ten million tons of asphalt. Its surface is firm enough for people to walk on, although gas escapes from below, forming bubbles here and there. For several decades huge loads of asphalt have been dug from this tar-like lake and shipped to all parts of the world for use in paving roads. No matter how large a hole is made in the pitch, it doesn't remain for long because it fills up from below. Shiploads of asphalt have been taken out of this crater for more than a hundred years, yet it never runs empty. The supply seems to be constant and endless.

In a small way this pictures God's infinite grace, which is superabundant and never diminishes. No matter how great our problems, His love is never exhausted!

Whatever our situation, God's marvelous grace is sufficient to give us the peace, power, and security we so desperately need.

Henry Bosch

**No matter how great our problems, God's
grace and love are never exhausted!**

GOD OF NEW BEGINNINGS

Psalm 25:1–12

God opposes the proud but shows favor
to the humble. —James 4:6

"How did you learn to skate?" someone asked the winner of a competition. "By getting up every time I fell down," was the reply.

The Christian life is also a series of new beginnings, of falling down and getting up again. When we stumble, we often think, "I've failed again. I might as well give up." But God is the God of new beginnings. He not only forgives our sins but He uses our failures to make us wiser.

Sometimes our pride can cause us to resist starting again. In Psalm 25, David showed a heart of humility by praying for forgiveness. He asked the Lord to forgive the sins of his youth (v. 7), and he rejoiced that God teaches sinners (v. 8), guides and instructs the humble (v. 9), and teaches His ways to those who fear Him (v. 12).

John Newton, the composer of "Amazing Grace," expressed a similar perspective: "Though I am not what I ought to be, nor what I wish to be, nor yet what I hope to be, I can truly say I am not what I once was. . . . By the grace of God I am what I am!"

Do you feel like a failure? Do you need a new start? A new year stands in front of you. Go to the Lord in humility, and He'll show you that He's the God of new beginnings.   *Joanie Yoder*

**Go to the Lord in humility, and He'll show you
that He's the God of new beginnings.**

THE WRITERS

James Banks Pastor, Peace Church, Durham, North Carolina. Author: *Prayers for Prodigals*, *Praying the Prayers of the Bible*, and *Peace through Prayer*.

Henry Bosch (1914–1995) Original managing editor, *Our Daily Bread* (1956–1981).

Dave Branon Former senior editor, Our Daily Bread Publishing. Author: *Beyond the Valley* and *Lands of the Bible Today*.

Dave Burnham Served at Our Daily Bread Ministries as a teacher for a dozen years after a thirty-year ministry as a pastor. Current chairman of Burnham Ministries International.

Anne Cetas Former managing editor, *Our Daily Bread*. Author: *Finding Jesus in Everyday Moments*.

Poh Fang Chia Country director, Our Daily Bread Ministries, Singapore.

Peter Chin Pastor, Rainer Avenue Church, Seattle.

Winn Collier Pastor, All Souls Church, Charlottesville, Virginia. Author: *Restless Faith* and *Let God*.

Bill Crowder Former vice president of ministry content, Our Daily Bread Ministries. Author: *Windows on Christmas*, *God of Surprise*, *Gospel on the Mountains*, *Wisdom for Our Worries,* and *King Solomon*.

Lawrence Darmani Novelist and publisher in Accra, Ghana. Author: *Grief Child*.

Dennis DeHaan (1932–2014) Former editor *Our Daily Bread*.

Mart DeHaan Former president, Our Daily Bread Ministries. Author: *A Matter of Faith: Understanding True Religion*.

M. R. DeHaan, MD (1891–1965) Founder and first president, Our Daily Bread Ministries.

Richard DeHaan (1923–2002) Former president, Our Daily Bread Ministries. Founder of the ministry's national television program *Day of Discovery* (on the air 1968–2016).

Xochitl Dixon Blogs at xedixon.com. Author: *Waiting for God* and *Different Like Me*.

David Egner Former editor, Our Daily Bread Ministries. Author: *Praying with Confidence*.

Estera Pirosca Escobar Romanian by birth but living in the United States, she is National Field Director for International Friendships, Inc. Through that outreach, she has seen many international students trust Jesus as Savior.

Tom Felten Current managing editor, *Our Daily Bread*. He has a leadership role at Forest Hills Bible Chapel in Grand Rapids and serves at Michigan's Upper Peninsula Bible Camp in the summers.

Asiri Fernando serves with Youth for Christ in the mountains of Sri Lanka.

Dennis Fisher Former senior research editor, Our Daily Bread Ministries. Former chairperson: C. S. Lewis Studies Consultation for the Evangelical Theological Society.

Vernon Grounds (1914–2010) Served as president of Denver Seminary. Author: *Radical Commitment* and *YBH: Getting Serious about Your Faith*.

Tim Gustafson Editor, Discovery Series of Our Daily Bread Ministries; former managing editor, *Our Daily Bread*. Author: *Brother to Brother*.

C. P. Hia Special assistant to the president, Our Daily Bread Ministries. Based in Singapore.

Kirsten Holmberg Speaker and author, residing in Idaho. Author: *Advent with the Word: Approaching Christmas through the Inspired Language of God*.

Adam Holz Director, Focus on the Family's website Plugged In. Author: *Beating Busyness*.

Karen Huang A book editor for many years in Singapore. Author: *Letters to a Single Woman*.

Arthur Jackson Midwest region urban director, PastorServe. Former pastor.

Cindy Hess Kasper Former senior content editor, Our Daily Bread Ministries; has written for *Our Daily Bread* since 2006.

Alyson Kieda Former editor, Our Daily Bread Ministries.

Randy Kilgore Writer and workplace chaplain. Founder of Desired Haven Ministries, Massachusetts. Author: *Made to Matter: Devotions for Working Christians*.

Leslie Koh Editor, Our Daily Bread Ministries, Singapore. Former journalist for *The Strait Times* newspaper in Singapore.

Monica La Rose Editor, Our Daily Bread Ministries. Has a master's in theology from Calvin Seminary, Grand Rapids, Michigan.

Albert Lee Former assistant to the president, Our Daily Bread Ministries, Singapore.

Julie Ackerman Link (1950–2015) Began writing for *Our Daily Bread* in 2000. Author: *Above All, Love* and *Hope for All Seasons*.

Kimya Loder is a researcher and scholar who seeks to embody Jesus's model of servant leadership.

David McCasland Longtime writer for *Our Daily Bread*, beginning in the late 1990s. Author: *Oswald Chambers: Abandoned to God* and *Eric Liddell: Pure Gold*.

Elisa Morgan Cohost of *Discover the Word* and *God Hears Her*, productions of Our Daily Bread Ministries. President emeritus, Mothers of Preschoolers (MOPS) International. Author: *Praying Like Jesus, You Are Not Alone*, and *Christmas Changes Everything*.

Keila Ochoa Works with Media Associates International to help train writers worldwide. Author of a number of books in the Spanish language.

Glenn Packiam Lead pastor, New Life Downtown, Colorado Springs. Author: *Blessed Broken Given: How Your Story Becomes Sacred in the Hands of Jesus, Discover the Mystery of Faith*, and *Secondhand Jesus*.

Katara Patton Executive editor for VOICES at Our Daily Bread Ministries. Author: *Successful Mothers of the Bible* and *Navigating the Blues*.

Kenneth Petersen Former publisher, Our Daily Bread Publishing. Author: *Farm Sweet Farm: 75 Devotions, A Bushel of Reasons to Love Country Living*, and *Oh Happy Day: Soul-Stirring Inspirations with a Gospel Music Twist*.

Karen Pimpo A project manager in marketing communications. Contributing writer for both *Our Daily Bread* and YMI, a youth outreach of Our Daily Bread Ministries. Sings in the Grand Rapids Symphony Chorus.

Amy Boucher Pye Writer, speaker, retreat leader. Lives in North London, England. Author: *Finding Myself in Britain* and *Transforming Love*.

Haddon Robinson (1931–2017) An expert of the ministry of preaching, served on the board of Our Daily Bread Ministries for many years. Author: *Biblical Preaching: The Development and Delivery of Expository Messages*.

David Roper Former pastor and founder of Idaho Mountain Ministries. Author: *A Man to Match the Mountain* and *Teach Us to Number Our Days*.

Patricia Raybon Writer, journalist, support of Bible-translation projects. Author: *I Told the Mountain to Move* and *My First White Friend*.

Lisa M. Samra Writer, facilitator of mentoring relationships with women, developer of focus groups focusing on spiritual formation.

Jennifer Benson Schuldt A technical writer living in the Chicago area. Has written for *Our Daily Bread* since 2015.

Joe Stowell Former president of both Moody Bible Institute (Chicago) and Cornerstone University. Author of more than twenty books.

Herb Vander Lugt (1920–2006) Author and longtime senior research editor for Our Daily Bread Ministries.

Paul Van Gorder (1921–2009) wrote for *Our Daily Bread* from 1969 until 1992. He was also associate Bible teacher for the ministry's Day of Discovery television program.

Sheridan Voysey Writer, speaker, broadcaster in Oxford, England. Author: *Resurrection Year* and *Resilient*.

Ruth Wan-Lau A longtime publishing industry veteran and a resident of Singapore, she has written more than thirty books. Writes for *Give Us This Day: Our Daily Bread for Families and Kids*.

Marvin Williams Pastor, Trinity Church, Lansing, Michigan. Author: *Loving God, Loving Others*.

Mike Wittmer Professor of Bible, Cornerstone Theological Seminary; pastor, Cedar Springs Baptist Church. Author: *Heaven Is a Place on Earth*, *The Last Enemy*, and *Despite Doubt*.

Joanie Yoder (1934–2004) Joanie and her husband, Bill, began a Christian rehabilitation center in England, helping people become God-dependent instead of drug-dependent. Author: *God Alone*.

Spread the Word
by Doing One Thing.

- Give a copy of this book as a gift.
- Share the QR code link via your social media.
- Write a review of this book on your blog, favorite bookseller's website, or at ODB.org/store.
- Recommend this book to your church, small group, or book club.

Connect with us. [f] [○]
Our Daily Bread Publishing
PO Box 3566, Grand Rapids, MI 49501, USA
Email: books@odb.org